The Search for
COMMON
GROUND

What Unites and Divides Catholic Americans

James D. Davidson, Andrea S. Williams,
Richard A. Lamanna, Jan Stenftenagel,
Kathleen Maas Weigert, William J. Whalen,
Patricia Wittberg, S.C.

Our Sunday Visitor Publishing Division
Our Sunday Visitor, Inc.
Huntington, Indiana 46750

International Standard Book Number: 0-87973-925-8
Library of Congress Catalog Card Number: 97-66310

Cover design by Rebecca Heaston

PRINTED IN THE UNITED STATES OF AMERICA

925

To Catholic Americans, especially those who participated in our personal interviews, focus groups, Indiana survey, and national poll.

Contents

Introduction
by Dean Hoge

T his is the book American Catholics need today. It gives a reliable picture of the beliefs of the Catholic community, and it does so in non-ideological terms. It clarifies the current debates about where American Catholicism is headed and what it should do. This will be a reference work for years to come.

Careful sociological research done by independent researchers offers a corrective to many statements made by spokespersons of the Catholic right or the Catholic left. For example, we hear it said that Catholic women are angry. Is it true? We hear it said that parish-sponsored education programs such as Confraternity of Christian Doctrine (CCD) have little effect. Is it true? This book tells us. With this new data, the debates will become more accurate and more productive. Fewer voices can spout off about how young Catholics today are turning their backs on the Church, joining cults, or whatever. Fewer can make brash statements about the effects of family influences, Catholic schools, or having nuns as teachers.

Of the many themes in this book, let me call attention to two.

Young versus old

Davidson and his team prove clearly what many priests and lay leaders have experienced for themselves: young Catholics are different from older

Catholics. The programs that served the spiritual needs of the older generation will not have the same effect in the future. Some of the underlying assumptions of the pre-Vatican II church practices need to be revisited. For researchers studying Catholicism, this is not a new finding. But this book gives us a new level of detail and a useful spelling-out of implications. The authors show that the major fault line in Catholic belief and commitment lies between the pre-Vatican II Catholics and the Vatican II Catholics; that is, between persons born before 1940 and those born after 1940. In 1997 this escarpment lies between persons about 57 and older, and those 56 and younger. The cliff is actually not as steep as this, but a definite slope is visible over a span of several years. Catholics older than their middle 50s are different from younger Catholics.

The authors also show that no additional fault line occurs among younger people. Catholics in their 30s, 40s, and early 50s are similar to one another in basic beliefs and commitments. The change from pre-Vatican Catholics to Vatican II Catholics was a onetime thing, not a steady trend that is continuing. There is no second fault line. Some people claim that there is a "rebound effect" today among young adult Catholics, so that they resemble the older generation more than the middle-adult generation. The book shows us that while this did occur on one of the measures, the overall picture is *no* rebound effect. The young Catholics have not changed in religious beliefs and commitments from those a decade or two older.

The authors also show that the much-discussed social conservatism of young Catholics on social issues does not exist at all. On the contrary, young Catholics are more committed to reaching out to the poor than any other age group. It is true that other research on priests has found a shift toward conservatism among the young, but such a shift did not take place in the laity.

The detailed description of the changing generations is, in my opinion, the main new lesson in this book. Today Catholics are fully accepted in all parts of American society. Catholics attend Ivy League universities like anyone else, and they are elected to Congress or the White House like anyone else. They intermarry with Protestants and Jews more than ever before, and they are more knowledgeable about Christian theology and history than ever before. They are also more independent-minded, and they expect more of their parishes, priests, and bishops. Davidson and his colleagues describe a "shift from an institutional approach to faith among pre-Vatican II Catholics to a more individualistic concept of faith among post-Vatican II Catholics."

Sociological studies have described an additional trend which is having an impact. Young Americans today are more skeptical of the claims of all major institutions, not just churches, than at any time since polling began in the 1950s. All American institutions are affected by this, which is a little like continental drift in that it has seismic proportions and affects everything else. The fall-off in trust is worst with Congress and other branches of government, but with churches it happened too, and it is bad enough.

In this new American setting, no one should expect traditional Catholic institutions to survive unchanged. A foremost example of pressure on our institutions is the growing shortage of priests. Because of the shortage, parish life cannot long continue as we know it. Something has to be done, and both laity and priests need to take part in making the decisions. We need to begin discussion and experimentation now.

The big task before us is to reconnect the Church with the people. We need to open communications. We need to reassess the centrality and necessity of every aspect of the institutions. Their crucial elements need strengthening at all cost, and others need adjusting. To every policy, practice, habit, and custom we must put a test question: "Will this strengthen the faith and spiritual life of the new Catholics in the twenty-first century?"

Polarization

News stories tend to tell us that Catholics are polarized, with one faction battling the other on issue after issue. This book gives an accurate assessment of divisions today. It tells us that polarization exists only on a few topics. On basic beliefs and practices there is none. The polarization that exists is mainly on questions of church leadership, priesthood, and moral teachings. It is not on doctrine, creed, or sacraments. Catholics are polarized on a few topics but unified on many others.

We must bear in mind that the American Catholic community is the fastest-changing religious group in America today. This change is a product of the immigrant history, rapid increases in education and wealth, the events of the '60s in America, and the Vatican Council. Every Catholic family has its own examples of religious change from grandparents to parents to children. Social change of this magnitude introduces tensions into any religious community, as factions endorsing the new do battle with factions holding fast to the old. American Judaism is a clear example. It has split into three main denominations, with a fourth now in formation, whose main differences are questions of how to relate to American society and modern culture. The orthodox Jews reject the new, and the reformed and reconstructionist embrace much of the new.

Similar tensions are facing Catholics. American Catholicism has not split institutionally along these lines, and let us pray that it will not. Catholics seem to have a genius for somehow holding together. The authors of this book analyze what keeps American Catholics together and what threatens to separate them. Preserving unity in the future will require all the efforts we can muster, and with the coming of a massive wave of Catholic immigrants from Latin America and Asia, it will require special sensitivity. A good beginning is defining and strengthening the common ground we have.

We all owe gratitude to Jim Davidson, his coworkers, and the Lilly Endowment for an accurate picture of where Catholics came from, where we are, and where we are going.

Preface

T his book describes how American Catholics approach faith and morals. It is based on a three-year research project that included in-depth interviews with lay people; focus groups with lay people belonging to different birth cohorts; a statewide questionnaire survey of Indiana parishioners; and a national sample of American Catholics. The project was funded by Lilly Endowment, Inc.

James D. Davidson was project director. Other staff persons in the project office were Andrea S. Williams, graduate research assistant, and Sherry Leuck, project secretary. In addition, the leadership team included a diocesan coordinator for each of Indiana's five dioceses; a diocesan advisor, appointed by each Indiana bishop; and five independent advisors, selected by the director for their expertise in the areas of theology and data analysis. A complete list of team members is presented in Appendix A. The coauthors of this book have served as members of the research team from the very beginning of the project.

The coauthors and other members of the leadership team have different personal and professional backgrounds and, hence, different views of the Church and its teachings. Rather than denying these differences, we have put them to use, making sure that our study reflects a wide variety of concerns and perspectives. We have tried to be evenhanded in our analysis of issues that often produce divisions between Catholics. As we have debated our differences, we have focused on our common goal of producing results that will be useful to all Church leaders.

James Davidson took the lead in drafting chapters one through six and Chapter 11. Sister Patricia Wittberg wrote Chapter 6; Andrea Williams, Chapter 7; Jan Stenftenagel drafted Chapter 8; Kathleen Maas Weigert was responsible for Chapter 9; and Richard Lamanna is the author of Chapter 10. William Whalen has offered substantive and editorial assistance on all chapters. Each chapter has been reviewed and critiqued by the entire writing team.

The project was authorized by each of Indiana's five bishops, who supported the project from beginning to end. We are especially grateful to Archbishop Daniel Buechlein (Indianapolis); Bishop William Higi (Lafayette); Bishop Gerald Gettelfinger (Evansville); Bishop John D'Arcy (Fort Wayne-South Bend); and Bishop Dale Melczek (Gary). Their unwavering support was a key ingredient in the success of the project.

We also thank the pastors and office staff persons of the 49 Indiana parishes that participated in the statewide survey. Their cooperation allowed us to conduct the largest and most accurate Catholic survey ever done in the state. We also are very grateful to the nearly 3,000 Indiana parishioners who agreed to be interviewed, participated in our focus groups, and responded to our questionnaire. We also extend our thanks to all the Catholics who participated in our national telephone poll. We want everyone to know that, in one way or another, your cooperation has made this book possible.

We also express our appreciation for the help we received from a number of people in Purdue University's department of sociology and anthropology. Bill Jones deserves special thanks for coordinating the coding and processing of the statewide survey. He also responded promptly and skillfully to all of our urgent requests for computer assistance. We could not have met our deadlines if it were not for the diligent efforts of graduate students Jennifer McKinney, Mee Sook Kim, Denise Baird, Melissa Farmer, and Donald Loiacano, who did most of the coding and data entry for the statewide survey. Graduate student Bill Stroup developed the lisrel analyses reported in Appendix J. Thanks, Bill. Pat Henady and Deborah Lee have helped us with our fiscal responsibilities to Lilly Endowment, Inc. We also have benefited from the fine work of Tonatiuh Melgarejo, who translated the English version of our statewide questionnaire into Spanish.

Response Analysis, a professional polling company in Princeton, New Jersey, conducted our national poll. We extend special thanks to Gwen Miller and Andrew Kulley for their professionalism and courtesy. We highly recommend Response Analysis to anyone who wants to conduct a custom survey such as ours.

Along the way, we have met and worked with many highly committed people whose ideas have shaped our thinking. These people include Reverend Eugene Hensell and other members of the faculty at St. Meinrad Archabbey, who met with us for a couple of days at the outset of the project, when we were reviewing life in the Church prior to Vatican II and developments in the Church since then. Religious eductors and catechists at the Office of Pastoral Ministry in Lafayette — especially Harry Dudley, Fidelis Tracy, C.D.P., Carl Wagner, Marilyn Winter, O.P., and Barbara Kerkhoff — have provided valuable feedback when we've asked for it. We also are grateful to religious educators in Gary and the archdiocese of Indianapolis who have invited us to share our findings. They have asked questions leading to important clarifications in our thinking. Father Anthony Pogorelc and Father Frank DeRego also have provided very helpful critiques of our work. Nearly 300 Indiana diocesan and parish leaders joined us for a day-long conference on December 15, 1995. Their enthusiastic participation and insights have contributed to the analyses in this book. We also have met many outstanding colleagues and made many good friends in the seven dioceses of Florida. Our participation in their meetings has contributed to our understanding of Catholic Americans. We also thank members of the North American Forum on the Catechumenate for their challenging questions and the insights we gained from participating in one of their conferences.

We also are grateful to Greg Erlandson and Jim Manney at Our Sunday Visitor for their interest in our work and their willingness to publish our results. Given our desire to share the findings with as many diocesan and parish leaders as possible, we could not have asked for a better publisher or a better pair of collaborators.

This whole project has been an exhilarating experience for all the members of the research team. It would not have been possible if it were not for generous funding from Lilly Endowment, Inc. We are especially grateful to Sister Jeanne Knoerle, Lilly's program director for our project. We also thank Mr. Fred Hofheinz for his long-standing and invaluable support of our work.

Each member of the research team has family members, friends, and colleagues who have made sacrifices so we could conduct this project. In a very personal way, we dedicate this book to all of these wonderful people.

1 • The American Church, 1930s-1990s

Increasing Diversity in Faith and Morals

The close relationship between religion and society explains why the changes in religion that have taken place in the recent past are often described as "revolutionary." The United States has experienced a major turning point in its history in the post-World War II era. . . . For American Catholics an era of their church history was also coming to an end. . . . This combination of changes turned American Catholicism inside out and radically transformed the church and the people.

Jay P. Dolan (1989:320)

As the historian Jay P. Dolan suggests, the relationship between the Church and American society has changed dramatically over the past 50 to 60 years. We contend that it has progressed from a largely, though not entirely, hostile and closed relationship in the 1930s, '40s, and '50s to one which is more tolerant and open in the 1970s, '80s, and '90s. We are particularly interested in one aspect of this change — the way the American Catholic laity views faith and morals.[1] A relatively unified system of belief and practice, with which the laity was more inclined to agree than disagree, has given way to a more pluralistic theology and an increasingly wide range of beliefs and practices which lay people are increasingly willing to express publicly.[2]

The 1930s-1950s: Unity Prevails Over Diversity

The 1929 stock market crash ushered in a decade of economic hardship in America. No matter what one's religious affiliation, it was hard finding work and making a decent living during the economic depression of the 1930s. On the heels of the depression came World War II. Though a noble war for many Americans and the basis of heightened patriotism in the 1940s, the war also caused great hardship. Thousands of American families lost fathers, sons, and daughters.

Protestants were the nation's economic, political, and cultural elite. A study of the religious affiliations of persons listed in the 1930-31 edition of the *Who's Who in America* shows that over half of the listees belonged to just three mainline denominations: Episcopal, Presbyterian, and Congregationalist (Davidson, 1994a; Davidson, Pyle, and Reyes, 1995). Catholics were under-represented among the nation's elites and concentrated toward the bottom of the socioeconomic ladder (Dolan, 1985; Herberg, 1960).

American society was quite hostile toward Catholicism. Anti-Catholic prejudice and discrimination, which was so evident in Al Smith's bid for the presidency in 1928, was still widespread in the 1940s and '50s (Blanshard, 1951, 1958; Kane, 1955; Zahn, 1955, 1957). The predominantly Protestant society harbored cruel stereotypes of Catholics as an uneducated and inferior, yet power-hungry, people who wanted to take over the country. When Catholics seized control, the myth went, they would do whatever the pope told them to do. Catholic beliefs would be imposed on everybody.

To prevent this from happening, Protestants used a variety of methods to keep Catholics from getting ahead. The 1924 Immigration Act slowed Catholic immigration, especially from eastern and southern European countries. The Ku Klux Klan was only one of many organizations which discriminated against Catholics in the workplace, neighborhoods, and other spheres of community life. Catholics could not find work as public school teachers or in predominantly WASP companies. They were discouraged from participating in civic associations. They were segregated into predominantly Catholic neighborhoods.

The Church, meanwhile, was turned inward, emphasizing the need for Catholics to stick together. Starting in the late nineteenth century, it built a Catholic "ghetto," consisting of a vast array of parishes, parochial schools, seminaries, convents, monasteries, magazines and newspapers, social service agencies, youth groups such as Catholic Boy Scouts and Catholic Girl Scouts, professional societies, fraternal groups such as the Knights of Columbus and the Daughters of Isabella, hospitals, book publishers, and book clubs (Cogley and Van Allen, 1986; Herberg, 1960; Dolan, Appleby, Bryne, and Campbell, 1989). Most Catholics married other Catholics, got married in the Church, and raised their children in the Church (Chancellor and Monahan, 1955; Kennedy, 1952; Lenski, 1963; Thomas, 1951a and 1951b).

Data from 1959 illustrate the size of the Catholic ghetto (*Official Catholic Directory*, 1960). The Church performed 319,992 marriages. There were 1,344,576 infant baptisms. Another 146,212 adults were baptized that year. There were 4,195,781 youngsters attending Catholic grade schools; another 520,128 attended Catholic high schools. Many more went to Sunday school for religious instruction.

Huge numbers of young Catholics went into seminaries and convents, where they studied for roles in the ghetto culture (Briody and Sullivan, 1988; *Official Catholic Directory*, 1960; Wittberg, 1994). As the 1950s came to a close, there were 53,796 priests and another 39,896 young men in seminary. There were 168,527 sisters and about 7,000 young women entered convents every year. These men and women worked in 16,896 parishes, 9,897 Catholic grade schools, 1,567 Catholic high schools, 945 hospitals and sanitoria, 347 nursing schools, 326 homes for the aged, 279 orphanages and infant asylums, 265 Catholic colleges and universities, and 131 protective institutions.

Throughout the 1930s, '40s, and '50s, the Church strove for uniformity in belief and practice. This emphasis emerged in the nineteenth century, when Vatican I (1869-70) concentrated authority in the papacy and proclaimed the doctrine of papal infallibility (Seidler and Meyer, 1989; Burns, 1992). The pope's role was to discern truth and communicate it through the bishops to local priests and sisters. Priests and sisters, in turn, transmitted the truth to the laity through the specifically Catholic organizations comprising the Catholic ghetto. They relied heavily on the *Baltimore Catechism*. The catechism asked basic questions and provided basic answers, which young Catholics were expected to memorize. Question: "Who made us?" Answer: "God made us" (McGuire, 1961:12). Young Catholics were taught that the Catholic Church is the one true Church, and they were expected to abide by its teachings (Rodriguez, 1982).

Priests and sisters produced compliance by stressing the concept of sin, generating a great deal of guilt, and communicating the image of a stern God who punishes people for their sins. Not agreeing with basic Church teachings and not complying with its primary behavioral expectations were seen as mortal sins resulting in eternal damnation unless one confessed them to a priest.

The Church's emphasis on unity also stood in relation to its view of Protestants as the "separated brethren." Protestants had rebelled against the Church during the Reformation and were seen as promoting false doctrines. Episcopalians were somewhat like Catholics, but most Protestants — especially "holy rollers" — were altogether different, and wrong. Catholics had a duty to accept Church teachings and stay away from Protestant churches and Protestant ideas.

> The theology passed on in the Catholic ghetto, then, was more often than not consciously anti-Protestant in content, determinedly defensive and apologetic in tone, and based on Ready Answers to questions which no one outside the walls was really asking (Cogley and Van Allen, 1986:144).

Catholics also learned that American society was a hostile place; it was run by Protestants, and there was a good chance Catholics would be discriminated against because of their religion. The Church was their refuge. Their dependence on the Church for social and spiritual benefits increased the likelihood that they would comply with Church teachings.

Unity Prevails

What emerged from this rather harsh and closed relationship between Church and society was a subculture that united Catholics (Cogley and Van Allen, 1986; Rodriguez, 1982). This culture included a unified and distinctively Catholic approach to faith and morals. All Catholics didn't think exactly the same about the Church and its moral stances, but there seems to have been extensive agreement on these issues. Though lay people dissented on some issues, which we will discuss below, for the most part they complied with Church teachings. With regard to faith and morals at least, unity prevailed over diversity.[3]

About three-quarters of Catholics attended Mass at least once a week; many went more often than that (Fichter, 1951, 1952, 1953, 1954; Lenski, 1963; Orbach, 1961). While this means that about one quarter of Catholics did not attend as often as the Church expected, the rate of Mass attendance among Catholics was about twice as high as Protestants' rate of attendance at worship (Moberg, 1962).

Though it is easier to document the extent of Catholics' compliance with the Church's behavioral norms, there is some evidence indicating that Catholics also tended to accept Church teachings. An early-1950s study of Catholics in a New Orleans parish revealed that 94 percent of Catholics agreed with the Church's teaching that they had a moral obligation to vote. Ninety-two percent agreed with the Church's opposition to mercy killing. Ninety-one percent supported the use of tax money for social welfare programs. Eighty-seven percent concurred with the Church's opposition to divorce. And 76 percent agreed with the Church's teaching that God punishes people for their sins (Fichter, 1951:259-271).

A late 1950s study in Detroit also showed that Catholics believed in a personal God, the divinity of Christ, and life after death. The study included an index of "doctrinal orthodoxy" which measured belief that there is a God; that God is "a Heavenly Father who watches over you"; that "God answers people's prayers"; that there is a life after death; that God expects people to worship every week; and that Jesus is the Son of God. The author concluded:

> As might be expected, doctrinal orthodoxy proved more frequent among Catholics than among Protestants. Sixty-two percent of the Catholic respondents took an orthodox stance on all items, compared with only 38 percent of the Negro Protestants and 32 percent of the white Protestants (Lenski, 1963:57).

Most Catholics also accepted the Church's emphases on authority and obedience. They believed that God speaks through the Church; that popes — and by extension, bishops, priests, and nuns — are God's representatives on earth. When the Church's National Organization for Decent Literature condemned books, and its Legion of Decency condemned movies, Catholics paid attention. It is not surprising, then, that researchers found that Catholics were more likely to have authoritarian and dogmatic personalities than Protestants (Adorno et. al., 1950; Fendrich and D'Antonio, 1970; Lenski, 1963; O'Dea, 1958; Rokeach, 1960).

Diversity in the Midst of Unity

Though the emphasis was on uniformity, Catholics did not all act or think the same.[4] There were well-known differences in the way Irish, Italian, Polish, German, and other ethnic Catholics approached faith and morals (Cogley and Van Allen, 1986). Although the Church sought adherence to its teachings, some Catholics clearly did not comply (Kane, 1960). Fichter's study of Catholics in New Orleans in the early 1950s revealed four types of Catholics: seven percent were "nuclear" Catholics (who engaged in virtually all of the religious practices the Church considered normative), 41 percent were "modal" Catholics (who fulfilled most, but not all, requirements), 13 percent were "marginal" Catholics (who conformed in some areas, but deviated from the norm in many others), and 39 percent were "dormant" Catholics (who were not practicing their faith at all).

The same study showed that only seven percent of Catholics agreed with the Church's emphasis on tightening fast and abstinence requirements. Only 11 percent agreed with the Church's goal of integrating racially segregated parishes, and only 26 percent concurred with its goal of integrating parochial schools. Only a third agreed with the Church's opposition to interfaith marriages. And only 38 percent agreed with its opposition to use of the atom bomb.

A 1950 study of first-grade children in 446 Catholic schools in 33 states revealed that many Catholic families were not providing their children with the type of religious education the Church wanted. Fifty-three percent of the children could make the Sign of the Cross, but only a third could say the Hail Mary or knew the real story of Christmas; only 23 percent could say the Lord's Prayer; and only 13 percent knew the story of Adam and Eve. Overall, the research concluded, "the formal religious education and training which the majority of Roman Catholic families give their preschool children seems very inadequate when judged by traditional expectations" (Thomas, 1951a:180)

In short, the best research available on Catholics' beliefs and practices between the 1930s and 1950s points to some diversity in the midst of overall unity. Catholics certainly did not comply with all Church teachings, but the Church produced comparatively high levels of agreement with its doctrines and participation in most of its rituals.

1960s and '70s: A Turning Point

The Church and society relationship began to change in the 1950s. In contrast to the economic hardships of the 1930s, Americans enjoyed a period of real economic prosperity in the 1950s and '60s (Galbraith, 1958). Catholics participated in this wave of prosperity. With the help of the G.I. Bill, they caught up with Protestants in education and occupational status. By the early '60s, Catholics had incomes which were virtually the same as Protestants' (Glenn and Hyland, 1967; Greeley, 1977). Catholics were upwardly mobile; they were making it into the American mainstream. They also were being assimilated into American culture, including its emphases on democracy and individual freedom (Weigel, 1959; Herberg, 1960; Dolan, 1985, 1989). Ironically, Catholic ghetto organizations such as parochial schools contributed to this enculturation (Dolan, 1985; Gleason, 1989; Rodriguez, 1982).[5]

Protestants also were becoming more tolerant of Catholics. Protestants appreciated Catholics' vigorous opposition to communism and their willingness to assimilate into society. They demonstrated increased tolerance by voting for the nation's first Catholic president. Though John F. Kennedy encountered anti-Catholicism and won by the narrowest of margins, his election in 1960 symbolized Catholics' ascendancy into the American middle class and demonstrated the nation's growing acceptance of Catholics.[6]

Social and Cultural Change

As this was going on, social and cultural changes swept the nation. Martin Luther King's civil rights movement evolved into a black power movement led by Malcolm X and the Black Panthers. Other minority movements sprang up among Latinos and Native Americans. Betty Friedan's 1963 book *The Feminine Mystique* launched the modern-day women's movement. At the University of California-Berkeley, Mario Savio became the spokesman for a counterculture movement that went far beyond the walls of the academy. College students also initiated protests against the war in Vietnam — protests which grew into a national revolt against political authority. Hugh Hefner and *Playboy* magazine articulated a more permissive attitude toward sex.

These changes raised questions about the American way of life Catholics were moving into. Conventional ways of doing things were called into question in virtually every sphere of life. African-Americans challenged institutionalized racism in the public sector: transportation, schools, housing, voting, and hotels and restaurants. Latino farmworkers organized against agribusinesses. Native Americans seized lands which they said the government had taken from them in illegal treaties. Women called attention to male chauvinism in every walk of American life. Young people seemed to question everything: norms against premarital sex, the meaning of marriage, the need to go to class, the duty to serve in the military, the value of work, parental authority, and laws against the use of drugs. A popular bumper sticker said it all: "Question Authority."

These changes affected Catholics. While many Catholics preferred traditional beliefs and practices, assimilation into the cultural mainstream increased other Catholics' interest in new approaches to faith and morals that were more compatible with American culture. The civil rights movement crystallized differences between Catholics who accepted racial segregation and those who felt the Church should lead the way toward a more integrated society. A grape boycott led by Cesar Chavez raised moral questions about the rights and responsibility of farm-owners and farmworkers. The women's movement challenged Catholics to rethink religious beliefs that contributed to their subordinate role in the Church; some resented the movement, others embraced it. Youth movements created sharp differences between young Catholics who preferred traditional faith and morals and those who wanted to experiment with new approaches. The *Playboy* philosophy revealed divisions between Catholics who upheld traditional sexual mores and those who favored more liberal views of sex.

Vatican II

The Church also was changing, as was its orientation to American society. While there had been some growing signs of change in the Church in the 1950s, even Pope John XXIII — who just wanted to open a window and let in some fresh air — could not have anticipated the dramatic changes which flowed from Vatican Council II (Burns, 1992; Ellis, 1969; Ebaugh, 1991; Seidler and Meyer, 1989).

The Second Vatican Council produced 16 documents, which sometimes challenged traditional Catholic concepts of faith and morals, proposing new interpretations (Abbott, 1966; Fesquet, 1967; Flannery, 1992; Foley, 1993; McCarthy, 1994).[7] The Council prescribed a new understanding of the Church's place in the world. Vatican II reversed the Church's traditional view of the world as a hostile place, arguing instead that the Church should be more fully integrated into modern society. Rather than viewing the Church as a haven from the evils of secular society, the Council urged Catholics to see the Church as a positive force in the world. As Catholic historian Jay Dolan has said, "Vatican II was largely responsible for forcing Catholics to rethink the meaning of Catholicism in the modern world" (Dolan, 1985:428).

Vatican II also ushered in an era of greater ecumenism. By acknowledging positive aspects of non-Catholic and non-Christian religions, the Church authorized appreciation of different religious traditions. The Council admitted that the Church was not without failings and acknowledged that religious truth could be found in other faiths.

The Council also made changes in the ecclesiastical structure of the Church. While a pyramidal model of the Church (with the laity subordinate to priests and bishops who, in turn, were subordinate to the pope) remained intact, there was to be more collegiality between the pope and the bishops. Bishops were encouraged to give the laity more voice through instruments such as parish councils. The laity, in turn, were encouraged to view themselves as "the people of God."

Vatican II asked the laity to take greater responsibility for their own faith. It turned away from its earlier emphasis on sin and punishment as means of social control, opting instead for greater emphasis on personal freedom and commitment (Dolan, 1989). At the same time that the Council was dispensing with traditions such as Latin Masses and meatless Fridays, it was asking Catholics to view their faith in more personal terms.

The Council also introduced striking liturgical changes. The Latin (Tridentine) Mass at which the priest faced the altar was replaced with a Mass at which the priest faced the people and spoke in their language. Liturgists were encouraged to experiment, and changes soon followed such as more singing, guitar music, the kiss of peace, and use of the common cup.

The 1980s and '90s: Increased Diversity

The more tolerant and open relationship between Church and society has produced many changes in the Church. Officially, the emphasis on absolute papal authority has been modified to permit greater collegiality between the pope and the bishops. Informally, it has led to closer collaboration between priests, sisters, and lay people. Many pieces of the organizational infrastructure which sustained the ghetto culture of the pre-Vatican II Church have been dismantled. As the number of priests and sisters has declined, so has the number of organizations which are run by clergy and religious. Though the number of Catholics has increased from about 40 million to nearly 60 million in the last 30 years, the number of Catholic seminaries, convents, grade schools, high schools, and protective institutions has declined. Parallel organizations (such as Catholic Boy Scouts and Catholic Girl Scouts) have all but disappeared (Dolan, 1985).

Fewer and fewer young Catholics go to Catholic schools. Whereas 4,195,781 youngsters attended Catholic grade schools in 1959, less than half of that number (only 1,949,989) did in 1995. While 520,128 teenagers attended Catholic high schools in 1959, only 378,847 were in parochial high schools in 1995. Far more young people (4,199,356) get their religious education through parishes. Today's young Catholics are usually taught by lay people who don't have as much theological training as priests and sisters do. There were only 45,506 lay teachers out of a total full-time teaching corps of 160,632 in 1960 (28 percent); by 1995, 150,726 lay teachers comprised 90 percent of all instructors.

Many Catholics still participate in fraternal groups like the Knights of Columbus and the Daughters of Isabella, but these groups do not generate as much interest as new special purpose groups led by an increasingly well-educated and socially diverse laity. Liberal groups such as Call to Action and Catholics Speak Out, and conservative groups such as Catholics United for the Faith, Catholic Campaign for America, and Right to Life express the ideological pluralism — some would say polarization — in today's Church (Dinges, 1983; Weaver and Appleby, 1995). Many Catholics read middle of the road publications like *St. Anthony Messenger* and *U.S. Catholic,* but many others read conservative literature such as *The Wanderer*, or liberal newspapers such as the *National Catholic Reporter.* According to one observer:

> Anyone who reads the Catholic press in the United States
> might legitimately wonder if the editors and readers of
> *The Wanderer* and the *National Catholic Reporter* belong
> to the same Church (McBrien, 1983:181).

Bishops have authorized more theological latitude in seminaries, convents, colleges, universities, and parishes — leading to a great deal more theological experimentation. Sister Joan Chittister describes the changes in her religious community this way:

> The spirituality before Vatican II was a spirituality of
> interchangeable parts — the Singer Sewing Machine
> Company could have done as well. Everybody in the
> Community was a potential fourth grade teacher; everybody in the Community was a potential high school
> teacher. What you did was send in warm bodies. After
> Vatican II, you began to ask, Who is this person, really?
> What gifts has she been given for the upbuilding of the
> Church? How can this Community affirm those gifts,
> and how can this person promote the charism of this Community? (Quoted in *Occhiogrosso*, 1987:9).

In some theological quarters, there was a movement from a world view which stressed universals and essences to one which stresses existence and particularity (Ryba, 1994). While pre-Vatican II theology never completely overlooked the context of human behavior, it emphasized natural law as the basis of judging right and wrong. Since the Council, many theologians, pastors, and lay people now pay more attention to the circumstances surrounding human actions and their effects on the parties involved. While the pope, many Church officials, and some lay people continue to emphasize moral universals and objective truth, a growing number of theologians and lay people feel moral judgments should be based on an understanding of specific human experiences in specific contexts (D'Antonio, Davidson, Hoge, and Wallace, 1989, 1996).

Parishes also do not exert as much control over Catholics' lives as they used to. As Catholics have assimilated into the American mainstream and achieved greater affluence, their lives have broadened to include many non-Catholic friends and access to civic groups which used to exclude them. These new networks satisfy many social needs which parishes used to meet. Thus, today's Catholics are no longer as dependent on their parishes as Catholics were in the 1930s and '40s, when parishes were their refuge from the harsh realities of anti-Catholicism (Dolan, 1989). Also, with the Church modifying its earlier emphases on sin and punishment, and stressing religious freedom, parish leaders no longer exercise as much control over the laity's attitudes and actions. Without the guilt attached to mortal sins and the fear of eternal damnation, Church leaders cannot command as much compliance with Church teachings as they used to.

Instead of memorizing the *Baltimore Catechism* and being drilled in doctrine the way their parents were, young Catholics learn to think for themselves (McNamara, 1992). They are taught that they are on their "personal faith journey," that Jesus loves them very much, and that they are supposed to "be nice" to other people (Markey, 1994; O'Malley, 1986). The emphasis on the "one true Church" has given way to the idea that Catholicism is one among many Christian faiths. The commonalities with other Christians are stressed, not the differences. What used to be considered a hostile world now seems friendlier.

These changes have had consequences for the laity's approach to faith and morals. As we show below, Catholics are still united on many matters, but less than in the past. New theological options have been added to the ones which already existed, and the laity are exercising their new-found freedom to draw their own conclusions on issues of faith and morals. Lay people now have a wider range of beliefs and practices to consider, and at least on some key issues, they seem to be making more diverse decisions.[8]

Persisting Unity

Church leaders have not abandoned their emphases on papal authority and compliance with Church teachings. Pope Paul VI (1968) reaffirmed the Church's opposition to artificial birth control in *Humanae Vitae*. More recently, Pope John Paul II has proclaimed the teaching authority of the Church and asserted his traditional views of faith and morals in encyclicals such as *Veritatis Splendor* (1993) and *Evangelium Vitae* (1994).

Researchers and persons in the media have not focused much attention on areas of theological agreement among Catholics. Though there has been virtually no research on issues such as belief in the Trinity, the Incarnation, and the Resurrection, there are no public confrontations between the pope and the laity over these core doctrines. The relative tranquility surrounding these issues suggests that there may be considerable agreement between the pope and the laity on these taken-for-granted tenets of faith.

There is some evidence of persisting unity among Catholics. Most Catholics remain loyal to the Church. Research has shown that they have difficulty imagining themselves being anything but Catholic (Greeley, 1990; Donahue, 1995; D'Antonio, Davidson, Hoge, and Wallace, 1996). Even when they disagree with the pope, they continue to respect him as Christ's vicar on earth. The throngs of American Catholics — including young Catholics — who enthusiastically cheer him and attend his public Masses during his visits to this country are a sign of this persisting loyalty to the Church.

Increased Diversity

However, the trend has been toward a greater variety of beliefs and practices and a widening range of views on particular issues. Research on the pluralism in today's Church points to many specific areas of disagreement related to faith and morals.

On two issues which were almost never considered in the 1930s and '40s, the percentage of Catholics favoring married priests has grown steadily from 49 percent in 1974 to 76 percent in 1993, as has the percentage favoring the ordination of women, which has gone from 29 percent in 1974 to 63 percent in 1993 (Edmonds, 1993). Mass attendance has declined from about 75 percent to 40 to 45 percent (Dolan, 1985; D'Antonio, Davidson, Hoge, and Wallace, 1989, 1996), though reception of Holy Communion seems to be on the rise (Sweetser, 1996). Failure to comply with Church teachings no longer produces long lines at the confessional. Only about one-fifth of today's Catholics go to private confession, a far cry from the hordes of people waiting for confession in the 1940s and '50s (Gallup and Castelli, 1987:30; Greeley, 1977:132). The Church has introduced a communal penance service, but the number of people participating in this form of the sacrament also seems to be small. An increasing number of Catholics don't feel they need to go to confession of any kind. Perhaps they no longer think in terms of sin as a violation of God's law; no longer believe that certain actions (e.g., birth control) are matters for confession; or feel they can talk things out with God whenever and wherever they want to.

With regard to morals, two-thirds of Catholics still believe life begins at conception and reject the idea of abortion on demand. However, now "American Catholics are part of a broad consensus that opposes abortion on demand but believes that abortion should be legal in some circumstances" (Gallup and Castelli, 1987:95). Opinions vary greatly about what to do under specific circumstances, and about four in 10 Catholics wonder whether their views on abortion are right or wrong (Gallup and Castelli, 1987:98).

In spite of Pope Paul VI's encyclical *Humanae Vitae,* a majority of American Catholics now disagree with the Church's opposition to artificial means of birth control (D'Antonio, Davidson, Hoge, and Wallace, 1989, 1996; Donahue, 1995; Gallup and Castelli, 1987). While Pope John Paul II continues to oppose artificial means of birth control on the grounds that their use is contrary to natural law, American Catholics are increasingly inclined to disagree. The same trend is occurring with regard to divorce and remarriage. Contrary to official Church teachings, Catholic lay people increasingly believe that remarriage after divorce is morally acceptable (D'Antonio, Davidson, Hoge, and Wallace, 1989, 1996).

While many religious educators talk a lot about "peace and justice," others hardly mention the Church's "social teachings." The few lay people who have read (or read about) the American bishops' pastoral letters on peace and economic justice are sharply divided over the bishops' teachings: a majority (especially black Catholics) seem to agree, but others (especially affluent executives and business managers) do not (D'Antonio, Davidson, Hoge, and Wallace, 1989).

Observing Catholicism's post-Vatican II years, Protestant scholar Martin Marty has written:

> While the Catholic church remained officially one after the Council, it divided between left and right in thought and action. . . . What everyone called "post-Vatican II Catholicism" was infinitely more diverse in appearance than what had gone before. The old idea that there existed a monolithic church that took signals from Rome and disrupted the Republic was buried. Catholic theology was no longer a single expression of official Thomism. Creative men and women worked with a variety of theologies and with diverse degrees of loyalty to the old ways. . . . (Marty, 1986:464-467).

Catholic theologian Father Richard McBrien sees the recent trend toward pluralism this way:

> Roman Catholicism has simply entered the modern world . . . and that world is an inherently pluralistic one. As the Second Vatican Council insisted in its Pastoral Constitution on the Church in the Modern World (Gaudium et Spes), the Church is itself a part of this pluralistic world, and not something over against the world . . . just as the world is pluralistic in character, so too is the Catholic Church (McBrien, 1983:179).

Priest-sociologist Andrew Greeley sums it up this way:

> . . . almost all Catholics identify with the Church but feel no constraint to keep all the rules. On the one hand, they're loyal to the Church. . . . On the other hand, Catho-

lics remain in the Church in their own style and on their own terms. And that is, I think, the biggest transformation in American Catholics in the years since 1960. They are now Catholics on their own terms, and there's nothing that their parish priests or their Bishops or the Pope can do to change that. By the way, the psychology behind their reasoning is that even if Church leaders don't approve, they think God does approve (quoted in *Cateura*, 1989:324-325).

Summarizing their 1993 study of Catholics, D'Antonio, Davidson, Hoge, and Wallace draw the following conclusion:

The lesson of the book is clear: a majority of the American Catholic laity is slowly moving in the direction of wanting a more democratic Church in which laypersons can participate at all levels. This desire is strengthening with the passage of time. . . . In the chapters on authority, human sexuality, changes across three generations, the role of women, post-Vatican II Catholics, the Church's most committed, and Latino Catholics, we have seen how growing numbers of the laity have been abandoning the traditional positions demanded by the magisterium (D'Antonio, Davidson, Hoge, and Wallace, 1996:160).[9]

Conclusion

As the relationship between the Church and American society has shifted from mutual suspicion and limited contact to greater tolerance and more openness, there also has been a change in the way Catholics approach faith and morals. In the 1930s, '40s, and '50s, there was some diversity of belief and practice in the midst of overall unity. By the 1980s and '90s, there seems to be some unity in the midst of increased diversity. While the trend toward pluralism is pretty clear, there are still a number of unanswered questions about the amount of diversity in today's Church and the reasons why today's Catholics have such different approaches to faith and morals. In the next chapter, we delineate these questions and indicate the theory and methods we have used in our search for answers.

2 • Questions Church Leaders Ask
What Do Lay People Believe and Why?

The pope and bishops are responsible for teaching gospel values to people in every country and culture. . . [T]he translation of Church teaching into the lived reality of people's lives is . . . the task of theologians and preachers. . . . The third and most important phase of the Church's teaching mission is the individual believer's response to Church teaching.

Nicholas Lohkamp, O.F.M. (1991)

Parish and diocesan leaders know there has been a trend toward pluralism in the American Catholic Church. They know that today's Catholics have a broader range of views about faith and morals than Catholics did back in the 1930s and '40s. They experience pluralism every day. Bishops experience it in visits to their parishes and their meetings with lay people. Priests have to deal with it every time they prepare homilies; they know they will be speaking to parishioners who have all sorts of attitudes about faith and morals. Religious educators confront it in classes for young people and in adult-education programs. Liturgists have to take it into account when they try to design worship experiences that will be meaningful to everyone. Catholic school teachers and administrators wonder about the most effective ways to handle the tensions between official Church teachings and young Catholics' views on issues such as premarital sex and birth control. Lay leaders on diocesan and parish committees wonder if there are beliefs that all Catholics must obey, or if it is okay for Catholics to make up their own minds on everything.

Like the late Cardinal Bernardin and other leaders of the "common ground initiative," parish and diocesan leaders want to identify the areas of greatest unity among Catholics and understand the processes that produce so much diversity in today's Church. They want to know what binds Catholics together and why, at the same time, they seem to have such different views of faith and morals. They say that understanding convergence and divergence will enhance their current ministries and their efforts to pass Catholicism on to future generations of American Catholics.

In their attempts to understand pluralism and its implications for the Church, these leaders try to keep up with studies of Catholics' beliefs and practices. While they are willing — often eager — to learn from these studies, they have reservations about some of them. For example, they question the validity of studies sponsored by Catholic organizations with distinctly liberal or conservative viewpoints. They suspect that these groups have theological axes to grind, ask loaded questions, and present biased interpretations of their data.

Leaders also are suspicious of academic research and media-sponsored studies focusing mainly on "hot" issues where there are serious conflicts between Church teachings and what the laity actually believe. They believe that studies focusing on issues such as abortion and the ordination of women exaggerate the divisions in the Church. While they understand that such research may sell books and newspapers and may improve TV ratings, they doubt that it yields accurate accounts of what Catholics actually believe about a broad range of issues. They suspect that there is more agreement among Catholics than these studies suggest.

Church leaders also question the usefulness of national surveys that include people who were raised Catholic but are no longer involved in the Church. They feel that studies including people who grew up Catholic, but who are no longer Catholic in any behavioral sense, exaggerate the amount of religious inactivity and theological dissent in the Church. They suspect that there is a great deal more unity among practicing Catholics than most studies indicate.

Thus, diocesan and parish leaders still have a number of questions about the extent of the diversity in today's Church.

In what areas of faith and morals is there the greatest

unity among parishioners? Where are parishioners' views most likely to be in compliance with Church teachings?

Are there issues on which Catholics hold dramatically different views? What topics seem to produce the most diverse approaches to faith and morals?

On which dimensions of faith and morals are parishioners least likely to agree with official Church teachings? On what issues are the Vatican and the laity most at odds?

Church leaders also wonder *why* Catholics have such different views of faith and morals. In their search for reasons why Catholics think and act so differently, they feel that studies are limited in three ways. Some are purely descriptive. While these studies provide statistics, they don't offer explanations for the different ways that Catholics think and act. Other studies reduce complicated patterns of faith and morals to just one or two factors, such as race or gender. Others employ theories that are so esoteric and statistics that are so complicated that they have little or no practical value. As a result, Church leaders still have a number of questions about the reasons why some of today's Catholics are more likely to agree with Church teachings than others are.

To what extent is today's diversity related to personal attributes, such as birth cohort, race, and gender? How similar, or different, are older, middle-age, and young Catholics' view of faith and morals? What about Anglos, Latinos, and blacks? Men and women? Which of these demographic characteristics produces the biggest differences among Catholics?

Can differences between Catholics can be traced to the different ways in which they were raised? How much of the diversity in adults' beliefs and practices goes back to their religious upbringing? Do people who went to Catholic schools and people who did not have different beliefs and practices later on in life?

What effect, if any, do parish religious education programs have? How much impact do parents' religious orientations have on their children's beliefs, as compared to the formal instruction Catholics get in parishes and parochial schools?

Is religious diversity due to experiences Catholics have during their adult years? How similar or different are the faith and morals of Catholics who are married to other Catholics and Catholics who are married to non-Catholics? Who complies with Church teachings the most: Catholics who are most aware of Vatican II, or those who are least aware of it? To what extent, and in what ways, do Catholics' economic and political views affect their approaches to faith and morals?

How much does one's Catholic identity affect one's beliefs and practices? What about benefits Catholics have derived from belonging to the Church — do they have any impact on people's approach to faith and morals? Are people who donate the most time and energy to the Church any more likely to agree with Church teachings than people who give very little to the Church? To what extent are people's beliefs and practices based on loyalty to the Church, or the rational calculation of costs and benefits?

In short, parish and diocesan leaders have a number of important questions about the extent of pluralism among today's parishioners, and the conditions that produce different approaches to faith and morals. As they search for answers to these questions, they look for unbiased information on Catholics' actual beliefs and practices; analyses that focus on the parishioners they work with nearly every day; and meaningful explanations that are presented in user-friendly ways.

Catholic Pluralism Project

With these questions and concerns in mind, we assembled a research team consisting of clergy and laity of different theological stripes. That team designed a three-year research project that would provide Church leaders with an accurate description of the different ways that parishioners approach faith and morals, and would explain these variations in ways that would be useful to people in diocesan and parish ministry. Data collection concentrated on practicing Catholics, but we also compare parishioners to Catholics without parishes.

Leadership Team

The project was directed by James D. Davidson, professor of sociology at Purdue University. Andrea S. Williams served as the graduate research assistant, and Sherry Leuck as the office manager and project secretary. Each of Indiana's five bishops appointed a "diocesan advisor" who served as a liaison between the bishop and the project. Five "diocesan coordinators," all selected by the project director, headed up the collection and analysis of data from their respective dioceses. Five "independent advisors" were chosen by the director because of their expertise in Catholic theology, data collection, and/or data analysis. Fifteen of the 18 team members were Catholic; 14 were lay persons; three were Catholic priests; one was a Catholic sister. All but one of the team members lived in Indiana because the early stages of the project focused on Indiana's five dioceses. See Appendix A for a complete list of persons on the research team.

Members of the research team had a wide range of views about faith and morals. Some were quite conservative; others were more liberal. Rather than denying our personal theological differences, we put them to work for us (a decision which produced many very lively meetings!). We made sure that our research was informed by our different theological orientations and included questions reflecting these differences. We did not assume that pluralism was either good or bad; we differed on that. Instead, we assumed that, whether it is good or bad, it needs to be understood.

Faith and Morals

Figure 2.1 shows that "faith and morals" are the focal points of our analysis. We want to provide the most accurate data we can, showing what Catholics actually believe and how they actually practice their faith. We also want to document as precisely as we can the different ways in which Catholics understand moral issues. Another goal is to identify the social and religious antecedents which contribute to these differences. According to our theory, Catholics' orientations to faith and morals are shaped by

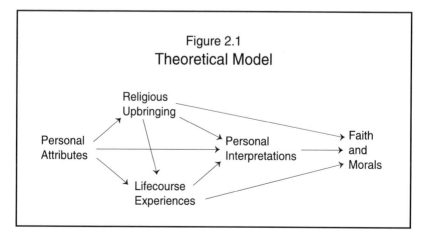

Figure 2.1
Theoretical Model

their "personal attributes," "upbringing," "lifecourse experiences," and "personal interpretations."

Faith

"Faith" encompasses Catholic doctrines about the supernatural and the Church. It also includes ideas which, though not necessarily taught by Church leaders, are rather widespread among lay Catholics. It also includes Catholic rituals and devotional practices. We distinguish between three types of beliefs and ideas (Ryba, 1994). Some beliefs, such as the Incarnation, the Resurrection, and Mary's role as the Mother of God, are considered "pan-Vatican II beliefs" because they were important before the Council and are just as important in Church teachings today. Other beliefs, such as belief in the Church as the "one true Church" and the need to obey Church teachings even when one doesn't understand them, were emphasized prior to Vatican II, but theologians and religious educators have not stressed them as much since then. We call these "pre-Vatican II beliefs." A number of other ideas were largely unheard of prior to the Council, but have become rather widespread in recent years. Some of these ideas (e.g., the ordination of women and the idea that one can be a good Catholic without attending Mass) are not considered Church teachings, but are held by some lay persons. We call these "recent ideas."

We also distinguish between three types of religious practices (Davidson, 1994b). "Pan-Vatican II practices" (e.g., Mass attendance, receiving Holy Communion) were emphasized prior to the Council and continue to be expected behaviors. "Pre-Vatican II practices" (e.g., saying the rosary, going to private confession) were normative during the 1940s and '50s but have been de-emphasized since Vatican II. Practices such as Bible reading and group penance have been emphasized more in the past 30 years than they were prior to the Council. That's why we call them "recent practices."

Morals

The concept of "morals" pertains to ethical norms of conduct. We consider two moral dimensions: sexual and reproductive ethics and social teachings.

The Church has specified positions on a whole range of sexual and reproductive issues (D'Antonio, Davidson, Hoge, and Wallace, 1996). In the pre-Vatican II Church, the emphasis was on natural law, stressing the intrinsic evil of abortion, birth control, premarital sex, and homosexual activity. Pope John Paul II has continued to emphasize the natural-law approach in recent encyclicals aimed at reaffirming Church teachings in these areas. However, in the wake of Vatican II, some theologians, parish priests, sisters, and religious educators have espoused a more "consequentialist" approach to sexual ethics. This approach interprets the rightness or wrongness of sexual acts in relation to the circumstances under which they occur and/or the effects they are likely to have on the persons involved. Thus, notwithstanding the pope's official teachings, post-Vatican II norms have down-played the natural-law approach to sexuality and stressed instead a greater appreciation of the effects that context has on our decisions regarding good and evil.

Social teachings comprise another dimension of Catholic moral thought (Burns, 1992; Fitzpatrick, 1991; Dorr, 1983; Holland and Henriot, 1983; Neal, 1990, 1987). These teachings concern the Church's role in society, especially with regard to issues of peace and social justice. Over the past 100 years, popes and bishops have published a long list of encyclicals and pastoral letters stating the Church's social teachings. These documents specify criteria for judging the morality of economic and political actions. They describe the Church's "preferential option for the poor." More specifically, they address topics such as business owners' responsibilities to provide workers with fair wages and benefits and workers rights to form unions. They examine the causes and consequences of poverty, its various manifestations (e.g., hunger and homelessness), and actions Catholics should take to remedy these problems. These documents are more prominent in Catholics' religious education since Vatican II than they were prior to the Council.

One of our goals is to learn to what extent American Catholics tend to agree or disagree with Church teachings in each of these areas. Agreement with Church teachings is a sign that the magisterium and "the people of God" share a Catholic worldview. Disagreement indicates the extent to which the magisterium and the laity are not on the same page at this point in American Catholic history. We make no assumptions about the spiritual maturity or immaturity of people who agree with Church teachings. Nor do we assume anything about the spiritual maturity or immaturity of people who disagree with official teachings. We leave such judgments to theologians and psychologists, who are far more qualified than we are to draw such conclusions.

Theoretical Framework

Figure 2.1 illustrates the theory we use to explain variations in Catholics' beliefs and practices.

Learning Theory

Learning theory calls attention to the processes by which people learn and the content of what they learn at various stages of their lives (Bandura, 1977; Lott and Lott, 1985; Lee, 1992). One way people learn is by imitating people they admire and want to be like. They also learn through reinforcement and rewards. People also learn through punishment; experiencing rejection is a painful way of learning what not to believe and how not to act. These processes occur throughout people's lives. Catholic children learn faith and morals from parents, relatives and friends, priests and sisters, and lay teachers. As they grow older, they learn from spouses, coworkers, parish and diocesan leaders, and persons whom they admire. Thus, Catholics' views of faith and morals at any given moment are, at least partly, the result of things they have learned to that point in life.

Self-concept Theory

This theory suggests that Catholics are not just products of their environment (Charon, 1989; Meltzer, Petra, and Reynolds, 1975; Rosenberg, 1981; Stryker, 1980; Stryker and Serpe, 1982; Turner, 1991; Wallace and Wolff, 1991; Wimberley, 1989). They are not just mirror images of the people around them. They interpret their experiences. They affirm certain aspects of their lives and reject others. They become their own persons; they develop a sense of "self"; they form their own identities. They also act according to these identities. Catholics' self-concepts shape their approaches to faith and morals. Persons with strong Catholic identities are more likely to comply with Church teachings than persons who do not attach as much importance to being Catholic.

Self-interest Theory

According to this theory, people tend to avoid settings, beliefs, and actions where costs outweigh benefits (Blau, 1964; Cook, 1987; Finke and Stark, 1992; Homans, 1974; Iannaccone, 1990; Lee, 1992; Turner, 1991; Wallace and Wolff, 1991; Willer and Anderson, 1981). They prefer situations in which benefits outweigh costs. Thus, Catholics are inclined to calculate the costs and benefits of being Catholic and shape their faith and morals accordingly. Catholics who feel they benefit a great deal from the Church relative to the sacrifices they make for it are likely to agree with Church teachings. Those who feel the costs far outweighf the benefits are less likely to conform to the Church's expectations.

These theories suggest that Catholics' faith and morals are partly the result of the ways in which they were raised and the kinds of experiences they have had over the course of their adult lives. They also are partly a product of Catholics' self-concepts and self-interests. The theories also suggest specific conditions which we need to consider at each stage of life. Thus, to explain how Catholics think and act today, we need to track the specific experiences they have had from birth to the present time.

Figure 2.1 indicates how we have done this. We assume individuals are born with a set of relatively ascribed qualities ("personal attributes") such as race, ethnicity, and sex. They also are born in particular years, making them members of different birth cohorts (a group of individuals born and raised in the same era). We distinguish between three cohorts. "Pre-Vatican II Catholics" were born in or before 1940; they were raised in the Church long before Vatican II. "Vatican II Catholics" were born between 1941 and 1960; they experienced the dramatic changes from the "old Church" to the "new Church" during their formative years. "Post-Vatican II Catholics" have grown up entirely in the wake of Vatican II. Since we were studying Catholics 18 years of age and older, we defined "post-Vatican II Catholics" as persons who were born between 1961 and 1977. (Williams and Davidson, 1996; D'Antonio, Davidson, Hoge, and Wallace, 1996.)

These personal attributes set people's lives in motion. They influence what is likely to happen to people during their childhood years. For example, pre-Vatican II Catholics raised in the 1930s and 1940s have shared social and religious experiences which set them apart from Vatican II Catholics, who are products of the 1950s and '60s, and post-Vatican II Catholics, who grew up in the 1970s and '80s.

We pay special attention to the way personal attributes affect people's "religious upbringing." We concentrate on the religious affiliations, beliefs, and practices of one's family and friends; closeness to parents; the nature of one's religious socialization at home, church, and school; and one's own religious beliefs and practices during childhood. Personal attributes and one's religious upbringing affect one's "lifecourse experiences." We examine adult Catholics' family lives, the religious beliefs and practices of their significant others, and their socioeconomic situations. We also address their social attitudes, focusing particular attention on their views about poverty and men's and women's roles in society. In addition, we consider the religious experiences they have had during their adult years. In particular, we explore their experiences of the holy and their awareness of Vatican II. These influences might affect Catholics' faith and morals directly, or they might have indirect effects through the next part of our model.

The fourth area in Figure 2.1 ("personal interpretations") includes self-concept theory's emphasis on personal identity. We pay special attention to the salience that Catholics attach to religion generally, to being Catholic, and to their parishes. The more committed Catholics are to their faith and their parishes, the more likely they are to embrace traditional Church teachings. The less they identify with their religious heritage, the less traditional they are likely to be with regard to faith and morals. Personal interpretations also include self-interest theory's emphasis on the costs and benefits of being Catholic. We examine the extent to which, and the ways in which, being Catholic has benefited people. We also consider what Catholics say about the costs and benefits of belonging to their particular parishes. The more Catholics stress the benefits of being Catholic, the more they are likely to be active in the Church and comply with its norms; the more they emphasize costs, the less active and less orthodox they are likely to be.

Methods

We started by interviewing individual Catholics, progressed to focus groups made up of parishioners from each of Indiana's five dioceses, and then did a statewide questionnaire survey of Indiana parishioners (see Appendix B for more details). After analyzing these results (Davidson, 1996, 1995, 1994b; Ryba, 1994; Lamanna, 1994; Weigert, 1994; Williams, 1994; Williams and Davidson, 1996), we conducted a national telephone poll.

This book is based largely on the national poll, but includes supplementary data and quotations from the other phases of our work. Our national sample included 1,058 persons 18 years of age and older who answered "Catholic" when asked: "What is your present religion, if any?" After persons were asked a series of questions about their religious beliefs and practices, they were asked: "Are you currently registered as a member of a Catholic parish near where you live?" Sixty-eight percent of all respondents said "yes." Thirty-one percent said "no"; one percent said "don't know." Persons who said "no" or "don't know" then were asked: "Is there one parish where you attend more often than any other?" Forty-seven percent of these respondents said "yes"; 52 percent said "no"; one percent said "don't know."

So, our first important finding is that two-thirds of those Americans who identify themselves as Catholics belong to parishes; one-third do not.[1] In chapters three through nine, we concentrate on the two-thirds of Catholics who are registered parishioners. These are the people diocesan and parish leaders are most likely to interact with on a regular basis. They also are the people who are likely to be the backbone of the Church in the years ahead. In Chapter 10, we examine the 31 percent of persons who say their present religion is Catholic but who are not registered with a parish. The results indicate that parishioners and Catholics without parishes have very different social characteristics and quite different orientations toward faith and morals.

Our analysis is based mainly on national data gathered at one point in time: between May and July 1995. Because we do not have longitudinal data, we cannot prove beyond a shadow of a doubt that one variable causes the other. However, we can establish the extent and nature of relationships between variables at the time of the study. We can indicate whether two variables tend to go hand in hand. In addition, the sequencing of variables in our theoretical model and the way we measure our key variables allow us to draw tenable conclusions about the effects variables have on one another.

Conclusions

In this chapter, we have specified a number of questions that Church leaders have about the increased pluralism in today's Church. Church leaders want accurate descriptions of the areas in which there is the most unity among Catholics and the spheres in which diversity tends to be most pronounced. They especially want data reflecting the beliefs and practices of Catholics who belong to parishes. For evangelization purposes, they also are interested in the characteristics of Catholics without parishes. They also want thoughtful analyses of the social and religious conditions which account for Catholics' different approaches to faith and morals. With these needs in mind, we designed a three-year study of the Catholic laity's orientations to faith and morals. One of our goals was to describe Catholics' beliefs and practices. Our other goal was to explain why some Catholics are more likely to agree with official Church teachings than others are. This book summarizes our findings.

3 • Faith and Morals
A Catholic Worldview?

I can understand the reasoning behind the Church's decisions. Therefore, it's easy for me to accept what the
Church teaches.

A respondent's comment
at the end of our questionnaire

I'm comfortable being a Catholic, but I have my own
mind and I don't believe in everything the Catholic
Church does.

A participant's comment
in one of our focus groups

In this chapter, we summarize parishioners' responses to our questions
about their faith and its moral implications. We begin with a review of
parishioners' religious beliefs and practices. After that, we turn to their
views about sexual and reproductive ethics and the Church's social teachings. We conclude the chapter with an analysis of the extent to which
these various dimensions of faith and morals comprise an integrated worldview.

Faith

We examine six components of faith: pan-Vatican II beliefs and practices, pre-Vatican II beliefs and practices, and recent ideas and practices.

Pan-Vatican II Beliefs

Doctrines such as the Trinity, Incarnation, and the Resurrection have been part of the Catholic tradition for centuries and remain essential Church teachings today. They were not subject to negotiation at Vatican II, nor were they changed. That's why we call them "pan-Vatican II" beliefs. They are still considered basics of the Catholic faith, just as they were before the Council. Pan-Vatican II beliefs are reaffirmed in the Nicene Creed at every Mass.

> We believe in one God, the Father, the Almighty,
>> maker of heaven and earth, of all that is seen and unseen.
>
> We believe in one Lord, Jesus Christ, the only Son of
>> God, eternally begotten of the Father, God from
>> God, Light from Light, true God from true God,
>> begotten, not made, one in Being with the Father.
>> Through him all things were made. For us men and
>> for our salvation
>>> he came down from heaven:
>
> by the power of the Holy Spirit
>> he was born of the Virgin Mary, and became man.
>
> For our sake he was crucified under Pontius Pilate; he
>> suffered, died, and was buried.
>> On the third day he rose again in fulfillment of the
>> Scriptures;
>> he ascended into heaven and is seated at the right
>> hand of the Father.
>> He will come again in glory to judge the living and
>> the dead,
>> and his kingdom will have no end.
>
> We believe in the Holy Spirit, the Lord, the giver of
>> life, who proceeds from the Father and the Son.
>> With the Father and the Son he is worshiped and
>> glorified.
>> He has spoken through the prophets.
>> We believe in one holy catholic and apostolic
>> Church.

> We acknowledge one baptism for the forgiveness of
> sins.
> We look for the resurrection of the dead, and the life of
> the world to come. Amen (*Catechism of the Catho-*
> *lic Church*, 1995:56-57).

Using the Nicene Creed as our guide, we included questions about the Trinity, the Incarnation, the Resurrection, Mary as the Mother of God, and Christ's presence in the Eucharist in our national telephone poll and our statewide questionnaire. Including questions about these issues is one of the things which sets our study apart from surveys which tend to overlook these beliefs and focus on issues of a more controversial nature.

Catholic parishioners attach considerable importance to all of the pan-Vatican II beliefs we examined. Ninety-two percent say that belief that "Mary is the Mother of God" is important to them personally. Ninety-two percent also say that belief that "Jesus was completely divine like God and completely human like us in every way except sin" is important. The same percentage of parishioners also report that belief that "Jesus physically rose from the dead" is salient to them. Eighty-eight percent attach real importance to belief that "In Mass, the bread and wine actually become the Body and Blood of Christ." Seventy-nine percent say that it is important to them that "There are three persons in one God."

In short, though pan-Vatican II beliefs are often overlooked in surveys and do not get much attention in news stories about American Catholics, they are a very salient dimension of faith for most parishioners.[1] The tendency for Catholics to value these beliefs suggests they are an important point of common ground among Catholics who may differ on other issues.

Pan-Vatican II Practices

Catholicism puts a lot of emphasis on religious practice — so much so that people in our interviews and focus groups were more likely to use the concept "practicing Catholic" than "believing Catholic" to describe a committed Catholic. Reflecting on their religious upbringing, they often said that "practicing" one's faith seemed more important than understanding it. When people think of Catholic practices, they think of attending Mass, receiving Holy Communion, praying privately, and attending Holy Days of Obligation. The Church stressed regular participation in these practices prior to Vatican II, and they remain normative today. That is why we call them "pan-Vatican II" practices. They are still used as indicators of the extent to which people are "practicing Catholics."

Catholics vary in their participation in these activities. Eighty-three percent of Catholics report praying privately at least once a week. Fifty-seven percent say they attend Mass at least once a week. Fifty-one percent attend Holy Days of Obligation regularly. Forty-eight percent receive Holy Communion at least once a week.

Pre-Vatican II Beliefs

In Chapter 1, we showed that the Church of the 1930s and '40s felt it was in a conflict relationship with American Protestantism. It viewed itself as "the one true Church" and Protestant faiths as purveyors of false doctrine. To produce as much unanimity as possible on Catholic teachings, Church leaders stressed hierarchal authority in areas of faith and morals and the laity's need to obey.

Bishops attending Vatican II did not totally reverse the Church's views on these matters, but they did make some important modifications. While reaffirming the truth of Catholic doctrines and the hierarchy's teaching authority, bishops reconsidered some of the Church's traditional emphases on authority and obedience. For example, they adopted a more ecumenical orientation toward other Christian faiths and reconceptualized the Church as "the people of God," placing more responsibility for faith in the hands of lay people.

Despite these official reinterpretations, we expected that traditional views of authority and obedience would persist among some older Catholics, and may have been passed on to a number of younger ones as well. Thus, we asked parishioners about three hallmarks of the pre-Vatican II Church: the Church as "the one true Church," the pope as the Vicar of Christ, and the laity's need to obey. Eighty-two percent of parishioners agree that "the Pope is the Vicar of Christ." Fifty-nine percent believe that "the Catholic Church is the one true Church." Fifty-two percent say "it's important to obey Church teachings even if I don't understand them." Thus, though the Church placed more emphasis on authority and obedience before the Council than it does these days, pre-Vatican II beliefs persist among a sizable number of Catholics.

Pre-Vatican II Practices

In addition to pan-Vatican II practices such as attending Mass and receiving Holy Communion, the Church offers lay people a variety of devotional opportunities to enhance their spiritual lives. In the 1930s, '40s, and '50s, the Church emphasized practices such as saying the rosary, starting and ending each day with prayer, practicing devotions to Mary and saints, and going to private confession. Many — though not all — of these practices were quite personal, could be done at home, and did not require much time or preparation. These practices were normative prior to Vatican II, but have not been emphasized as much since the Council. That's why we call them "pre-Vatican II" practices.

We wanted to see how widespread these practices are among today's Catholics, so we asked about them. Seventy-two percent of parishioners say they start and end the day with prayer at least once a week. However, only a minority of parishioners engage in other pre-Vatican II practices. Only 35 percent practice devotions to Mary or a special saint at least once a week; only 27 percent of Catholics pray the rosary at least once a week; and even fewer (25 percent) go to private confession several times a year.

Recent Ideas

In contrast to the Church's pre-Vatican II emphases on hierarchical authority and obedience, the post-Vatican II years have seen increased emphasis on freedom of conscience and personal responsibility for one's own faith. Authorization for greater freedom and individual responsibility is embedded in Council documents such as *Dignitatis Humanae*.

The post-Vatican II emphasis on freedom of conscience and personal responsibility has given rise to a number of new ideas, some of which are at odds with official Church teachings (D'Antonio, Davidson, Hoge, and Wallace, 1996). As Catholics have experimented with their new-found freedoms and responsibilities, some have questioned behavioral norms such as the need to attend Mass on a regular basis. Some people in our focus groups suggested that one can be a good Catholic without going to Mass. Questioning why the priesthood should be reserved for celibate males, some concluded that the Church ought to ordain women and married men.

Though ideas such as these were not authorized by the Council and are not promulgated by the pope or other Church officials, they have gained considerable attention in surveys, newspaper stories, and television reports about American Catholics. We felt it was important to find out how widespread these ideas are among parishioners. We examined two "recent ideas" in our national poll: one having to do with the need to attend Mass, the other concerning the ordination of women. Fifty-seven percent think "one can be a good Catholic without going to Mass." Fifty-seven percent also feel "women should be allowed to be priests."

Recent Practices

In the 1930s and '40s, Church leaders encouraged devotional activities such as rosaries and novenas. They did not encourage lay people to read the Bible or participate in Bible study, which were considered forms of Protestant spirituality. Things have changed in post-conciliar years. Church leaders have lessened their emphasis on traditional practices such as novenas and rosaries, and introduced a variety of new, scripture-oriented devotional activities. Catholics are now encouraged to read the Bible, participate in Bible study, and belong to prayer groups. Most of these practices — though not all — require preparation and meetings at church or in other people's homes. We call them "recent practices" to reflect the new-found emphasis the Church has given to these devotional forms.

Though Church leaders have urged Catholics to participate in scripture-oriented practices, not many parishioners are doing so. Twenty-two percent read the Bible at least once a week; only 14 percent attend prayer groups or faith sharing groups at least once a month; and only eight percent attend Bible study at least once a month. We suspect there are a number of reasons why so few Catholics participate in these practices, including the fact that they require more time and preparation than most pre-Vatican II practices.

To sum up, responses to our faith items fall into three clusters. There is considerable consensus on the pan-Vatican II beliefs we studied. The vast majority of Catholic parishioners embrace ideas such as the Incarnation and the Resurrection; relatively few parishioners deny the importance of such beliefs. There is more variation on pan-Vatican II practices, pre-Vatican II beliefs, pre-Vatican II practices, and recent ideas such as the ordination of women. On the average, for every one parishioner who accepts these ideas or participates in these practices, there is another one who does not. Finally, very few Catholics are attracted to recent practices such as Bible reading and prayer groups. These behaviors have not taken hold, at least not yet.

Morals

We also addressed two main areas of moral concern: sexual and reproductive ethics and the Church's social teachings.

Sexual and Reproductive Ethics

Burns (1992) has shown that, at least since the centralization of papal authority in the later nineteenth century, issues of sexual and reproductive ethics have been key elements in the hierarchy's concept of morality. Over the past century, popes have stressed a natural-law approach to sexual and reproductive issues, differentiating between behaviors which are "natural" (and therefore inherently right) and ones which are "unnatural" (hence, always wrong). In the natural order of things, according to the Church, couples should not have sexual intercourse until they are married. Though the Church has modified its traditional emphasis on procreation over conjugal love — now giving the two factors equal emphasis — it continues to teach that all acts of intercourse should permit the transmission of life, and that all pregnancies should be carried to term. Homosexual activity, premarital sex, artificial birth control, and abortion are considered unnatural and inherently wrong (Kosnik, et al., 1977; Fox, 1995; D'Antonio, Davidson, Hoge, and Wallace, 1996).

While these remain the Church's official teachings, a different view has gained some credence in recent years. This view — which we call "consequentialism" (Kelly, 1991; Ryba, 1994) — suggests that there is nothing intrinsically right or wrong about sexual and reproductive acts. Rather, their rightness or wrongness depends on the circumstances and their consequences for the persons involved. From this point of view, it is up to individuals to decide whether their actions are right or wrong.

To make sure our study addressed the Church's concerns about sexual and reproductive issues, we asked Catholics what they believe about premarital sex, the use of condoms and pills for birth control, abortion, and homosexual acts. To reflect both the natural-law and consequentialist approaches to these issues, we asked parishioners to select one of three possible responses: "Always wrong," "wrong except under certain circumstances," and "completely up to the individual."

Here's what we found, starting with the area where Catholics are most in agreement with the Church and ending where they tend to disagree with the Church most. Forty-one percent of parishioners agree with the Church's teaching that homosexual acts are always wrong. Three percent say such acts are wrong except under certain circumstances. Forty-six percent say the decision to engage in homosexual acts is entirely up to the individual.

Thirty-nine percent agree with the Church on abortion, saying it is always wrong. Thirty-three percent say abortion is wrong, but that it might be all right under certain conditions. Twenty-seven percent feel the decision to have an abortion is completely up to the individual.

Thirty-three percent of Catholics say premarital sex is always wrong. Nine percent say it is usually wrong, but might be acceptable under certain circumstances. Fifty-eight percent say it is up to the individual to decide whether premarital sex is right or wrong.

Only nine percent agree with the Church's view that use of condoms and pills for birth control is always wrong. Ten percent think it is wrong, but would tolerate it under limited circumstances. The vast majority (81 percent) of Catholics say it is strictly up to the individual.

Social Teachings

The Church also has well-established views about the morality of social, economic, and political conditions (Gremillion, 1976; Henriot,

DeBerri, and Schultheis, 1987; Neal, 1990; Fitzpatrick, 1991). Though rooted in scriptural texts about the charity, justice, and peace, the Church's modern social teachings date back to 1891, when Pope Leo XIII issued his encyclical *Rerum Novarum* on the rights and responsibilities of business owners and workers. Ensuing encyclicals such as Pius XI's *Quadragesimo Anno* and Pope John XXIII's *Mater et Magistra* elaborated the Church's concerns about the distribution of economic resources, access to political power, and the need to end violence and pursue peace. More recent encyclicals, such as *Laborem Exercens* (1981) and *Centesimus Annus* (1991), and the American bishops' pastoral letters on peace (1983) and economic justice (1986) are modern-day extensions of this tradition of social concern.

In our national telephone poll, we concentrated on the core issue of concern for the poor. This issue lies at the heart of the "preferential option for the poor" and most parish outreach programs. One item in our poll tapped the general principle of being concerned for the poor. It stated: "Helping needy people is an important part of my religious beliefs." Seventy-seven percent of parishioners strongly agree, and another 20 percent agree somewhat. Two percent disagree somewhat, and only one percent strongly disagree. Another item addresses a more concrete expression of social concern: "Catholics have a duty to try to close the gap between the rich and the poor." Parishioners views on this item are more diverse. Thirty-three percent of parishioners strongly agree; another 25 percent agree somewhat. Twenty-one percent disagree somewhat, and another 21 percent strongly disagree.

In short, sexual and reproductive issues are focal points of considerable diversity in today's Church. Approximately four out of 10 Catholics agree with Church teachings on homosexual acts and abortion, and almost as many believe that individuals, not the Church, must decide what is right or wrong with regard to these behaviors in any given set of circumstances. There is even more consensus among Catholics that individuals must make up their own minds about premarital sex and the use of artificial means of birth control; most parishioners disagree with the Church's teachings on these two issues. With regard to social teachings, there is considerable agree on the general principle of helping the needy, but more diversity among parishioners regarding the need to close the gap between the rich and poor.

Unity and Diversity: Another Look

Our next step is to combine these survey items into indices, or scales, summarizing parishioners' attitudes and behaviors (see Appendix C for the statistical relationships among items used in each index).[2] To simplify

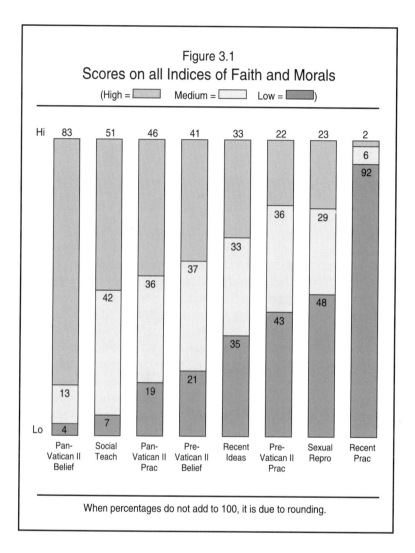

Figure 3.1
Scores on all Indices of Faith and Morals
(High = ▨   Medium = ☐   Low = ■)

When percentages do not add to 100, it is due to rounding.

presentation of the data, we divide each index into three equal segments: "high," "medium," and "low."[3] High scores indicate a clear tendency to accept beliefs and participate regularly in religious practices; medium scores indicate intermediate levels of belief or practice; low scores indicate a clear tendency to disagree with the ideas and not participate in the practices. Figure 3.1 indicates the extent of agreement and disagreement on each index.

The highest scores occur on our measure of pan-Vatican II beliefs. Eighty-three percent of Catholics attach a great deal of importance to beliefs such as the Trinity, the Incarnation, and the Resurrection; 13 percent do not give quite as much importance to them; and only four percent do not think of them as salient. Clearly, these beliefs represent a common ground of faith for most Catholics.

Next come three indices on which 41 to 51 percent of Catholics score high: social teachings, pan-Vatican II practices, and pre-Vatican II beliefs. Fifty-one percent of parishioners score high on our index of social teachings. Another 42 percent have medium scores; only seven percent score low. On the index of pan-Vatican II practices (measuring Mass attendance, reception of Holy Communion, and the frequency of private prayer), 46 percent score high, 36 percent score medium, and 19 percent seldom if ever engage in these practices. Forty-one percent embrace preconciliar emphases on authority and obedience; 37 have mixed feelings about these matters; and 21 percent tend to reject them.

These indices are followed by three others, where there is an even greater range of ideas and actions. Thirty-three percent of Catholics score high on our index of recent ideas such as ordaining women and not having to attend Mass. Another third of Catholics are not as convinced; and 35 percent disagree with such ideas. pre-Vatican II practices come next, with 22 percent of parishioners regularly engaging in traditional devotional practices, such as saying the rosary or starting and ending each day with prayer. Thirty-six percent do these things from time to time; and 43 percent hardly ever do them. Twenty-three percent score high on the index of sexual and reproductive ethics, indicating their agreement with the Church's natural-law approach to issue such as premarital sex and abortion. Twenty-nine percent are not as certain; and 48 percent are more inclined to say it is up to individuals to decide the rightness or wrongness of such behaviors.

The lowest scores of all are on recent practices. Only two percent of parishioners are actively involved in practices such as Bible study and prayer groups; six percent are somewhat active; and 92 percent seldom if ever participate in these devotional practices. Though these new forms of devotion have been promoted by Church leaders in the last 25-30 years, most Catholic lay people do not think of their faith in these terms.

Thus, unity is most evident on pan-Vatican II beliefs, such as the Incarnation and Mary as the Mother of God, which were not changed by Vatican II. Though there is some variation on these items, what is more impressive is the extent of parishioners' agreement on these beliefs. There is more diversity on other dimensions of faith and morals. Catholics have more diverse views on social teachings; pan-Vatican II practices such as Mass attendance and Holy Communion; and pre-Vatican II beliefs about tradition and obedience. Their views on recent ideas such as the ordination of women, pre-Vatican II practices such as the rosary, and sexual-reproductive ethics are even more diverse. It is interesting to note that there is more agreement on unauthorized ideas such as the ordination of women than there is on the Church's sexual and reproductive ethics. Finally, most Catholics have not responded to Church leaders' encouragement to participate in practices such as reading the Bible and participating in Bible study and prayer groups. Catholics are still more likely to engage in pre-Vatican II practices such as saying the rosary.

An Integrated Worldview?

Many theologically-inclined clergy and lay leaders talk of a Catholic worldview. The concept of a worldview suggests a system of ideas and actions forming a coherent whole and standing over against competing worldviews. It implies that beliefs and practices are based on a set of consistent principles and follow logically from one another. They are incompatible with beliefs and practices based on conflicting views, resulting in the rejection of these alternatives.

Whether there is such an integrated worldview at the level of Catholic doctrine is a matter of theological debate, not sociological inquiry. Our question is this: Does such an integrated worldview exist among Catholic parishioners? To what extent do Catholic parishioners who adhere to one set of beliefs also embrace others which are based on the same principles? To what extent do they reject views which express opposing principles? To what extent do they act in accordance with these views — participating in those rituals which are compatible with their beliefs and avoiding those which are not?

Previous research on individuals' religious beliefs and practices indicates that people's attitudes and actions tend to be rather loosely connected (Davidson, 1975; Davidson and Knudsen, 1977; Roberts and Davidson, 1984; Myers and Davidson, 1984; D'Antonio, Davidson, Hoge, and Wallace, 1989, 1996). Though there tends to be some order and continuity in their beliefs and practices, people are not strictly logical or meticulously consistent in their actions or beliefs. Human beings seem quite capable of expressing one idea while simultaneously holding onto another which seems rather inconsistent, or acting in ways which seem quite contrary to their attitudes.

The descriptive data we have presented so far also suggest that Catholics tend to accept some matters of faith and morals, without necessarily agreeing with others. They seem quite capable of valuing the Church's pan-Vatican II beliefs while, for example, disagreeing with its rule of ordaining only celibate males. They seem to accept the idea of helping the needy, but balk at the idea of closing the gap between the rich and poor. The data we have presented so far suggest that Catholics' beliefs and practices are either loosely integrated or, in some cases, may even be at odds with one another. Before we know for sure, we need to examine the relationships among our various measures of faith and morals.[4]

Faith

Four of the six dimensions of faith are rather tightly woven together (see Appendix D for statistics). Pan-Vatican II beliefs and practices tend to go hand and hand. Parishioners who say that beliefs such as the Incarnation and the Resurrection are important to them personally also tend to go to Mass and receive Holy Communion on a regular basis. Pre-Vatican II beliefs and practices also are quite compatible. Catholics who believe the Church is the one true Church and emphasize the importance of obedience also tend to say the rosary and regularly practice devotions to Mary or other saints. Finally, pan-Vatican II beliefs and practices also tend to correlate with pre-Vatican II beliefs and practices. Catholics who tend to embrace beliefs such as the Resurrection also tend to believe in the one true Church and say the rosary. Similarly, those who go to Mass most regularly also tend to adhere to traditional doctrines and participate in traditional devotional activities.

The correlations among these indices indicate a pattern of faith which we think of as "traditional beliefs and practices." People who tend to score high on the items in any one of these dimensions also tend to score high on the items in the others. The overlap is not 100 percent, but it is significant. Thus, in analyses which we report in upcoming chapters, we combine these four measures into one index of "traditional beliefs and practices" and avoid unnecessary repetitiveness.[5] Forty-six percent of parishioners score high on our index of traditional beliefs and practices; 45 percent have moderate scores; only nine percent score low (see Figure 3.2).

The four dimensions of "traditional beliefs and practices" correlate with recent practices. These findings suggest that rather traditional Catholics tend to accept the scripture-oriented forms of devotional life that have emerged in the post-Vatican II years. These results may be a bit surprising to those who assume that traditional Catholics are likely to oppose change, but they are not surprising to those who assume that traditional Catholics are open to any and all opportunities to deepen their faith.

The one dimension of faith which is at odds with all the others consists of recent ideas. As expected, Catholics who score "high" on traditional beliefs and practices tend to reject rather recent ideas such as ordaining women and not needing to attend Mass. The inclination to comply with traditional Church teachings fosters an unwillingness to accept ideas which are clearly at odds with Canon Law. Conversely, parishioners who are attracted to recent ideas conflicting with official Church teachings are not as inclined as other Catholics are to comply with traditional Church teachings, though they do not reject traditional ideas altogether.

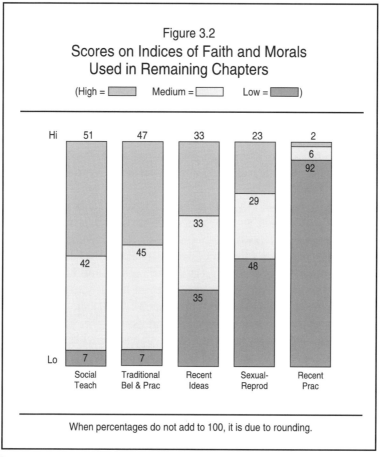

Figure 3.2
Scores on Indices of Faith and Morals
Used in Remaining Chapters

(High = ☐   Medium = ☐   Low = ☐)

	Social Teach	Traditional Bel & Prac	Recent Ideas	Sexual-Reprod	Recent Prac
Hi	51	47	33	23	2
					6
					92
				29	
			33		
		45			
	42			48	
			35		
Lo	7	7			

When percentages do not add to 100, it is due to rounding.

Morals

The late Cardinal Bernardin (Bernardin, 1984; 1988a; 1988b; 1988c; 1990) has suggested that Catholic morals can be thought of as a seamless garment held together by a consistent life ethic. This image of a seamless garment suggests a holistic view in which sexual-reproductive ethics and social teachings form an integrated whole the same way threads of different colors and textures combine to make a single sweater.

Our data show that there is some tendency for the two dimensions of morality to overlap (see Appendix D). Catholics who accept the Church's sexual and reproductive teachings also are inclined to accept its social teachings, and vice versa. However, the correlation is quite modest, indicating only about a seven-percent overlap between the two. Thus, Catholics who accept one set of moral norms tend to have widely varying views on the other, suggesting an ethical perspective that is loosely, rather than tightly, integrated.

Faith and Morals

There are rather significant relationships between five dimensions of faith and the Church's sexual and reproductive teachings. Catholics who are inclined to score "high" on pan-Vatican II beliefs and practices, pre-Vatican II beliefs and practices, and recent practices also tend to accept the Church's teachings on sexual-reproductive issues such as birth control and abortion. They also tend to agree with the Church's social teachings, though the connections between faith and social teachings are somewhat looser. Parishioners who are not as inclined to adhere to these five dimensions of faith also struggle with the Church's sexual and reproductive norms and its social teachings.

Recent ideas represent the one sphere of faith which is most at odds with the Church's sexual and social teachings. Catholics who question traditional issues of faith also question the Church's sexual and reproductive norms. They are also a bit more likely to question the Church's social teachings, though there is not a great deal of connection between these dimensions. It is those who reject unauthorized recent ideas such as ordaining women who tend to support the Church's sexual and reproductive ethics and, to a lesser extent, its social teachings.

Overall, these findings suggest a rather loosely integrated Catholic worldview. That worldview seems to be grounded in agreement with pan-Vatican II beliefs and practices, pre-Vatican II beliefs and practices, and to a lesser extent with recent practices. Agreement on these issues tends to be accompanied by agreement with the Church's sexual and social teachings, though the overlap among these dimensions is often modest.

A sizable minority of parishioners do not feel compelled to accept traditional norms about ordination and the obligation to attend Mass. While they dissent on these issues, they do not reject the Church and all it stands for. They are more likely to agree with the Church on some matters (e.g., the Church's social teachings) than to agree with its views on others (e.g., sexual and reproductive ethics).

For the most part, then, Catholic parishioners seem to be faithful people who develop a variety of beliefs and practices as they live out their lives in the context of a Catholic Church situated in an American culture. As Wilkes (1996: xvi) has noted, the "vast majority of Catholics . . . find themselves at odds with certain teachings and practices of the Church, but are unable to stay away from what has been the single most formative influence in their lives."

It seems more accurate to conclude that parishioners share a rather loosely integrated worldview than to say they are sharply polarized around conflicting worldviews.[6]

Conclusions

Pan-Vatican II beliefs are the area of greatest unity among Catholics. Church leaders are not creating controversies around these central faith issues; and, regardless of their views on other matters, the laity are not quarreling with the Church over these matters. As a result, researchers are not attracted to them, and people in the media hardly ever cover them. Though they don't attract much attention, they are a crucial dimension of faith for Catholics. They are the single most important basis of Catholic unity. They are the issues on which Catholics agree most. They are the glue that holds Catholics together. They are the reason why Catholics remain loyal to the Church, even when they disagree with it on other matters.

Social teachings represent another area of common ground. Most Catholics embrace the principle of concern for the poor. Parishioners may disagree on specific social policies, but very few reject the Church's emphasis on a "preferential option for the poor."

Pan-Vatican II practices and pre-Vatican II beliefs are other spheres of convergence. Close to half of parishioners score "high" on these indices, and about one-third score "medium." Though there are important variations in pan-Vatican II practices, Catholics link their faith to practices such as prayer, Mass attendance, and Holy Days of Obligation. Though Catholics certainly do not agree on all matters of authority and obedience, they respect the Church's role as teacher and the laity's need to take Church teachings into account.

Variations are more pronounced in the areas of recent ideas, pre-Vatican II practices, and sexual and reproductive ethics. Because the laity's views in some of these areas — especially recent ideas and sexual-reproductive ethics — are often at odds with official Church teachings, they are flash points of conflict between the Vatican and the laity. Because they are areas of tension between the hierarchy and the people, they also attract the attention of researchers and members of the media.

For many Catholics, these are hotly contested, but are not essential, components of faith. Agreement on pan-Vatican II beliefs — and, to a lesser extent, social teachings, pan-Vatican II practices, and pre-Vatican II beliefs — allows many Catholics to quarrel over other flashpoint issues without becoming schismatic. It's as if accepting teachings such as the Incarnation and practices such as Mass attendance gives them permission to fight over other issues, the same way family members know they will always "be family" even when they disagree about specific issues. Other Catholics feel these areas of great debate also are of great significance. Their loyalty to the Church hinges on these issues. Though some Catholics attach so much importance to these issues that they have threatened to leave the Church if the issues are not resolved to their satisfaction, some recent research suggests that such defections are not likely to occur (Donahue, 1995).

The area where Catholics score lowest of all is post-Vatican II practices. Despite Church leaders' efforts to institutionalize practices such as Bible reading, Catholics have been slow to embrace them. Parishioners are not inclined to think of these forms of devotion when they think of practicing their faith.

When we examine the relationships among these spheres of faith and morals, we see that four areas (pan-Vatican II beliefs and practices, and pre-Vatican II beliefs and practices) cluster together rather nicely, forming a relatively distinct pattern of traditional belief and practice. If there is an integrated worldview among today's Catholics, these are its core elements. That is why, in upcoming chapters, we combine these four indices into an overall measure of "traditional beliefs and practices." These traditional beliefs and practices are loosely connected to Catholics' sexual and reproductive ethics and their views of the Church's social teachings. They are negatively linked to recent ideas and practices, which seem like theological particles that parishioners have difficulty attaching to other elements of their Catholic worldview.

In the remaining chapters, our goal is to explain why Catholics have such different beliefs and practice their faith in such diverse ways. We begin with the "personal interpretations" part of our theoretical model. In Chapter 4, we examine the extent to which Catholics' religious self-concepts and their self-interests affect their approaches to faith and morals.

4 • Self-concept and Self-interest
Bases of Faith and Morals

> [Most] of the time people's beliefs and actions express both their self-concepts and benefits received from involvement in social groups. Most of the time they are linked to people's identities and self-interests.
> *Davidson and Pyle (1994:184)*

Now that we have described the different ways in which Catholics orient themselves to faith and morals, our main task is to account for these variations. Why do some Catholics embrace the Church's official teachings, while others spurn them? Why are some active in the Church, while others do almost nothing? Why do some engage in private devotional activities, such as saying the rosary or reading the Bible, while others do not? Why do some agree with the Church's social teachings, while others vehemently disagree? What social and religious conditions produce such different patterns of faith and such different approaches to the Church's moral stances?

Theoretical Framework

We begin our search for answers to these questions in the "personal interpretations" cell of the theoretical model we outlined in Chapter 2. According to our theory, Catholics' orientations to faith and morals are at least partly explained by their religious self-concepts and their self-interests.

Self-concepts

All Catholics have some sense of who they are religiously. In their interactions with family members, friends, and church leaders, they formulate religious identities. They think about who they are, who they want to be like, and who they don't want to be like. They create a sense of self. For example, they choose to think of themselves as more or less religious. They decide whether they are good Catholics or not. They come to think of their parishes as relatively important, or relatively unimportant, parts of their lives.

Here are some comments Indiana parishioners made about their religious identities:

> I was born, raised, and always will be a Catholic.

> We were different. We were special.

> I grew up as a Catholic and now I joined the military and haven't been going to church much but I still consider myself Catholic. My dogtags say I am.

> I feel like I am a representative of my church out there in the community.

> I've thought about becoming an Episcopalian but have decided to be part of the loyal opposition.

> [I used to be Catholic] because my parents baptized me Catholic. . . . Right now I'm Catholic because I have chosen to continue in the faith that I was baptized into.

> I'm old, fat, bald-headed, black, and a Catholic.

> I am a good person and a Catholic. I guess that makes me a good Catholic.

It's not so important that a person be a good Catholic. It's more important to me that a person be a good Christian.

I was born Catholic. I didn't choose.

Self-interests

Catholics also think about the costs and benefits of being Catholic. They think about the price they have paid (not just in terms of money) and the advantages they have gained. They ask questions such as the following: To what extent have I received a sound moral foundation? Has the Church contributed to my education in any way? Does it help me with my spiritual needs? To what extent does it help me in my family life and at my job? Have I met my friends through the Church? Do I get anything out of being Catholic? How much time and money should I give to the Church?

Here's what a few Indiana Catholics said about the costs of being Catholic:

After Vatican II, I quit going to church because it seemed so foreign to everything familiar that I had grown up with. The music was impossible to sing. I couldn't find my place in the missal. I spent the whole Mass turning pages and came out so mad I thought it was better to stay home.

I have never become "involved" with the Church because I've always felt that once they had you to do the volunteer work, they just kept sucking you in for more. I found this to be true from my mother's experiences. Therefore, I have steered away from becoming active.

The church and parish have made me feel discriminated against because of my low income.

Pardon me, but I'm not going to pay for a babysitter so I can go to Mass.

Other Catholics talked about the benefits they derive from being in the Church. Here are just two examples:

I am proud to be a Catholic. I was raised a Baptist and I feel there is no greater strength than the Catholic church. I feel great unity and acceptance in my Catholic church which I did not feel as a Baptist.

> I never thought of the Church having a negative effect on
> my life.

Though we can make a rather sharp conceptual distinction between
self-concept and self-interest, the two are often closely related. The connection between identity and benefits is evident in some comments made
by Indiana Catholics:

> My parish: that's my spiritual home.

> It's not so much the church playing a role in my life; it's
> me playing a role in the church.

> I could be happy in a lot of different churches.

> The Catholic Church is a place to call home.

> It's my parish. It's my church. I've been through three
> superintendents. They go and I stay here. I've been
> through three, four, five priests. They go and I stay here.

Catholics act on the basis of these interpretations. As they formulate a
sense of who they are, they tend to act in accordance with their religious
identities. The more they think of themselves as good Catholics, the more
they are likely to choose beliefs and practices that are consistent with
Church teachings. As they calculate costs and benefits of being Catholic,
they also tend to act accordingly. The more they feel they benefit from
being Catholic, the more likely they are to agree with Church doctrines
and behavioral expectations.

These theoretical propositions guide our analysis in this chapter. First,
we report parishioners' answers to a set of questions about their religious
identities and the benefits they associate with being Catholic. Then, we
examine the relationships between Catholics' self-concepts and self-interests and each of our six dimensions of faith and morals. On the basis of that
analysis, we combine self-concepts and self-interests into a more general
measure of parishioners' commitment to the Church. Finally, we show how
commitment to the Church relates to each dimension of faith and morals.

Self-concept and Self-interest:
A Descriptive Overview

Here's what parishioners in our national poll said in response to our
questions about their religious self-concepts and self-interests.

Self-concept

We used four items to measure self-concept (see Appendix E). There was a close connection between items tapping a general religious identity (e.g., "How religious are you now?") and ones relating more specifically to Catholic identity (e.g., "I cannot imagine being anything other than Catholic"). That's why we combined all four items into an overall index of religious self-concept.

Seventy-nine percent of parishioners say "my parish is an important part of my life"; only 21 percent disagree with that statement. Seventy percent say "I cannot imagine myself being anything other than Catholic"; only 30 percent disagree. Sixty-four percent reject the idea that "I could be just as happy in some other church; it wouldn't have to be Catholic"; 36 percent agree with that idea. Finally, we asked: "How religious would you say you are now?" Thirty percent say "very religious"; 41 percent say "fairly religious"; and 29 percent say "somewhat" or "not very religious."

Self-interest

Next, we asked two questions about the benefits of being Catholic, five others dealing with parishioners' satisfaction with their parishes, and two about the extent to which parishioners feel they have a stake in the Church. Overall, parishioners feel that being Catholic works to their advantage.

Ninety-four percent say "being Catholic has given me a solid moral foundation"; only six percent disagree. Seventy-three percent say "there is something special about being Catholic which you can't find in other religions"; 27 percent disagree. These two items are combined into a measure of the benefits Catholics feel they derive from being Catholic (see Appendix E).

We also asked respondents to evaluate their parishes on five dimensions: "friendliness of the people"; "quality of the homilies or sermons"; "quality of the music at Mass"; "meeting your spiritual needs"; and "helping you make decisions in work or family." Respondents were asked to rate their parishes as excellent, good, fair, or poor on each dimension. Responses indicate high levels of parish satisfaction. Eighty-five percent of Catholics rate their parishes as excellent or good in terms of friendliness. Eighty percent are satisfied with the homilies or sermons. Seventy-eight percent rate their parishes as excellent or good in meeting their spiritual needs. Seventy-three percent like the music at Mass. Sixty-five percent say their parishes are excellent or good when it comes to helping them with daily decisions in work or family.

We also wanted to find out how much of a stake parishioners feel they have in the Church. Sixty percent of parishioners say "I give more than my fair share of money to the church"; 40 percent disagree. Forty-two percent say "I donate a lot of time to the church"; 59 percent disagree. Overall, then, approximately half of parishioners (42 to 60 percent) feel they have a stake in the Church; the other half do not.

These feelings of having a stake in the Church correlate with parishioners' actual donations. When we examine the relationship between respondents' judgments about their financial contributions and their actual giving, we find that the two are positively related.[1] Fifty percent of parishioners who feel they give more than their fair share of money to the Church give $600 or more, whereas only 36 percent of those who do not feel they give their fair share give $600 or more. Thus, we built a two-item index of how much Catholics feel they have a stake in the Church (see Appendix E), knowing that it tends to reflect parishioners' actual contributions.

Relationships with Faith and Morals

As expected, all four measures have sizable and similar effects (see Appendix F). They all increase the tendency to accept traditional beliefs and practices, engage in recent practices such as Bible reading, and agree with the Church's moral teachings. Adherence to Church values and norms is highest among parishioners who have the strongest Catholic identities, feel they have benefited from being Catholic, are the most satisfied with their parishes, and invest the most time and money in the Church. Disagreement with the Church's views is most widespread among parishioners who only weakly identify with the Church, do not feel they have benefited from the Church, are unhappy with their parishes, and feel they have little or no stake in the Church.

Strong religious self-concepts and self-interests also stifle tendencies toward the dissident ideas included in our measure of recent ideas. The tendency to accept recent ideas that are at odds with Church teachings is greatest among parishioners who have difficulty identifying with the Church, see few advantages to being Catholic, feel they get very little out of their parishes, and do not feel heavily invested in the Church.

Commitment to the Church

There is a positive relationship between self-concept and self-interest.[2] The stronger one's Catholic identity, the more likely one is to benefit from being in the Church; and, the more one benefits from being Catholic, the more one tends to identify with the Church. We also have shown that self-concept and self-interest have similar effects on parishioners' approaches to faith and morals. The more parishioners think of themselves as strong Catholics and the more they benefit from being Catholic, the more they tend to accept Church teachings on faith and morals, and the less likely they are to embrace recent ideas such as the ordination of women or not needing to attend Mass on a regular basis. Weaker religious identities and a lack of benefits go hand and hand with lower levels of adherence and higher levels of dissent.

With these findings in mind, we combined the two strongest items in our self-concept index with the two items in the self-interest index measuring parishioners' stake in the Church. Together, these four items form an excellent index of parishioners' overall commitment to the Church (see Appendix E). Here's the breakdown on parishioners' commitment: 38 percent "high"; 44 percent "medium"; 18 percent "low."

When we examine the link between parishioners' commitment to the Church and their beliefs and practices, we see even more clearly how commitment affects parishioners' faith and morals (see Table 4.1). The more parishioners are committed to the Church, the more they think and act in accordance with its norms. The less committed they are the less active they are, and the more willing they are to disagree with Church teachings.

Seventy-seven percent of all parishioners who are highly committed to the Church adhere strongly to traditional beliefs such as the Incarnation and participate regularly in traditional practices such as Mass attendance, receiving Holy Communion, and saying the rosary. Thirty-nine percent of those who score "medium" in commitment to the Church comply with its traditional approach to faith. Only five percent of those who don't think of the Church as important abide by its traditional beliefs and practices.

Commitment also fosters agreement with the Church's sexual and reproductive ethics. Forty-four percent of Catholics scoring "high" in commitment strongly agree with the Church's sexual teachings, compared to only 12 percent of those scoring "medium," and only four percent of those scoring "low." Agreement with the Church's social teachings also increases with commitment. Highly committed parishioners are almost twice as likely to accept the Church's social teachings (63 percent) as are parishioners who score "low" in commitment (35 percent).

As we indicated earlier, very few Catholics are highly involved in practices such as Bible reading and attending Bible study classes. Therefore, to get a more stable picture, we cross-tabulated commitment with a combination of "high" and "medium" scores on our recent practices index. The results indicate that commitment also leads Catholics to participate in these practices, though to a lesser extent. Thirteen percent of parishioners who are highly committed to the Church are at least somewhat active in post-Vatican II devotional activities. On the other hand, among

Table 4.1
Faith and Morals by Commitment to the Church
(percent)

Commitment	Faith			Morals	
	Traditional Beliefs/ Practices	Recent Ideas	Recent Practices	Sexual/Rep. Ethics	Social Teachings
	(High)	(High)	(High,Med)	(High)	(High)
High	77	19	13	44	63
Medium	39	34	5	12	44
Low	5	59	4	4	35
r=	.53	-.36	.13	.39	.23

those Catholics with little or no commitment to the Church, only four percent engage in these forms of spiritual life.

While commitment is positively associated with these four dimensions of faith and morals, it is negatively linked with recent ideas. Catholics low in commitment are most inclined to accept dissident beliefs such as the ordination of women (59 percent). Among those with "medium" levels of commitment, 34 percent agree with such ideas. Among the most highly committed parishioners, only 19 percent accept ideas such as not needing to attend Mass to be a good Catholic.

Though commitment is a very strong influence, one must be careful not to overstate the positive link between commitment and adherence to Church teachings. Even among those who are most committed, there is some variation in belief and practice. Though only two percent of parishioners scoring "high" in commitment do not accept the Church's traditional beliefs and practices, 31 percent don't agree with its sexual-reproductive ethics, 33 percent disagree with its social teachings, and 74 percent do not engage in the devotional activities it has been promoting since the Council. Conversely, while 53 percent of the most committed tend to reject recent ideas such as the ordination of women, 19 percent of the most Church-oriented Catholics score "high" on this index (another 28 percent score "medium"). Clearly, commitment to the Church enhances compliance with its teachings, but it does not preclude dissent.

Four Case Studies

To illustrate the complex relationship between commitment and the way Catholics approach faith and morals, we want you to meet four people from our statewide survey of Indiana Catholics. *Fatima* is highly committed and tends to comply with Church teachings. *Brandon* also is a committed Catholic, but he disagrees with many more of the Church's views on faith and morals. *Dinah* is not as committed as either Fatima or Brandon, but her views of faith and morals are generally in accordance with Church teachings. *Elizabeth* is neither committed nor in compliance with Church teachings.

Fatima

Fatima is a 46-year-old woman of Puerto Rican descent. She was born and raised in Indiana. She was raised by both her mother and father and was quite close to both of her parents. Her mother is still alive; her father is not. Neither of her parents went to high school. Her mother has been a homemaker; her father was a blue-collar worker. Her mother is Catholic; her father was not.

Religion was more important to Fatima's mother than it was to her dad. Her mom went to Church about once a month; her dad seldom if ever went. Neither her mother nor her father talked to her very much about religion. She was never encouraged to be nun, and never gave it serious thought. As a child, Fatima went to Mass and received Holy Communion on a regular basis. She also went to confession, had religious education classes, and said her prayers. She says she was fairly religious. She says her religious upbringing was very positive, giving her parish especially high marks.

Fatima attended public grade school and public high school. She still lives in her hometown and still has the same best friend she had when she was 18 years old. She has never married. She has a white-collar job that pays between $15,000 and $20,000 per year.

Fatima is quite committed to the Church. She says she cannot imagine being anything but Catholic. She describes herself as fairly religious and says her parish is an important part of her life. She also says attending Mass on a weekly basis and contributing to the Church financially are important parts of her personal religious outlook. She gives $100 to $500 a year to the Church.

Fatima is quite traditional in her approach to faith and morals. She believes the Catholic Church is the one true Church, and wishes it put more emphasis on tradition. She says it is very important to obey Church teachings even when she doesn't understand them. She fully accepts doctrines about heaven, hell, the Trinity, and the Real Presence. She believes that suffering is God's way of testing our faith. Although quite traditional, she likes the post-Vatican II practice of drinking from the common cup at Mass. She opposes the recent idea of ordaining women and is not sure she likes the idea of ordaining married men.

She believes, as the official Church does, that abortion and artificial birth control are always wrong. She also thinks that premarital sex is usually wrong. She is not sure what to think about homosexuality and euthanasia. With regard to social teachings, she says helping the poor and ending racism, sexism, and other forms of injustice are very important to her personally.

Brandon

Brandon is a 24-year-old white male whose ethnic background is German. Both of his parents went to high school. His dad has a blue-collar job; his mother's is white-collar. He was close to both of his parents, especially his mother.

He was raised in a largely Catholic town in Indiana, and his whole family was Catholic — both of his parents and all of his grandparents.

Religion was more important to his mom than it was to his dad. His mother attended Mass weekly; his father went two or three times a month. His mother talked with him about religion frequently; his dad did sometimes, but not as often. Although they talked about religion, Brandon doesn't recall ever being encouraged to consider the priesthood, and he says he never really gave it serious thought.

In his childhood years, Brandon went to Mass and received Holy Communion weekly. He also attended Holy Days of Obligation on a regular basis. He says he was fairly religious. He reports that his religious upbringing was very positive and that his family approved of his religious beliefs and practices.

Brandon attended both Catholic and public schools. He is a high school graduate, and has a white-collar job that pays him between $10,000 and $15,000 per year. He is still single. He lives in the same town he grew up in; still lives in the same neighborhood; and attends the same parish. Both of his parents are still alive.

Brandon has a strong Catholic identity and donates both time and money to the Church. He says he cannot imagine himself being anything other than Catholic. His parish is important to him, and he is somewhat active in its social life, religious education programs, and social outreach activities. He feels it is important to attend Mass regularly, which he does. Though he gives less than $100 a year, he says it is important to support the Church financially.

And although he is committed to the Church, he is not nearly as traditional as Fatima. He agrees with some teachings, but is more likely than Fatima to disagree with what the Church has to say about faith and morals. For example, he accepts doctrines about heaven, hell, and the Trinity, but he does not believe that the bread and wine used at Mass actually become Christ's Body and Blood. He does not believe the Catholic Church is the one true Church. Nor does he think he should obey Church teachings if he doesn't understand them. He says he needs to exercise his own conscience. He is not sure what to think about papal infallibility. He objects when people refer to God as "Her," but he thinks both women and married men ought to be ordained. He has mixed feelings about using the common cup at Mass.

With regard to sexual teachings, he does not accept the Church's teaching that abortion, homosexuality, premarital sex, and artificial birth control are always wrong, but he thinks they usually are. He is not sure whether euthanasia is right or wrong. Brandon seems more convinced of the Church's social teachings. He says helping the poor and working to end racism, sexism, and other injustices are very important to him personally, but he is not especially actively involved in social concerns.

Dinah

Dinah is a 43-year-old African-American female. She was born in Indiana and raised by her parents. Her mother is a high school graduate and homemaker. Her father went to grade school and is a blue-collar worker.

Neither of Dinah's parents was Catholic, so she was not raised in the Church. Although not Catholic, both of her parents thought religion was important. They attended worship services on a regular basis, and because she was very close to both parents, they talked with Dinah about religion quite frequently. She says she was fairly religious and tended to be rather conservative in her faith as a child. Her parents approved of her religious outlook.

Dinah went to public grade school, public high school, and a state-supported college. With her college degree, she has gone on to a professional career, which pays her $20,000 to $30,000 a year. She is separated from her husband and has a five-year-old child. She still lives in her hometown, though she no longer lives in her old neighborhood. Her mother is still alive, but her father has passed away.

Dinah is now Catholic and considers herself quite religious. She says she often talks to God and often listens to Christian music on the radio. She says that she cannot imagine being anything but Catholic and that her parish is an important part of her life. But she is not as highly committed to the Church as either Fatima or Brandon. She says it is not important to attend Mass every weekend, and she doesn't. She is not very active in her parish. She does not attach much importance to supporting the Church financially and didn't give any money to the Church in 1993.

Although her commitment to the Church is somewhat limited, her beliefs and practices tend to coincide with Church teachings. She believes in heaven and hell. She believes there are three persons in one God and that the bread and wine used at Mass actually become the Body and Blood of Christ. She accepts the idea of papal infallibility. She does not accept the idea of ordaining women, though she thinks it would be good if married men were allowed to be priests. She thinks it is important to read the Bible, though she doesn't do so very often. She says premarital sex, abortion, and euthanasia are always wrong or usually wrong. She's not sure whether homosexuality is right or wrong, and — contrary to Church teachings — she believes people should use condoms and pills for birth control. With regard to social teachings, she says helping the poor and ending racism, sexism, and other injustices are extremely important to her personally, and they are. She is actively involved in social concerns, though not through her parish.

Elizabeth

Elizabeth is a 54-year-old white female. She was born and raised in Indiana. Her ethnic ancestry is part English and part Italian. Her parents are high school graduates. Her father has a blue-collar job, while her mother's is white-collar.

Her mother's side of the family is all Catholic. Her father's side doesn't belong to any particular church. Although religion was only somewhat important to her mother, and not at all important to her dad, her mother saw to it that Elizabeth was raised a Catholic. Elizabeth's mom sometimes talked to her about religion; her father never did. As a child, Elizabeth attended church and received Holy Communion regularly. Her family and friends never encouraged her to become a nun, but she thought about it. She says she was quite religious and rather conservative back then. When she assesses her religious upbringing, she says it was neither especially positive, nor especially negative.

Elizabeth attended Catholic grade school and public high school. She went to a publicly supported college, but never graduated. She has moved away from her hometown, her neighborhood, her parish, and her child-hood friends. She is married to a relatively active and rather traditional Catholic. She has three children, all in their early twenties now. She and her husband have white-collar jobs and a family income of $70,000 to $80,000 a year.

She is not very committed to the Church. She says she can imagine belonging to another faith. She says she is not very religious, and her parish is not important to her. She's not involved in any of its programs or activities. She doesn't think it is important to attend Mass, and doesn't feel any obligation to support the Church financially. She gives no money to the Church.

In terms of faith and morals, Elizabeth and the Church are not on the same page. Elizabeth rejects the concept of the Real Presence; does not believe there is a hell; does not believe in papal infallibility; disagrees with the idea that the Catholic Church is the one true Church; and hardly ever attends Mass or receives Holy Communion. She is not sure whether there is a heaven; nor is she sure whether there are three persons in one God. She rejects the idea of obeying teachings she doesn't understand; she says it is extremely important to follow her own conscience. She approves of ordaining both women and married men. She disagrees with the Church's sexual and reproductive ethics. Instead, she feels that abortion, homosexuality, artificial birth control, premarital sex, and euthanasia are quite acceptable. In terms of social teachings, she says ending social injustices such as racism and sexism is extremely important, but she does not attach much personal importance to helping the poor.

Conclusions

This chapter yields three important conclusions, each having its own implications for parish and diocesan leaders.

First, though we can make a rather clear conceptual distinction between religious self-concept on the one hand and religious self-interest on the other, in the real world the two tend to go hand and hand. Parishioners with the strongest Catholic identities also are likely to feel they gain from being part of the Church; those who feel they have benefited from being Catholic are inclined to think of themselves as Catholic. People who do not identify with the Church also do not feel they derive as many benefits from being Catholic; those who don't feel they've gained much from being Catholic don't attach much importance to being in the Church.

Our experience has been that when Church leaders examine the reasons behind parishioners' approaches to faith and morals, they are more inclined to think in terms of self-concepts than self-interests. Church leaders are more likely to talk about people's religious identities than the costs and benefits people associated with involvement in the Church. Identity and self-concept tend to be seen as legitimate and noble motivations; self-interests are often viewed as inappropriate and selfish considerations that should discouraged.

We share the idea that identity is a valid consideration when examining the bases of faith and morals. Self-concepts are one reason why parishioners and Church leaders alike choose to act in certain ways and not in others. But, we warn against the view that self-interest is not a legitimate consideration. Whether Church leaders like to admit it or not, they — like most parishioners — prefer ideas and actions that work to their advantage over ones that do not. Though people are sometimes motivated by self-sacrifice, they are more likely to act on the basis of what they consider to be in their best interest. Thus, when assessing the reasons why parishioners think and act as they do, Church leaders would be wise to treat self-interests as legitimate considerations, along with self-concept.

Second, there is a strong and consistent relationship between commitment to the Church and a tendency to embrace its teachings and behavioral norms. Commitment turns out to be one of the strongest influences in our whole analysis. When parishioners have strong Catholic identities and feel they have a stake in the Church, they are highly motivated to support the worldview it promotes. This is illustrated by our profile of Fatima. When being Catholic is not important to people and they do not feel they have any reason to invest their time and money in the Church, they do not feel as obligated to accept its doctrines and codes of conduct. Our case study of Elizabeth exemplifies this pattern.

These findings are consistent with our theory that people act in accordance with both their identities and their interests. They confirm our hypothesis that Catholics' self-concepts and self-interests affect their approaches to faith and morals. They also have two important implications for Church leaders. First, they offer one possible explanation for why there is so much dissent in the Church today: many parishioners lack strong Catholic identities and do not feel they benefit much from being in the Church. Parishioners who lack Catholic identities and have little or no stake in the Church have little reason to support the Church's approach to faith and morals. The second implication is that Church leaders who stress a general Christian identity over a specifically Catholic self-concept and are unwilling to address parishioners' self-interests will tend to foster increased levels of disagreement with Church teachings. Leaders who encourage specifically Catholic identity and find ways to increase parishioners' feeling that they have a stake in the Church will promote compliance with Church teachings.

Finally, the correlation between commitment and agreement with the Church is by no means perfect. There are Catholics, such as Brandon, who are committed to the Church but disagree with many of its teachings and morals stances. Likewise, parishioners such as Dinah are less committed but tend to accept what the Church says about faith and morals.

These seemingly paradoxical findings lead to several questions. For example, why are some people more committed to the Church than others? What experiences in one's early years and later on in one's lifecourse lead some people to see the Church as important, while others do not? Also, why do some highly committed parishioners accept Church teachings, while others do not? Why do some committed Catholics disagree with its teachings, while some who are less committed tend to accept them?

To answer these questions we need to explore other parts of our theory. We begin that exploration in the next chapter, where we examine parishioners' lifecourse experiences and the effects they have on Catholics' approaches to faith and morals.

5 • Lifecourse Experiences
Their Effects on Faith and Morals

I am more spiritual now than when I was younger. Also, I am more interested in what being a Catholic is about than ever before. Maturity has a lot to do with this.

An Indiana parishioner

My husband and I are dependent on Social Security and have a lot of health problems and are not able to do what we would like to toward being active in our church. We're doing a lot of suffering.

An Indiana parishioner

Catholics have all sorts of lifecourse experiences. Some marry and have children; others do not. Some remain happily married, while others end up in nasty divorces. Some enjoy good health; others suffer. Some are in high-paying, white-collar careers, while others are in blue-collar jobs and earn much less money. Some feel God is watching over them; others have little or no sense of God's presence in their lives.

Our theory suggests that these lifecourse experiences affect the way Catholics approach faith and morals. According to learning theory, lifecourse experiences foster relationships with different types of people, some of whom become so significant that they shape the way people think about life. According to self-concept theory, these experiences also affect the way people come to think of themselves. And, according to self-interest theory, they affect the way people estimate the costs and benefits of being Catholic.

Our personal interviews and focus groups gave early indications that lifecourse experiences would be important. So did comments parishioners wrote on the back page of our Indiana survey. Two respondents indicated that marital status might be important. One said:

> I would like to see the Catholic church and parishes be more sensitive to the single vocation. I am older, never been married, and have never felt a place in the church.

The other person, who had been married, said:

> My drop in participation in the Church is the direct result of my divorce (which I did not seek or desire). I feel unwanted and shunned from my Church at the very time I most need the support.

Several married parishioners indicated that their family circumstances affect their religious outlooks. Here are four examples:

> My spouse is a recovering alcoholic who retired at age 55 because he could no longer perform his duties at work. . . . He never goes to church or takes part in church activities. Of our six children, only the two who live out of town are active Catholics. The other four do not attend church except on rare occasions. . . . It does seem rather unfair to spend your whole life trying to be a good practicing Catholic, send your children to a Catholic school, and then end up alone, because your spouse and married children do not share your faith and values.

> My involvement in church-related affairs, attendance at Holy Day Masses, and participation in the Mass has decreased since marriage and having a child. This is not because I personally feel it is less important or necessary, but with working, household chores, and caring for

a child, there just isn't the time and energy left to do all I should toward promoting my religious practices. Also, my husband, although Catholic by birth, was not raised Catholic because his parents divorced just after he was born. My husband does not see the necessity that I do in going to Mass when required, giving alms, going to confession, participating or working at, for, or toward church social benefits, etc. He also does not truly believe in some of our practices, I feel.

I am married to a man who was raised in the United Church of Christ. We attend both churches and participate in both churches. The children were baptized Catholic but they too attend both churches. It is upsetting to know that as of right now we feel more at home at St. John's United Church of Christ than at Blessed Sacrament.

Two other parishioners said their occupations affect their views of faith and morals. One man said:

As a professionally trained economist, I do not believe the Church has any business making official statements in matters where it lacks appropriate expertise (e.g., "greedy" capitalist, the efficiency of one economic system relative to another, minimum wage, health care reform, etc.). . . . More than one of my non-Catholic friends have remarked that they would consider becoming Catholic except for its "left-of-center" economic and political pronouncements (encyclicals).

A woman wrote the following:

I am a nurse and am very concerned about sharing a "common cup" when drinking the wine at church. I don't take part in this and will not allow my children. . . . With the chance of contracting some serious illness (TB and AIDS are on the rise), we can not take this chance. Wiping off the cup doesn't always wipe away potential viruses.

These comments certainly suggest that lifecourse experiences can have important effects on the way Catholics think about faith and morals. But, we cannot assume that all lifecourse experiences are of equal importance.

Nor can we assume that lifecourse experiences affect all dimensions of faith and morals in the same way. Some may affect faith in one way, but morals in another way. To find out what effects lifecourse experiences really have, we have to examine our national data. This investigation confirms some of our expectations, but it also produces some surprises.

We consider four sets of lifecourse experiences: family lives and significant others; socioeconomic status; relationships with God and the Church; and social attitudes. Table 5.1 provides a summary profile of parishioners on these issues. After describing Catholic parishioners, we examine the effects each of the circumstances has on parishioners' approaches to faith and morals.

Family Lives and Significant Others

Previous research shows that adults' family lives can have important effects on their religious orientations (Glock, Ringer, and Babbie, 1967; Wilson, 1978; D'Antonio and Aldous, 1990; Chalfant, Beckley, and Palmer, 1994; Hoge, Johnson, and Luidens, 1994). These studies suggest three family circumstances that have especially important effects: marital status, the religious affiliation of one's spouse, and the presence or absence of school-age children. Research in social psychology also suggests that our "significant others" (i.e., people we admire and want to emulate, not just spouses and boy- or girlfriends) affect our attitudes and actions (Stryker, 1980; Stryker and Serpe, 1982; Wimberley, 1989).

The average parishioner in our national poll is married, has a Catholic spouse, has no preschool or school-age children living at home, and admires someone who is a religiously active, traditional Catholic. However, parishioners' family circumstances and significant others vary widely. Sixty-two percent are married. Twenty-one percent have never married. Eight percent are widowed; seven percent are divorced; and two percent are separated. Eighty percent of married Catholics are (or were) married to Catholics. Twenty percent are (or were) married to persons who are not Catholic. Sixty percent do not have any preschool or school-age children living at home. Forty percent do. When asked to identify someone whom they admire and want to be like, 57 percent named Catholics who they say are religiously active and have a traditional religious outlook. Forty-three percent named people who are not Catholic, are not religiously active, and/or are not traditional.

Socioeconomic Status

Previous research leads us to believe that socioeconomic conditions also might affect parishioners' views of faith and morals (Demerath, 1965;

Table 5.1 — Profile of Parishioners' Lifecourse Experiences	
	Percent
Family Lives and Significant Others	
Are married	62
Are married to a Catholic	80
Do not have preschool or school-age children	60
Have significant other who is an active, traditional Catholic	57
Socioeconomic Status	
Have more than high-school education	57
Have spent most of lives in labor force	67
Have white collar jobs	70
Have incomes > $30,000	68
Social Attitudes	
Sex roles	
Believe there are still many laws and customs that are unfair to American women	79
Do not feel that it is more important for a wife to help her husband's career than to have a career herself	77
Do not feel that most men are better suited emotionally for politics than most women are	77
Feel most leaders of the women's movement are too radical	65
Feel that when children are young, it is better if the husband is the breadwinner and the wife stays home and takes care of the home and children	53
Poverty	
Believe poverty is mainly due to social conditions such as lack of jobs and low wages	77
Believe poverty is mainly due to poor people's own behavior, such as not managing their money well or lack of effort	23
Religious Experiences	
Closeness to God (many times)	
Feel God has forgiven your sins	70
Feel God has taken care of you when you really needed help	57
Feel God has answered your prayers	49
Have felt presence of God in a very special way	24
Awareness of Vatican II (many times)	
Have heard priest talk about Vatican II from pulpit	18
Have talked with other people about Vatican II	10
Have read books or articles about Vatican II	8

Glock, Ringer, and Babbie, 1967; Stark, 1972; Mueller and Johnson, 1975; Davidson, 1977; Alston and McIntosh, 1979; Roof and McKinney, 1987). These studies suggest that people with lower levels of education, lower status jobs, and lower incomes have more traditional religious orientations than people with higher educations, more occupational prestige, and loftier incomes.

To explore this possibility, we collected background information on four factors: education, employment history, occupation, and family income. The "typical" parishioner is a high-school graduate who is in the labor force, has a white-collar job, and has a family income between $30,000 and $49,999. However, parishioners' socioeconomic circumstances differ greatly. Twenty-seven percent are college graduates or have gone to graduate or professional schools. Thirty percent have been to vocational or trade school, or have attend college without graduating. Forty-three percent have high-school educations or less.

Two-thirds of parishioners have spent most of their adult lives in the labor force. Twenty-two percent are homemakers. Eleven percent are students. People in the labor force are in an array of careers and jobs which census officials and researchers rank in the following order. Starting at the top, 12 percent are executives or managers. Twenty-four percent are white-collar professionals (e.g., doctors, lawyers, teachers). Thirty-four percent are lower white-collar workers (e.g., sales people, technicians, and administrative support people). Twenty-two percent are in semiskilled jobs (e.g., people in precision production, machine operators, service workers). Nine percent are in unskilled work (e.g., transportation, farming, fishing, forestry).

There are sizable numbers of Catholics in every income category. Sixteen percent of parishioners have family incomes of $80,000 or more. Twenty-three percent are between $50,000 and $79,999. Twenty-nine percent are between $30,000 and $49,999. Twenty-two percent are between $15,000 and $29,999. Eleven percent have incomes below $15,000. Thus, distribution of Catholic family income tends to be diamond-shaped, with the largest percentage of Catholics in the middle-income range and smaller percentages toward the top and bottom of the income ladder.

Social Attitudes

Previous research suggests that adults' views on important social issues can affect their religious orientations (Glock, Ringer, and Babbie, 1967; Roberts and Davidson, 1984). Different social outlooks often serve as lenses through which people come to see faith and morals in different ways. Pursuing this line of inquiry, we examine two of today's more salient social concerns: the roles men and women play in society, and the origins of poverty.

Sex Roles

In the last 25 to 30 years, Americans have been engaged in a serious consideration of the roles that men and women have played historically and the roles they should play in the future. At one end of the spectrum is the view that society should reaffirm traditional roles calling for men to be the breadwinners and leaders of virtually every other sphere of social life. This view also gives primacy to women's traditional roles of caring for their homes and raising their children. We expect that people with this view would find it relatively easy to accept the Church's sexual teachings. At the other end of the spectrum is the view that historical sex roles are no longer appropriate. This view claims that men and women should share domestic responsibilities, have equal access to careers and incomes, and participate equally in all spheres of public life. We think people who stress sexual equality might have the most difficulty agreeing with the Church's views on sexual and reproductive ethics.

We asked Catholic parishioners to respond to five items having to do with sex roles. Responses to three items indicate a willingness to question some traditional views. For example, 79 percent of parishioners agree that "there are still many laws and customs that are unfair to American women"; only 21 percent disagree. Likewise, 77 percent do not feel that "it is more important for a wife to help her husband's career than to have a career herself"; only 23 percent agree with that statement. Seventy-seven percent also disagree with an item stating that "most men are better suited emotionally for politics than are most women"; 23 percent agree.

On the other hand, a majority of parishioners seem reluctant to identify with leaders of the women's movement. In response to the following item, "most leaders of the women's movement are too radical for me," 65 percent agree and 35 percent disagree. Some of that reluctance may be tied to parishioners' images (accurate or not) of radicalism among movement leaders. Some of it also seems linked to mixed feelings about sex roles. Fifty-three percent of parishioners agreed that "when children are young, it is better if the husband is the breadwinner and the wife stays home and takes care of the home and the children." Forty-seven percent disagree.

Poverty

Americans have two main theories about the origins of poverty (Feagin, 1975; Ryan, 1981; Davidson, 1985; Kluegel and Smith, 1986). One view is that poverty is caused by societal, or structural, conditions over which the poor have little or no control. These conditions include the quality of education that youngsters have access to; the number of job opportunities in a given community; the extent to which companies use factors such as race, ethnicity, religion, and gender when screening job applicants; and the wages companies pay.

The other view is that the poor are largely responsible for their own poverty. This theory suggests that poor people lack the personal qualities that are needed to get ahead in our society. Rather than saving their money, they spend it foolishly. Rather than being highly motivated to find work and succeed, they are lazy. Instead of leading moral lives, they tend to be promiscuous, have children out of wedlock, and use alcohol and drugs. They have too many kids. Instead of spending their money on nutritious foods, they waste it on junk food. When given opportunities to get ahead, they tend to blow them by missing work and goofing off on the job.

While most people's views of poverty are combinations of both structural and individual explanations, Americans tend to emphasize individual explanations (e.g., Kleugel and Smith, 1986). We asked Catholics which of these two explanations they think is more valid. Seventy-seven percent of parishioners believe that poverty is mainly due to "social conditions such as lack of jobs and low wages." Only 23 percent say it has more to do with "poor people's own behavior, such as not managing their money well or lack of effort on their part."

Religious Experiences

Catholics also have religious life histories. During their adult lives, some parishioners develop close personal relationships with God; others do not. Some also learn a great deal about major developments in the Church; others do not. We are impressed with the extent to which Catholics have had very personal experiences of the holy, but we are unimpressed with parishioners' awareness of major developments such as Vatican II.

Closeness to God

We asked four questions about parishioners' closeness to God during their adult years. One question concerns the frequency with which parishioners have felt "the presence of God in a very special way." One-fourth of Catholics say "many times"; 21 percent report "several times"; 40 percent indicate "a few times"; and 14 percent say "never." A second item asked how often parishioners have felt that "God has taken care of you when you've really needed help." Fifty-seven percent report "many times"; 18 percent, "several times"; 22 percent, "a few times"; and only three percent, "never." On the third item, we asked how often "God has answered your prayers." Forty-nine percent indicate "many times"; 21 percent, "several times"; 28 percent, "a few times"; and, again, only three percent, "never." The fourth question asks how often "God has forgiven your sins." Seventy percent say "many times"; 16 percent, "several times"; 11 percent, "several times"; and once again, only three percent, "never."

Awareness of Vatican II

We asked three questions about Vatican II. One concerned the frequency with which parishioners have heard priests talk about the Council from the pulpit. Eighteen percent said "many times"; 46 percent said "a few times"; and 35 percent said "never, or almost never." A second item asked how often parishioners have read articles or books about the Council. Eight percent said "many times"; 34 percent said "a few times"; and 58 percent said "never, or almost never." With a third item, we learned how often parishioners have talked with other people about Vatican II. Ten percent said "many times"; 26 percent said "a few times"; and 65 percent said "never, or almost never."[1]

Relationships with Faith and Morals

Our next step is to see if there are any relationships between these lifecourse experiences and Catholics' scores on our indices of faith and morals.[2] The results are shown in Table 5.2.

Family Lives and Significant Others

Three of these four variables are consistently related to faith and morals. Parishioners with Catholic spouses, no school-age children, and significant others who are religiously active and traditional Catholics are more likely to comply with Church teachings in faith and morals and less inclined toward recent ideas than persons with non-Catholic spouses and school-age children, and with significant others who are not active and traditional Catholics. Marital status makes no consistent difference.

Socioeconomic Status

Two socioeconomic circumstances are important influences on faith and morals: employment history and family income. Homemakers are more traditional on most of our indices than students and persons in the labor force. They also are less inclined to agree with the items in our index of recent ideas. Students are similar to homemakers in their tendency to embrace the Church's social teachings and to participate in recent practices but, unlike homemakers, they are inclined toward recent ideas about

Table 5.2 — Faith and Morals by Lifecourse Experiences (percent)

	Faith			Morals	
	Traditional Beliefs/Practices (High)	Recent Ideas (High)	Recent Practices (High,Med)	Sexual/Rep. Ethics (High)	Social Teachings (High)
All Parishioners	47	33	8	23	51
Family Lives and Significant Others					
Marital Status					
Married	47	33	6	23	49
Single	43	41	13	18	57
Widowed	66	18	10	38	53
Divorced	41	18	8	21	45
Separated	27	27	22	30	46
Religion of Spouse					
Catholic	50	29	9	28	50
Not Catholic	38	34	-	12	45
School-age Children					
Yes	40	35	8	16	49
No	51	31	8	28	52

Significant Others					
Catholic, active, and traditional	58	27	10	28	58
Other	31	40	5	17	41
Socioeconomic Status					
Education					
>College	37	26	13	31	53
College	42	40	4	14	51
Voc/trade, some college	44	28	10	25	45
High school	53	25	4	29	48
<High school	70	30	3	33	46
Employment history					
Labor force	43	33	6	21	47
Student	40	50	11	12	61
Homemaker	65	22	12	37	57
Occupation					
Executive/manager	33	46	1	20	45
Professional	44	31	13	17	59
White collar	37	34	2	17	42
Semiskilled	59	23	15	28	59
Unskilled	50	33	2	30	28
Income					
>$80,000	32	35	11	18	49
$50,000-$79,999	41	37	5	19	46
$30,000-$49,999	44	37	8	19	51
$15,000-$29,999	53	27	9	28	51
<$15,000	69	23	3	42	59

Table 5.2 — Faith and Morals by Lifecourse Experiences — continued (percent)

	Faith			Morals	
	Traditional Beliefs/Practices (High)	Recent Ideas (High)	Recent Practices (High,Med)	Sexual/Rep. Ethics (High)	Social Teachings (High)
Social Attitudes					
Sex Roles					
Unequal	57	16	15	50	66
Mixed	53	28	7	23	45
Equal	32	48	7	8	49
Poverty					
Blame society	48	33	9	24	53
Blame poor	45	31	6	19	39
Religious Experiences					
Closeness to God					
High	62	27	13	30	60
Medium	34	35	4	17	43
Low	15	57	-	6	33
Awareness/Vatican II					
High	72	20	27	41	72
Medium	48	30	6	25	49
Low	31	45	3	12	43

women's ordination and not needing to attend Mass. Persons who have spent most of their adult lives in the labor force score lowest on social teachings and recent practices and have intermediate scores on the other dimensions we studied.

Parishioners with relatively low family incomes tend to be traditional in their religious beliefs and practices and have a tendency to agree with the Church's moral teachings. They also are a bit more likely to reject the recent ideas we examined. Higher-income Catholics, on the other hand, are not as inclined toward traditional beliefs and practices; nor are they as keen on the Church's sexual and social teachings. They are more inclined to accept recent ideas such as ordaining women. Income was not linked with any distinctive scores on our index of recent practices. Education and occupational status have selected effects, but overall do not predict parishioners' views of faith and morals as consistently as employment status and income do.

Social Attitudes

Sex role attitudes are highly related to faith and morals. As expected, Catholics who favor traditional sex roles the most also tend to score highest on our various measures of traditional faith and morals and lowest on our index of recent ideas. Those who are more inclined to question traditional sex roles tend to accept recent ideas such ordaining women and do not score as high on our other measures of religious belief and practice. Parishioners' views of poverty affect their views on the Church's social teachings in the way we expected, but they have only limited effects on the other dimensions of faith and morals.

Religious Experiences

As expected, our measures of parishioners' closeness to God and their knowledge of major developments in the Church are consistently and significantly related to faith and morals. The closer parishioners have been to God over the course of their lives, and the more aware they are of Vatican II, the more they tend to agree with Church teachings and the more they disagree with recent ideas such as ordaining women and not having to attend Mass.

So far, then, the data lead us to believe that eight factors play special roles in fostering compliance with Church teachings: having a Catholic spouse; not having school-age children; admiring a Catholic who is religiously active and traditional; being a homemaker; having a lower family income; having traditional views about the roles men and women should play in society; having had experiences of being close to God; and being aware of Vatican II. Parishioners who are least traditional in their orientations to faith and morals have non-Catholic spouses; have school-age children; do not mention a religiously active and traditional Catholic when asked whom they most admire; are students or members of the labor force; have relatively high incomes; tend to question traditional sex roles; have not felt especially close to God; and are not aware of Vatican II. Four other factors (marital status, education, occupational status, and views of poverty) have selected effects but, overall, are less important.

Further Analysis

Some of the eight variables that seem most important are correlated with one another. For example, people who feel close to God also tend to be aware of Vatican II. Those (somewhat older) Catholics who have traditional views of men's and women's roles in society tend not to have school-age children.[3] Therefore, we looked to see how much, and what kind of, effect each of the lifecourse factors has when all the others are taken into account. Table 5.3 summarizes our findings.

Looking at the Rows

When the effects of other lifecourse factors are controlled, two variables have the largest and most consistent effects on all five dimensions of faith and morals: having had close relationships with God and having heard or read about Vatican II. These two influences foster traditional belief and practice, participation in relatively new devotional practices, adherence to the Church's sexual and reproductive norms, compliance with its social teachings, and a tendency to reject recent ideas such as ordaining women.

Having a significant other who is a religiously active and traditional Catholic matters on four of our five faith and morals indices. People who admire someone who has these Catholic traits are inclined toward traditional beliefs and practices and compliance with the Church's sexual and reproductive ethics and its social teachings. They also tend to reject ideas such as being a good Catholic without going to Mass on a regular basis.

Traditional sex-role attitudes also are important four out of five times. Parishioners with the most traditional views about men's and women's roles in society also tend toward traditional beliefs and practices, agreement with the Church's sexual and reproductive norms, and adherence to its social teachings. They also tend to reject recent ideas. Sex-role attitudes have no significant impact on recent devotional practices.

Having a Catholic spouse affects three of four dimensions. Parishioners with Catholic spouses tend to have traditional beliefs and practices,

Table 5.3
Relative Importance of Lifecourse Factors
Regression Analyses (Betas)

	Faith			Morals	
	Traditional Beliefs/Practices	Recent Ideas	Recent Practices	Sexual/Rep. Ethics	Social Teachings
Family Lives and Significant Others					
Spouse Catholic	.08	ns	.09	.15	ns
School-age Children	ns	ns	.07	ns	ns
S.O. is Catholic, active, traditional	.19	-.07	ns	.06	.13
Socioeconomic Status					
Homemaker	.07	ns	.10	ns	ns
High income	-.15	ns	ns	-.10	ns
Social Attitudes					
Traditional sex role attitudes	.10	-.41	ns	.34	.11
Religious Experiences					
Closeness to God	.50	-.12	.30	.15	.22
Awareness of Vatican II	.10	-.23	.30	.21	.14

Only betas with significance levels equal to or greater than .001 are shown; ns means not significant participate more than others do in recent devotional practices, and tend to agree with the Church's sexual and reproductive ethics. Spouse's religious affiliation does not affect recent ideas; nor is it linked with social teachings.

Employment status and income affect two dimensions. Being a homemaker increases one's tendency to have traditional beliefs and practices and the likelihood that one participates in recent practices. High-income parishioners tend to score lower on our index of traditional beliefs and practices and tend to disagree with the Church's sexual views. Employment status and income have no appreciable effect on either recent ideas or social teachings.

Having school-age children has a small tendency to increase participating in recent practices, but has no significant effect on any of the other dimensions of faith and morals.

Looking Down the Columns

Reading down the columns in Table 5.3, we see which lifecourse factors have the most impact on each dimension of faith and morals. Experiences that God has intervened in one's life explain parishioners' traditional beliefs and practices far more than any other lifecourse experience. They are followed — in descending order of importance — by having a significant other who is a religiously active and traditional Catholic; a smaller income; awareness of Vatican II and traditional sex-role attitudes; having a spouse who is Catholic; and being a homemaker. The parishioners who struggle the most with traditional Catholic beliefs and practices are those who have not felt God's presence in their lives; do not have a religiously active and traditional Catholic at the top of their list of significant others; have relatively high family incomes; have not heard much about Vatican II; have the most doubts about the traditional roles of men and women; have non-Catholic spouses; and are more likely to be students or members of the labor force than homemakers.

Of the eight lifecourse variables, the tendency to question the traditional roles of men and women in society has the most effect on parishioners' agreement with recent ideas such as ordaining women and not needing to attend Mass on a regular basis. Three other lifecourse factors also contribute to recent ideas: not having much knowledge of Vatican II, not feeling close to God, and not having a significant other who is a religiously active and traditional Catholic. Parishioners who tend to reject the recent ideas we examined have traditional sex-role orientations, are most aware of Vatican II, feel closest to God, and have a significant other who is an active and traditional Catholic.

The two lifecourse factors that have the most effect on recent devotional practices are awareness of Vatican II and feelings of being close to God. Being a homemaker also contributes. So does having a Catholic spouse and school-age children, but these factors have smaller effects. Practices such as reading the Bible and attending Bible studies are least common among parishioners who have little knowledge of Vatican II, the fewest personal experiences of God, spouses who are not Catholic, and no school-age children.

Parishioners' views of men's and women's roles in society have more impact on their views of the Church's sexual and reproductive ethics than any other lifecourse factor we examined. People with traditional views of men's and women's roles are most likely accept the Church's sexual teachings; those who question traditional sex roles tend to disagree with the Church's views on sexual and reproductive issues. Five other factors have smaller effects. Parishioners who are most likely to agree with the Church's sexual norms are aware of Vatican II, feel God has taken care of them, have Catholic spouses, have relatively low incomes, and have significant others who are active and traditional Catholics.

Closeness to God has more bearing on parishioners' views of the Church's social teachings than any of other eight lifecourse factors in Table 5.3. Catholics who have had frequent feelings of being close to God tend to agree with the social teachings; those who have not had such experiences of God are more likely to disagree. Three other factors also matter. Agreement with social teachings is more common among parishioners who are aware of Vatican II, have traditional views of sex roles, and have significant others who are active and traditional Catholics than they are among church members who do not know much about Vatican II, question traditional sex roles, and have a significant other who is not an active and traditional Catholic.

Conclusions

In this chapter, we have shown that lifecourse experiences have considerable effect on the way Catholics think about faith and morals. Two factors seem especially important: being close to God and being informed about major developments in the Church. These two factors have significant effects on all five outcomes. Catholics who have known God's love and care for them and those who are most aware of Vatican II are most inclined to agree with Church teachings. Those who have had very few experiences of the holy and who are not as well-informed are most likely to have views that differ from official teachings. Two other factors also are important on four of five dimensions: parishioners' views of men's and women's roles in society, and having a significant other who is an active and traditional Catholic. One's family income, having a Catholic spouse, being a homemaker, and having school-age children have selected effects but are not as important across the board.

We also have specified which lifecourse experiences have the most impact on specific dimensions of faith and morals. Knowing that God has intervened in one's life increases one's support of traditional beliefs and practices, recent practices, and social teachings. Sex-role attitudes have the most impact on recent ideas and sexual and reproductive ethics.

These findings suggest that the more Church leaders cultivate experiences of God and knowledge of major developments such as Vatican II in worship and adult education, the more they are likely to promote appreciation of and compliance with the Church's teachings. To the extent that leaders ignore these two important influences or — worse yet — undermine them, they will contribute to religious outlooks that are at odds with Church norms.[4] At this point at least, it appears that leaders are having somewhat more success in nurturing close relationships with God than they are informing lay people about events such as Vatican II. There is room for improvement in both areas, but especially with regard to fostering knowledge of Vatican II.

Though Catholics in the 1930s and '40s tended to interact with other Catholics and were not likely to have significant others who were non-Catholic, about half of today's parishioners say the person they admire most is not an active and traditional Catholic. Having made it into the middle class, and having been encouraged by the Church to become full participants in American society, parishioners now have religiously heterogeneous social networks and quite often respect people who have ideas that are not in sync with official Church teachings. Church leaders cannot reverse the trend toward more heterogeneous social relationships; nor do we think they should try. The wiser course, we think, is to accept this social diversity and to tolerate some of the dissenting views that accompany it, while encouraging relationships that foster a Catholic worldview.

The trend toward more egalitarian sex roles is formidable and likely to persist. It will continue to foster ideas such as the ordination of women and disagreement with the Church's sexual teachings well past the turn of the century. In light of this projection, we think Church leaders ought to explore ways in which Catholics with different views of sex roles can contribute to parish and diocesan life as the Church and American society try to sort out the positive and negative implications of changing sex roles in society and in the Church.

In Chapter 11, we examine the way the most important lifecourse variables interact with commitment to the Church (and other factors that also might affect Catholics' views of faith and morals. Among other factors that also might make a real difference are the experiences Catholics have during their childhood years. In Chapter 6, we examine the different ways in which Catholics are raised and identify the childhood influences that are most closely linked to their religious beliefs and practices later in life.

6 • Religious Formation
The Impact of Families, Catholic Schools, and Religious Education

I didn't choose. I was born Catholic — I was fortunate.

I don't think I'm going to do research into my heart and soul until I have children, and then I'm going to try and learn my faith.

Indiana parishioners

How does a person learn to be a Catholic? For most of the history of Catholicism, such a question would have made little or no sense. One could no more "learn" to be a Catholic than one could "learn" to be a member of one's family or village — in fact, one was automatically a Catholic precisely *because* one was born into a Catholic family or village. Religion was inextricably woven into the very fabric of family and community life: in home rituals and household shrines, in seasonal festivals for the village's patron saint, in folk beliefs and popularly revered holy places (Orsi, 1985; Diaz-Stevens, 1994). In most people's minds, being a Catholic did not require any knowledge of official doctrine or even regular attendance at Mass. "Indeed, precisely because the official Christian structure of society guaranteed that everybody was leading Christian lives, it was not so necessary to stress personal devotion. It was the structure itself that was religious, not necessarily the personal lives that people lived within it" (Casanova, 1994:16).

The Protestant Reformation, however, challenged this concept of religion. Mere membership in a family or community was no longer enough (Luria, 1989; Bruce, 1995:418). For many of the reformers, each adult was expected to make a free and informed choice to accept the teachings of Jesus Christ. Parents were to train their children to make this choice, and their efforts were to be supplemented by formal religious training in the churches.

The Catholic Church took on expanded educational responsibilities at least partially in response to these ideas. New teaching orders such as the Jesuits and the Ursulines established large numbers of primary and secondary schools to ensure that young Catholics — and especially young Catholic *girls* who, as mothers, would one day be expected to instruct their children — were provided with the basic teachings of their faith.[1] Other evangelization tools — catechisms, parish missions, and the Catholic popular press — also were developed in European Catholicism after the 1600s, to enkindle in Catholics an informed commitment to their faith (Dolan, 1978:13).

How did *Americans* learn to be Catholic? Over the past two centuries, we have developed our Catholic identity as a result of both familial/cultural and educational processes. Many of the newly arrived immigrant groups considered their Catholic faith a precious and valued part of their family and ethnic identity — an identity that was frequently threatened and attacked in the predominantly Protestant United States of the nineteenth century. Immigrants often clustered together in "institutionally complete" communities with their own schools, shops, athletic clubs, and newspapers, in an attempt to counteract the hostility which they experienced in the Protestant-dominated, "secular" institutions. As two of our respondents noted, there were few opportunities, and no incentives, to come into contact with outsiders:

> In my time, you were taught that it was even almost a sin
> to look into a church of a different denomination.

> My parents categorize people according to what Catho-
> lic parish they belong to.

Like medieval villagers, one was a Catholic in this environment because everyone one knew was a Catholic. Over time, however, the children and grandchildren of the immigrants did assimilate to American culture — a process, paradoxically, which may actually have been facilitated by the Catholic school system (McNamara, 1992:52). With cultural assimilation, however, came the danger of *religious* assimilation: the "loss" of Catholic children to the dominant Protestant faith. Parochial schools, therefore, were also expected to perform the important task of training Catholic children in the basic doctrines of their faith. The council of U.S. bishops which met in Baltimore in 1884 mandated that every parish construct a school for its members' children, and all Catholics were strongly encouraged to see that their sons and daughters attended it.

To what extent do familial, communal, and educational experiences influence the beliefs and values of today's Catholics? If today's young Catholics hold increasingly pluralistic views on faith and morals, is this because their parents were less likely to stress religion than parents of former generations? Or is it due to the fact that fewer Catholics send their children to Catholic schools, and CCD is an inadequate substitute?[2] Or have Catholic schools themselves become so secularized that they no longer effectively pass on the faith? Have lay teachers and administrators been as effective in instilling the Catholic faith as were the religious sisters, priests, and brothers of former decades? Or has the larger world which Catholics now inhabit changed so that no school system, no family, no religion teacher, can counteract its influence?

A Descriptive Overview

Our national survey included several questions which measured the familial aspects of religious formation: whether or not a respondent's parents were Catholic, how frequently the parents had attended church services or talked to their children about religion, and how close the respondents felt to their parents. Still other questions measured the amount of formal instruction our respondents had received in the faith: how much education they had had in Catholic schools, whether they had had priests, sisters, or Catholic lay religion teachers, and how many years of CCD they had attended. The survey also asked respondents to report how often they themselves had attended Mass, received Communion, and prayed privately when they were children.

Table 6.1 reports the responses to these questions *only for the subset of Catholic parishioners who were raised in the Church.* This is a different subsample than has been used in the other chapters of this book, which include converts. To study religious upbringing, however, it is better to study converts and "cradle Catholics" separately. (Converts are discussed later on in the chapter.)

The majority of cradle Catholics report that both of their parents were also Catholic; for those with only one Catholic parent, that parent was usually the mother. The respondents also report that their mothers attended church more frequently than did their fathers, and they are more likely to report feeling close to their mothers. Over half (59 percent) say that their

Table 6.1 — Religious Upbringing of Parishioners
(Cradle Catholics Only)

Question	Answer	Percent
Father Catholic?	Yes	87
	No	12
Mother Catholic?	Yes	94
	No	6
Father attended church?	Weekly or more	62
	At least monthly	15
	Rarely or never	23
Mother attended church?	Weekly or more	83
	At least monthly	11
	Rarely or never	6
Parents talked about religion?	Frequently	59
	Occasionally	30
	Rarely or never	11
How close to father?	Close or very close	77
	Somewhat close	16
	Not close	7
How close to mother?	Close or very close	9
	Somewhat close	6
	Not close	3
Childhood practices: Mass attendance	Weekly or more	91
	At least monthly	7
	Rarely or never	2

Table 6.1 continued — Religious Upbringing of Parishioners
(Cradle Catholics Only)

Question	Answer	Percent
Communion	Weekly or more	80
	At least monthly	15
	Rarely or never	5
Private prayer	Weekly or more	88
	At least monthly	7
	Rarely or never	5
Years of Catholic schooling?	None	32
	1-3	7
	4-6	11
	7-9	17
	10-12	22
	More than 12	10
Amount of CCD (for persons with 0-3 years of Catholic schooling)?	None	6
	Some	38
	Quite a bit	33
Catholic religion teachers?	Yes	88
	No	10
Type of religion teachers?	Mostly priests & sisters	57
	Mostly lay people	11
	Equal mix of both	32

parents talked to them "frequently" about religion while they were growing up, but a substantial minority report that such conversations happened
only occasionally (30 percent) or rarely (11 percent).

While they were growing up, over 90 percent of the respondents attended Mass at least weekly, and they received Communion and prayed
privately almost as often. Two-thirds have attended Catholic schools for at
least part of their education. Of those who report having no or only a few
years of Catholic schooling, over half state that they received either "a
great deal" or "quite a bit" of religious instruction in CCD classes. Almost all (88 percent) had Catholic religion teachers: slightly over half (57
percent) had mostly priests and sisters, 11 percent had mostly lay teachers, and 32 percent report having had an equal mixture of both.

Family Upbringing

> My upbringing was about rituals, not about understand-
> ing the faith.

> I was taught about personal spirituality by my father.
> *Indiana parishioners*

What effects have these childhood experiences had on the beliefs and
practices of adult Catholics? We first created summary measures of parents' religiosity (a combination of the two questions measuring how often
the respondent's father and mother attended religious services), and of
childhood religiosity (the three questions measuring how often the respondents had attended Mass, prayed privately, and received Communion
as a child, as well as their own estimation of their childhood religiosity).
Appendix H describes these indices in greater detail. We then related these
two indices and the other upbringing questions to the faith and morals
indices developed in Chapter 3. Table 6.2 reports the results.

Looking at Table 6.2, we can see that almost all of the family upbringing variables have a strong effect on the respondents' tendency, as adults,
to accept traditional Catholic beliefs and practices and to agree with the
Church on sexual and reproductive ethics. The strongest predictor of a
high score on both of these indices is the respondent's level of childhood
religiosity: respondents who report frequent Mass attendance, Communion, and prayer as children are over eight times more likely to report high
levels of traditional beliefs and practices today. Strong effects can also be
seen for two other childhood influences. Respondents who were close to
their parents or whose parents frequently talked to them about religion are
twice as likely to report high levels of traditional beliefs and practices

than those who were not close to their parents or whose parents "rarely" or "never" talked about religion. Similar patterns can be discerned for the effect of maternal closeness and childhood religiosity on our respondents' agreement with the Church's sexual and reproductive teachings. These findings echo those of previous research, which report similar familial influence on adults' beliefs and practice (Myers, 1996:863; Stolzenberg et al., 1995:98; Sherkat and Wilson, 1995:1008-1009; Wilson and Sherkat, 1994:155; Rossi and Rossi, 1990:29, 339; Hoge, 1988:55).

Parental influence had fewer consistent effects on our other indices. Agreement with the Church's social teachings and engaging in recent practices such as Bible study and prayer groups are actually slightly higher when one parent was *not* Catholic and (at least for the social teachings scale) when respondents did *not* have a high level of religiosity as children. Agreement with the Church's social teachings is highest among respondents whose parents were only moderately religious, or who were moderately close to their fathers.

For recent ideas about not attending Sunday Mass and the ordination of women (both of which, of course, are against official Church teaching), our respondents' childhood experiences seem to have had little consistent effect. Whether or not their parents were Catholic did not affect our respondents' propensity to agree with recent ideas, but *closeness* to parents made them less likely to do so (see Myers, 1996:864). The one consistent finding is that childhood religiosity seems to have the expected effect on recent ideas: those who report high levels of childhood Mass attendance, Communion, and prayer, and report that religion was important to them in childhood, are the least likely to score high on this index.

Catholic Education

> We learned by doing. We went to Mass. We went to confession. . . . It was a wonderful regimentation.

> We just shot paper wads in religion class.

> The Catholic Church did not, and still does not, emphasize nearly enough spirituality. When we were growing up, there were answers to every question, as long as it was in the *Baltimore Catechism*. . . . Religious education was not about the development of spirituality.

> Throwing out the *Baltimore Catechism* was the dumbest thing the Church ever did.
>
> *Indiana parishioners*

Table 6.2 — Effects of Family Background, Cradle Catholics Only (percent)

	Faith			Morals	
	Traditional Beliefs/Practices (High)	Recent Ideas (High)	Recent Practices (High,Med)	Sexual/Rep. Ethics (High)	Social Teachings (High)
All Cradle Parishioners	47	33	7	22	50
Mother Catholic?					
Yes	47	34	7	22	50
No	44	32	16	19	56
Father Catholic?					
Yes	49	33	7	22	49
No	41	34	9	22	56
Closeness to Mother					
Very Close	51	34	8	24	50
Moderately Close	37	33	4	17	52
Not Close	10	44	3	0	34
Closeness to Father					
Very Close	53	31	6	24	48
Moderately Close	43	36	8	20	55
Not Close	28	40	11	20	41

Parents' Religiosity					
High	54	29	7	25	49
Moderate	32	45	5	16	53
Low	38	38	6	17	47
Childhood Religiosity					
High	59	28	8	26	54
Moderate	28	44	5	16	41
Low	7	54	4	—	61
Parents Talk About Religion					
Frequently, Very Frequently	57	28	8	27	52
Occasionally	37	44	6	14	52
Rarely, Never	19	32	7	21	38

What about the effect of Catholic education? Are respondents who attended Catholic schools more actively Catholic as a result? Several authors (e.g. McCready, 1981; Greeley and Brown, 1970) have argued passionately for the Catholicizing effect of Catholic schools. However, the number of years our respondents spent in Catholic grade and high schools does not appear to have a consistent effect on whether they score high on the indices measuring traditional beliefs and practices, recent beliefs and practices, or agreement with the Church's teachings on social and sexual ethics — except when one has 12 or more years of Catholic schooling (see Table 6.3). This finding is consistent with a wide range of previous studies, which reported only "small and inconsistent" effects of Catholic schooling (D'Antonio et al., 1996:95-96; Walch, 1996:232; McNamara, 1992:135; Fichter, 1973:221-222; Lenski, 1963:270-271). Parishioners with more than 12 years of Catholic schooling *are* more likely to agree with the Church's teachings on social and sexual-reproductive ethics, more likely to engage in recent practices such as Bible study and prayer groups, and more likely to score high on our index of traditional beliefs and practices. Parishioners with more than 12 years of Catholic schooling are also *less* likely to agree with heterodox recent ideas on the ordination of women and not attending Sunday Mass (See McNamara, 1992:133; D'Antonio et al., 1996:95-96, for similar findings).

This, of course, does not necessarily mean that Catholic schools have failed in their mission of passing on the faith. The effect of Catholic schooling may be mediated through its effect on other variables. In other words, Catholic schools may influence their students to marry Catholic spouses, or to feel closer to God, or to participate more actively in their parishes (McCready, 1981). As chapters four and five have already pointed out, these lifestyle and commitment variables are strongly correlated with Catholic beliefs and practices. Appendix J explores the indirect effects of Catholic schooling in greater detail.

A frequently expressed assumption is that at least Catholic schools do a better job of passing on the faith than parish-based religious education classes do. Many of our focus group members seemed to share this view.

> I went through CCD from kindergarten all the way through high school. . . . It was watered down. If you really wanted to know something you would have to read about it on your own.

> In the CCD classes I went to, they kind of talked about being nice to each other. It wasn't a real dogmatic approach or anything.

Table 6.3 — Effects of Religious Education, Cradle Catholics Only (percent)

	Faith			Morals	
	Traditional Beliefs/ Practices (High)	Recent Ideas (High)	Recent Practices (High, Med)	Sexual/Rep. Ethics (High)	Social Teachings (High)
Number of years in Catholic Schools					
0	45	35	4	25	52
1 to 3	30	38	11	17	59
4 to 6	49	35	10	14	45
7 to 9	47	34	7	24	42
10 to 12	51	32	4	17	48
over 12	53	26	23	33	64
Amount of CCD					
None	38	36	3	16	48
Some	42	37	8	20	46
Quite a bit	54	29	7	26	53
A great deal	55	29	11	27	59
Catholic Religion Teachers?					
Yes	48	34	8	23	52
No	43	27	3	20	50
Type of Religion Teachers					
Priests/Sisters	55	27	7	28	50
Some of Each	39	43	10	16	49
Lay	37	46	9	14	60

Table 6.4 — Effects of Type of Religion Teacher For Each Birth Cohort (percent)

	Faith			Morals	
	Traditional Beliefs/ Practices (High)	Recent Ideas (High)	Recent Practices (High,Med)	Sexual/Rep. Ethics (High)	Social Teachings (High)
Pre-Vatican II Cohort:					
Priests/Sisters	68	21	8	44	56
Vatican II Cohort:					
Priests/Sisters	41	33	6	16	40
Some of Each	35	43	9	8	42
Lay	28	9	16	24	40
Post-Vatican II Cohort:					
Priests/Sisters	53	33	9	13	57
Some of Each	37	46	10	15	51
Lay	37	60	5	7	65

> I am appalled with how little I was taught in CCD.

But our survey respondents who received most of their religious instruction in CCD classes do not score noticeably worse than the Catholic school alumni on our indices. In fact, the pattern for CCD is more consistent than it is for Catholic schooling: those who report having "quite a bit" or "a great deal" of CCD generally agree with Church teachings more than those with little or none.

Another widespread assumption is that priests and sisters are better religion teachers than lay people are. Results from our focus groups were inconclusive, as the following comments indicate:

> I wasn't taught Church doctrine. The lay people that taught us had a very secular perspective.

> The education slacked off when we got older. . . . The priest that taught us in high school was interesting, but he didn't really teach us anything.

According to our national data, there is a strong tendency for those who had mostly priests and nuns as religion teachers to score more highly than those who had mostly lay teachers or a mixture of both. This pattern holds true for all of the indices except social teachings, where the respondents having lay religion teachers score the highest.

Is this an indictment of lay religion teachers? Are the differences on the indices due to what kind of a teacher a respondent had, or to what birth cohort a respondent belongs to? Table 6.4 reports these figures for each cohort of our respondents. Very few of the oldest cohort report having anyone but priests and nuns as religion teachers: only 12 were taught predominantly by lay people, and only 34 by a mixture of priests, nuns, and laity. Consequently, it is impossible to make valid comparisons between these few individuals and the over 400 older respondents who were taught by priests and nuns.

The other two cohorts, however, report having a wider variety of religion teachers. For both groups, those who report being taught by priests and sisters are more likely to score high on traditional beliefs and practices than those who were taught by lay persons or a mixture of the two. On the other hand, those middle-age respondents who were taught by *lay* teachers are *more* likely to engage in recent practices, *more* likely to agree with the Church's teachings on sexual ethics, and *less* likely to agree with heterodox recent ideas.

Among the respondents under 30, those who report a mixture of religion teachers are the most likely to agree with Church teachings on sexual issues. The youngest respondents who were taught by lay teachers are the most likely to agree with the Church's social teachings, but they are also more likely to agree with recent ideas such as the ordination of women and optional Sunday Mass attendance. Priests and sisters, therefore, seem to do a better job of passing on traditional beliefs and practices to their students, but evidence for the other aspects of faith and morals is mixed at best.

Comparing the Importance of the Upbringing Factors

Which of all these variables have the most impact on Catholics' religious beliefs and practices? In Appendix I, we weigh the impact of each upbringing variable while controlling for the effects of the other variables.

Overall, the most important factor is childhood religiosity. Its effects are felt on all five dimensions of faith and morals. Learning to be religious as a child increases adherence to Church teachings and diminishes dissent later in life. Religious education outside of Catholic schools affects four dimensions. It promotes traditional beliefs and practices, recent practices, and agreement with the Church's views on sexual and reproductive issues. It also stifles interest in unauthorized, recent ideas.

Two other religious-education factors also are significant on three dimensions. The more years of Catholic schooling one has, the more one tends to participate in recent practices such as Bible reading and the less one tends to accept recent ideas. However, parishioners with the most Catholic schooling also are a bit more likely to disagree with the Church's sexual and reproductive norms. Having priests and sisters for religious education (whether in Catholic schools or in CCD) fosters traditional beliefs and practices and agreement with the Church's sexual teachings; it also is an antidote to recent ideas.

Family influences also are important. Parents who talk frequently with their children about religion increase their offsprings' tendency to accept traditional beliefs and practices and social teachings; they also stifle interest in recent ideas such as ordaining women. Being close to one's mother predisposes one to traditional beliefs and practices, recent practices, and agreement with the Church's views on sexual and reproductive issues — findings that support previous research (Sandomirsky and Wilson, 1990:1222; Dudley and Dudley, 1989:366; D'Antonio, 1988:96).

Having religious parents and having a Catholic mother also promote traditional beliefs and practices and participation in recent practices. Being close to one's father also fosters traditional beliefs and practices, but tends to stifle recent practices such as Bible study. Father's religious affiliation has no significant effect on any of the five dimensions.

Persons Not Raised as Catholic

What about our respondents who converted to Catholicism as adults? The vast majority did not experience Catholic schooling (92 percent did not); nor did they have Catholic mothers (86 percent did not) or fathers (92 percent did not). What effect did high levels of parental or childhood religiosity in other faiths have on their Catholic beliefs and practices as adults?

Comparing Table 6.5 with Table 6.2, we notice that our convert respondents score higher than cradle Catholics in recent practices, and in their agreement with the Church's teachings on social and sexual ethics. The relationships between the family upbringing variables and these scales, however, are much less regular than they were for the cradle Catholics. Childhood religiosity and how frequently one's parents talked about religion show only weak or inconsistent relationships with most of the scales when we looked at converts. For example, converts reporting *low* levels of childhood religiosity are the *most* likely to score high on traditional beliefs and practices and agreement with the Church's sexual teachings. The middle category — persons whose parents talked about religion "occasionally," who were "moderately" close to their parents, who report "moderate" levels of parental or childhood religious practice — often register the highest or the lowest on the indices. Few of the relationships show patterns similar to those found among our cradle Catholic respondents.

Why might this be the case? For respondents from some denominations, converting to Catholicism may involve a complete break with one's past — including one's family and former religious upbringing. For these respondents, we might expect less correlation between upbringing variables and one's adult Catholic beliefs and practices. In fact, *lack* of closeness to one's parents, or having irreligious parents, may make the break easier. Some authors (e.g. Glock et al., 1967; Kirkpatrick and Shaver, 1990; Taylor and Chatters, 1988) advance a "family surrogate theory" whereby church membership is thought to be most attractive to those deprived of family ties. Other authors, however, (e.g. Christiano, 1986; Marler, 1995) have argued against this hypothesis. Perhaps *conversion* to churches is most attractive to those who have weaker family ties, while *remaining active* in one's childhood church is more attractive to those with strong family connections.

Conclusions

For cradle Catholics the most important upbringing factor influencing adult beliefs and practices is level of childhood religiosity. Having parents who talked about religion also is an important influence.

Table 6.5 — Effects of Family Background and Religious Education on Those Not Raised Catholic (percent)

	Faith			Morals	
	Trad. Beliefs/ Practices (High)	Recent Ideas (High)	Recent Practices (High,Med)	Sexual/Rep. Ethics (High)	Social Teachings (High)
All Converts	45	28	14	31	53
Closeness to Mother					
Very Close	45	32	10	35	48
Moderately Close	40	23	30	30	72
Not Close	71	24	—	24	33
Closeness to Father					
Very Close	47	35	16	35	51
Moderately Close	30	27	6	21	57
Not Close	62	—	32	38	58
Parents' Religiosity					
High	47	36	15	27	46
Moderate	40	29	10	34	68
Low	48	31	20	36	60
Childhood Religiosity					
High	40	60	—	26	38
Moderate	43	15	21	29	56
Low	48	35	—	42	56
Parents Talk About Religion					
Frequently, Very Frequently	56	17	20	47	59
Occasionally	17	27	7	18	46
Rarely, Never	44	26	11	24	53

Catholic schooling and CCD also have noteworthy effects, especially among persons with considerable religious education. Their main effects are in the area of faith, where they foster traditional beliefs and practices, encourage participation in recent devotional practices, and reduce interest in recent ideas such as the ordination of women. They have more limited effects in the area of morals. They have mixed effects on sexual and reproductive ethics and little or no impact on adherence to the Church's social teachings.

What are the implications of these findings? First of all, since childhood religiosity is such an important influence on adult beliefs and practices, parishes and Catholic schools should actively encourage high levels of religious participation by children and adolescents. Special Eucharistic liturgies appealing to these age groups are one good approach; others include youth choirs, retreats, young people's prayer or Bible study groups, and perhaps paraliturgical rituals. Efforts also might be made to encourage parents to create family prayer rituals and to feel comfortable talking about religion to their children. Perhaps a parish could provide classes or workshops on these topics — especially for the parents who come to register their children for baptism, CCD classes, or entrance into the parish school. Curricula in religion classes also might be strengthened to include more emphasis on Catholic beliefs and practices. We say much more about all of these implications in Chapter 11. Before that, however, we turn to the "personal attributes" part of our theory to see how birth cohort, gender, race, and ethnicity relate to Catholics' religious orientation.

7 • The Impact
of Generations
Pre-Vatican II Catholics, Vatican II
Catholics, and Post-Vatican II Catholics

The Catholic Church is the true Church that was founded
by Christ.

Pre-Vatican II Catholic

My spirituality is more important to me than my religion, and I can be spiritual anywhere. In fact, I am more
spiritual walking in the woods than I am walking down
the main aisle of the Church.

Vatican II Catholic

Your religion is within you. It's your relationship between
you and God. It doesn't matter if you're Catholic, Jew-
ish, or Protestant.

Post-Vatican II Catholic

We've all heard the stereotypes: older Catholics are conservative
and are longing for a return to the "good old days." Baby-
boomers practice a cafeteria-style Catholicism, picking and
choosing the aspects of Catholicism which most resonate with their world-

view and lifestyle, while at the same time maintaining a commitment to social-justice issues. Today's young Catholics have largely rejected Church teachings, are generally apathetic toward issues of faith and social justice, and lack a strong sense of what it means to be Catholic. There are, of course, many exceptions to these generalizations, as well as many individuals who fit these stereotypes almost perfectly.

But what's the real story — the "big picture"? Do the stereotypes largely reflect what's really going on within contemporary Catholicism? Or is the story much more complex? With each successive generation is there a general decline in acceptance of Church teachings and a weakening of Catholic identity? Is it true that the majority of older Catholics maintain fairly traditional beliefs and adhere to conventional practices? Are baby-boomer Catholics less committed to the Church than those belonging to their parents' generation? Do they maintain a greater commitment to social-justice issues? Have young Catholics rejected the faith, or is there a "rebound" effect with many of them yearning for the structure and guidance of the pre-Vatican II Church?

From the very beginning of the study, we were enticed by these questions. Church leaders with whom we spoke voiced similar concerns. So at every stage of data collection we kept these questions in mind. We found in the end that no discussion of diversity and unity among contemporary American Catholics is complete without consideration of generational variation.

A Theory of Generations

Karl Mannheim (1952) pioneered the study of generational variation when he argued that persons are shaped and molded during their adolescence in ways that forever impact their behavior and attitudes. His point was that persons born during the same time period and in a similar geographical area share a collective understanding of the world. Having been exposed to similar historical and cultural phenomena during their adolescence, persons born during a specific time period share a worldview that is likely to be vastly different from those born during different time periods. Thus, Mannheim argued, persons belonging to a particular generation, or birth cohort, have a shared vision of the world.

In his book *Frameworks*, Walrath (1987) lays out his interpretation of Mannheim's theory. According to Walrath, persons are forever affected by the historical and cultural phenomena to which they are exposed between the ages of 13 and 22. When persons are in this age range, they are experiencing their "formative years." The political, economic, and social events occurring during people's formative years continue to influence their attitudes and behaviors for the remainder of their lives. Despite the fact that persons of all generations eventually go through similar lifecourse experiences such as marriage, the raising of children, and retirement, one cohort's worldview at any particular stage in the lifecourse may be dramatically different from another's view at that same stage because of the experiences that occurred during its formative years. In Walrath's words (1987:35; italics in original text):

> [Persons] move chronologically through childhood, youth, and so forth on into old age like the generations that preceded them. But their experiences of the world are qualitatively very different at similar life stages . . . they never let go of the experienced differences . . . they continue to perceive and define the world in terms of that unique framework as they progress throughout their lives . . . *they perceive the same experiences differently from those socialized previously, who are now side by side with them in the same period.* In important respects they never grow up to take on the same perspectives their elders hold. They become a "cohort."

Three Cohorts: Pre-Vatican II Catholics, Vatican II Catholics, and Post-Vatican II Catholics

Using the theory of generations laid out by Mannheim and Walrath, we distinguish between three generations of Catholics (Williams, 1994, 1995; Williams and Davidson, 1996; D'Antonio, Davidson, Hoge, and Wallace, 1996). The oldest cohort was born in or before 1940, and experienced its formative years in the 1920s, '30s, and '40s. We refer to persons belonging to this cohort as pre-Vatican II Catholics, because they went through their formative years prior to the Second Vatican Council. The middle generation was born between 1941 and 1960, and came of age in the 1950s and '60s. We refer to these baby-boomer Catholics as the Vatican II generation because the Council took place during their formative years. This cohort includes the young Catholics that Fee, Greeley, McCready, and Sullivan (1981) studied nearly 20 years ago. The youngest generation was born after 1960, and came of age in the 1970s and '80s. We call this generation post-Vatican II Catholics because they came of age after the Council.

These three generations have had very different experiences during their formative years. Some experiences are societal in nature, uniting all members of the generation, regardless of their religious persuasions. Others are specifically Catholic, such as the Second Vatican Council, and set Catholics apart from non-Catholics in the same birth cohort. Together, these societal and specifically Catholic experiences have differently impacted the faith and morals of each generation.

Societal Influences

Older pre-Vatican II Catholics witnessed the affluence and prosperity of the roaring '20s during their formative years. Slightly younger pre-Vatican II Catholics grew up in the 1930s and '40s, and were influenced by the Great Depression and World War II. They knew what it was like to suddenly lose their jobs, incomes, and ability to provide for their families. They were called upon to defend their own nation from attack, and to defend the world against the evils of Nazism. They needed to pull together as a nation — to help one another economically and to win a world war. They turned to their families, government, and one another for help. They learned that their parents, political leaders, and other institutional authorities would do all they could to end economic hardship and bring peace. They complied when these authorities asked them to do their part in promoting the common good.

Catholics who grew up in the 1950s and '60s experienced dramatic changes during their formative years. When they were coming of age, they knew both the tranquillity of the post-war Eisenhower years and the radical social movements of the 1960s. During the 1950s, they learned to have confidence in established institutions. In the '60s, influenced by the civil rights movement, Betty Freidan's *The Feminine Mystique*, and Vietnam War protests, they learned to challenge them. In the 1950s, they learned to respect authority; in the '60s, adhering to the adage "don't trust anyone over 30," they questioned authority. These "baby boomers" went from acceptance of established institutions to an insistence on individual rights in determining their own lifestyles, including their own religious beliefs and practices.

Catholics who experienced their formative years in the 1970s and '80s have experienced a decrease in overt racial prejudice and discrimination, increased concern for the environment, and greater opportunities for women. Despite these positive experiences, post-Vatican II Catholics have known political corruption from Watergate to Whitewater; scientific and technological debacles from Three Mile Island to Chernobyl to the Challenger explosion; high rates of unemployment and an increased income gap between the rich and the poor; increased divorce among their parents; and fear of AIDS (Williams and Davidson, 1996; D'Antonio, Davidson, Hoge, and Wallace, 1996; Ludwig, 1995; Arkinson, 1995). Disillusioned and fearing the future, members of so-called Generation X have learned to distrust institutional authorities.

There also has been a decline in confidence in religion as a social institution. Whereas older generations were taught to emphasize the importance of religion and to respect religious authorities, today's youth stress the prevalence of religious hypocrisy, using Jim Bakker and Jimmy Swaggart as evidence for their case. "If religious leaders can't be trusted," young people say, "then we have no one to rely on but ourselves."

While these societal conditions have certainly impacted the faith and morals of today's Catholics, we must also appreciate the role that specifically Catholic experiences have had on members of the three generations.

Specifically Catholic Influences

Unlike members of mainline Protestant denominations, most Catholics growing up in the 1920s, '30s, and '40s were immigrants, or the children or grandchildren of immigrants. They had limited educations, blue-collar jobs, and modest incomes. They were distinctly working class. But, by the 1950s and '60s, Catholics were upwardly mobile; they were making it into the American mainstream and many were achieving the "American dream." By the 1970s and '80s, there was no doubt that the success of Catholics in the social, economic, and political arenas paralleled that of Protestants (Greeley, 1977, 1989, 1990). With socioeconomic success came assimilation into American culture (Herberg, 1960; Dolan, 1985), one aspect of which is an emphasis on the freedom to pick and choose one's own religious beliefs (Hoge, 1986; D'Antonio et al., 1989, 1996).

In the 1920s, '30s, and '40s, a vast network of specifically Catholic organizations inspired a distinctly Catholic worldview; stressed the importance of obeying Church teachings; and produced levels of doctrinal orthodoxy and religious practice which exceeded those of most Protestant denominations (e.g., Catholic Mass attendance rates were often as high as 75 percent on any given Sunday). Catholics growing up in the 1920s, '30s, and '40s were socialized into a "ghetto mentality" which assumed that the world was a relatively hostile place, and that Catholics would be safe if they stayed in the Church and participated in its large array of Catholic organizations. Pre-Vatican II Catholics grew up surrounded by traditional symbols and liturgies: Benedictions, Forty Hours Devotions, Stations of the Cross, Latin Masses, and Gregorian chants. They were taught that priests and nuns are holy persons who deserve respect.

Baby boomers grew up with one foot in the "old Church" and one in the "new Church." In the 1950s, they were taught their faith by priests and nuns who relied heavily on the *Baltimore Catechism*. Like the generation that came before them, they also learned a dogmatic approach to faith and morals. They were to do what the priests and nuns told them to do. When they did not, they were to go to confession seeking absolution for their sins.

Then came the Second Vatican Council. Vatican II was a uniquely Catholic experience in the mid-1960s; no other American faith group experienced the anticipation, formulation, and implementation of such dramatic changes. No other group experienced the radical change in religious worldview that the Council promulgated.

The Second Vatican Council prescribed a new understanding of the Church's place in the world. Vatican II reversed the Church's traditional view of the world as a hostile place, arguing instead that the Church should become part of the modern world. Rather than viewing the Church as a haven from the evils of secular society, the Council urged Catholics to see the Church as a positive force in the world.

Vatican II also ushered in an era of greater ecumenism. By acknowledging positive aspects of non-Catholic and non-Christian religions, the Church authorized appreciation of different religious traditions. Using a more relative than absolute approach to religious truth, and a more open than closed model of Christian identity, the Council admitted that the Church was not without failings and acknowledged that religious truth could be found in other faiths.

While the pyramidal model of the Church (with the laity subordinate to priests and bishops who, in turn, are subordinate to the pope) remained intact, there was to be more collegiality between the pope and the bishops. Bishops and priests were encouraged to give "the people of God" more voice through instruments such as parish councils. At this same time, priests and nuns came to be seen as more "human," or fallible. They were no longer viewed with the reverence and awe that the pre-Vatican II Church had encouraged.

Vatican II also asked the laity to take greater responsibility for their own faith. At the same time that the Council was telling Catholics that traditions such as Latin Masses and meatless Fridays were no longer important, it was asking them to view their faith in more personal terms. Prior to Vatican II, Catholics were told to look first to the Church for guidance. The Council placed more emphasis on one's own conscience. In the *Pastoral Constitution on the Church in the Modern World*, the Council argued that:

> Deep within the conscience man discovers a law which he has not laid upon himself but which he must obey . . . For man has in his heart a law inscribed by God . . . *Man's dignity therefore requires him to act out of conscious and free choice, as moved and drawn from a personal way from within, and not by . . . mere external restraint* (Flannery, 1992:916-917).

Whereas Vatican II Catholics experienced the changes of the Council during their formative years, those who grew up in the 1970s and '80s know relatively little about the Council itself, but have had a very different type of religious upbringing because of it. Instead of memorizing the *Baltimore Catechism*, they have been taught a more experiential approach to faith. They have been told that they are on personal "faith journeys" and that they must take responsibility for their own religious beliefs and practices. Instead of attending Latin Masses, post-Vatican II Catholics are attending guitar Masses that are more experientially based than the traditional liturgies their parents and grandparents experienced. They have learned a very individualistic approach to faith that is ultimately about one's personal relationship with God (see Williams and Davidson, 1996; McNamara, 1992; Markey, 1994; O'Malley, 1986). In Ludwig's (1995:4) words, they have grown up in a "deconstructed" context and seek "a constructive worldview."

So what does this mean? In considering the formative experiences of the three generations, we believe that the societal and specifically Catholic changes have combined to impact each generation's approach to faith and morals differently. Based on this, we predicted that those belonging to the oldest cohort, the pre-Vatican II generation, would be the most likely to embrace conventional beliefs and practices. Those belonging to the Vatican II generation would maintain beliefs and practices that reflect a socialization in both the pre-Vatican II Church as well as the post-Vatican II Church. The youngest cohort of Catholics, the post-Vatican II generation, would be inclined to reject the traditional ways of their grandparents' generation. Because they have been raised entirely in the post-Vatican II Church, with its decreased emphasis on ritual and obedience, it makes sense that this cohort of parishioners would be the most likely of the three generations to espouse beliefs and practices that are counter to traditional Church teachings. In exploring these hypotheses, we have learned that generation, or birth cohort, is a powerful predictor of one's approach to faith and morals.

Individual Interview and Focus-Group Findings

In talking with Catholics in both individual interviews and focus groups, we found support for our predictions regarding generational differences. The most striking difference among the generations was their general approach to faith and morals: pre-Vatican II Catholics tended to embrace conceptions of faith and morality which are consistent with conventional Church teachings; post-Vatican II Catholics expressed understandings of faith and morality that reflect an emphasis on individual choice and a decreased emphasis on what the Church prescribes. Those belonging to the middle cohort described views of faith and morality that are consis-

tent with conventional Church teachings, as well as those that are disso-
nant with Church teachings.

Pre-Vatican II Catholics

Pre-Vatican II Catholics generally espoused understandings of faith
which indicated that the Church is an important mediator in one's relationship with God. When asked why they are Catholic, the pre-Vatican II
generation often said that it is because the Catholic Church is the "one
true Church." The obvious implication of this statement is that the best
way one can relate to God is through the Church. For most participants of
this generation, their relationship to the Church and self-definition as
Catholic are central to their faith. The following focus group excerpt illustrates this.

> *Person 1*: Being Catholic is a very important part of my
> life. I can't imagine what I would do without the Church
> being there for me. It gives me a solid foundation.

> *Person 2*: Yes. I agree. I think we are the true Church.

> *Person 3*: The Catholic Church is the true Church that
> was founded by Christ.

> *Person 4*: Yes. It has truth. I can't imagine being any-
> thing other than Catholic.

Pre-Vatican II Catholics also emphasize sacraments and rituals. When
asked in an individual interview why it is that she is Catholic, a woman
belonging to the pre-Vatican II generation responded saying "because of
the ritual of the Mass and the prayers."

Similarly, when asked about the essentials of being a "good Catholic,"
most pre-Vatican II persons answered with statements such as "participate in the sacraments," "abide by the commandments and rules of the
Church," and "be active in the Church in some way." A 62-year-old woman
answered, "It's important to attend Mass regularly. . . . The more [Church]
teachings you accept, the better you can be." Almost all pre-Vatican II
participants also agreed that it is important to support the Church financially.

In terms of sexual morality, the majority of pre-Vatican II Catholics
argued that it is important for a "good Catholic" to follow Church teachings regarding premarital and homosexual relations. This cohort over-
whelmingly voiced opinions opposing abortion, but was divided on their

opinions of artificial birth control. A pre-Vatican II male who accepts the birth-control teaching said a good Catholic must:

> . . . accept the Pope as our leader and take his word and follow what the Pope teaches and what the Church teaches. Do a minimum as far as receiving sacraments and obey rules. I don't think you can just do your own thing and still call yourself a Catholic. Follow teachings of the Catholic Church . . . not pick and choose like a cafeteria . . . there are people who disagree with Church teachings and call themselves Catholic, but they're not.

The majority of the pre-Vatican II persons had very little to say in regard to social justice and the Church's social teachings. Even when asked if they believe it is important for a "good Catholic" to support the Church's stance on social issues, most pre-Vatican II Catholics supplied only vague responses. It seems that most Catholics of this cohort have no clear sense of the social teachings beyond the importance of being kind to other people. An exception to this was a 70-year-old widow who stated that a good Catholic is "someone who really cares about people, who witnesses to the justice issues too, who is not afraid to speak up when necessary."

Post-Vatican II Catholics

Post-Vatican II Catholics tended to respond very differently from pre-Vatican II Catholics to questions about their faith and morals. When asked why she is Catholic, a woman belonging to the post-Vatican II generation stated: "I think it's important to me mainly because I was raised Catholic. I think if I had been raised in another faith then I don't think I would [be] Catholic." Similarly, in the focus groups post-Vatican II Catholics tended to state that they are Catholic because they were born and raised Catholic and have never considered being anything else. Unlike the pre-Vatican II generation, these younger Catholics didn't see their Catholic identity as a commitment to the institutional Church. As one participant explicitly stated, "It's not really important that I'm Catholic."

These younger Catholics also responded to the question of what it takes to be a "good Catholic" differently than did the pre-Vatican II respondents. Most stated that they did not want to judge others according to criteria set forth by the Church because "what really counts is what's in your heart," that what is important is "that you're doing the right thing for you," and that "whether a person is a good Catholic or not is between the person and God." Many respondents of this generation indicated that participation in the sacraments, Mass attendance, and contributing to the

Church financially are not important when considering the essentials of being a "good Catholic." When asked whether a "good Catholic" needs to attend Mass weekly, one focus-group participant answered, "No . . . why have the middle person when you have a direct line to God. . .? I'm a good Catholic because I'm a good person." In an individual interview, a 26-year-old woman answered this question by saying, "I think being a 'good Catholic' is not necessarily going to Church every Sunday, but being good to other people and loving people, and being the best person you can be doing God's acts and work." Another interview respondent said:

> "I think being a 'good Catholic' is like your personal behavior more than following the rules and regulations of the Church. . . . I don't really think God distinguishes on religions and there are lots of different religions, but I think we all have the same God. So I don't really think being a good Catholic is any different than being a good person."

On various sexual and reproductive issues, the majority of post-Vatican II focus-group participants openly disagreed with Church teachings. Only one post-Vatican II participant voiced agreement with the Church's stance on birth control; all other participants either explicitly or implicitly disagreed with *Humanae Vitae*. A 26-year-old mother-to-be addressed the issue by saying that "As far as the social aspects and the Church's view on abortion and birth control: that has nothing to do with my view of the Church. It does not affect me whatsoever."

Conventional teachings regarding premarital and homosexual relations were also questioned by post-Vatican II Catholics, with more participants disagreeing with the Church's position on premarital sex. Referring to homosexuality, a post-Vatican II participant stated that "any type of love that someone wants to display to another person should really be respected." Just as with the pre-Vatican II cohort, post-Vatican II participants were relatively uninformed about the Church's social teachings.

Vatican II Catholics

With Vatican II-generation Catholics, the story was not as clear. Whereas the pre-Vatican II participants clearly tend toward conventional understandings of faith and morals and the majority of post-Vatican II participants maintain faith and morals that are largely at odds with traditional teachings, the Vatican II cohort varied from conventional to unorthodox conceptions of faith and morals. With this middle cohort, some participants clearly reflected pre-Vatican II beliefs and practices;

others tended to give responses similar to those provided by post-Vatican II participants.

When asked why they are Catholic, many Vatican II generation Catholics voiced explanations that were very similar to those given by the pre-Vatican II participants. For example, some focus-group members stated that they are Catholic because Catholicism is the "best" or "true" religion. One participant stated that he is Catholic because he is "convinced that the Catholic Church is going to get [him] to heaven." The articulation of opinions such as these indicate that some persons of this generation are similar to pre-Vatican II Catholics in that they view the Church as a central component to their faith. Others in this age group, however, voiced opinions which differ greatly from those commonly heard from the pre-Vatican II participants. For example, some Vatican II participants stated that they could be just as happy belonging to some other faith tradition. They just "happen" to be Catholic; they were born and raised Catholic and remain Catholic out of convenience or habit. Some of these respondents stressed the importance of a "personal" relationship with God over their identification with the Catholic faith. As one Vatican II focus-group participant stated: "Faith is my relationship to God, personally." A 36-year-old woman told us in an interview that "it all has to do with the

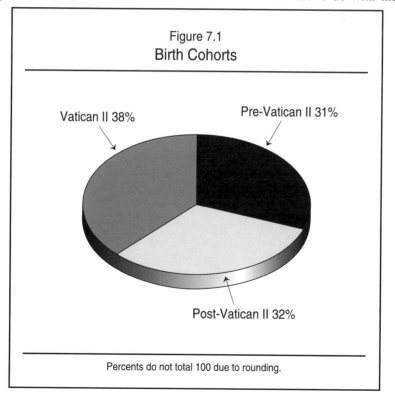

Figure 7.1
Birth Cohorts

Vatican II 38%

Pre-Vatican II 31%

Post-Vatican II 32%

Percents do not total 100 due to rounding.

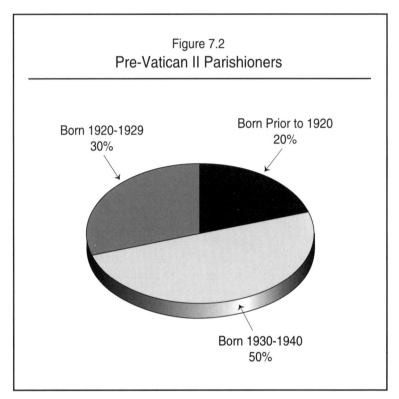

Figure 7.2
Pre-Vatican II Parishioners

Born 1920-1929
30%

Born Prior to 1920
20%

Born 1930-1940
50%

personal relationship with God." This attitude is more reflective of what we heard from the post-Vatican II participants.

Responses to the question of what is required to be a "good Catholic" also indicate that while some Vatican II respondents maintain pre-Vatican views of faith, others embrace attitudes more similar to the younger generation. Many Vatican II Catholics argued that it is important for a "good Catholic" to support the Church financially, adhere to Church teachings, and participate in the sacraments. Others, however, hold very different views, saying that obedience to teachings and support of the Church are insignificant in comparison with being a "good person." A Vatican II woman indicated this line of thinking in her individual interview when she said that being a "good Catholic" means "helping people when you can, sort of like going out of the way to help if you can."

For the most part, we found that in interviews and focus groups the Vatican II participants were more liberal than the pre-Vatican II generation on social-justice issues. As one focus-group participant said: "We're the children of the '60s and on the social issues we may be ahead of the Church." Some reflected progressive attitudes toward social-justice issues when asked about what it takes to be a "good Catholic." An interviewed woman in her late 30s told us that "a 'good Catholic' is concerned about ... social justice, and about being involved with hunger, homelessness, and racism."

In terms of sexual and reproductive morality, participants of this generation tended to be much more liberal than those of the pre-Vatican II generation. In fact, they often sounded more like post-Vatican II Catholics in that they frequently questioned Church teachings regarding abortion and birth control. As one woman stated, "I think *Humanae Vitae* sounds like two men talking to each other about a woman and the woman not having a voice."

Survey Findings

Using the same schema for categorizing birth cohorts, we find that 31 percent of the registered parishioners responding to our national survey belong to the pre-Vatican II cohort; 38 percent are Vatican II Catholics; and 32 percent are post-Vatican II Catholics (see Figure 7.1). Of the pre-Vatican II parishioners, 20 percent were born prior to 1920, 30 percent were born from 1920 to 1929, and 50 percent were born between the years 1930 and 1940 (see Figure 7.2). Thirty-four percent of the Vatican II parishioners were born between 1941 and 1949; 66 percent were born between 1950 and 1960 (see Figure 7.3). Of the youngest cohort, 61 per-

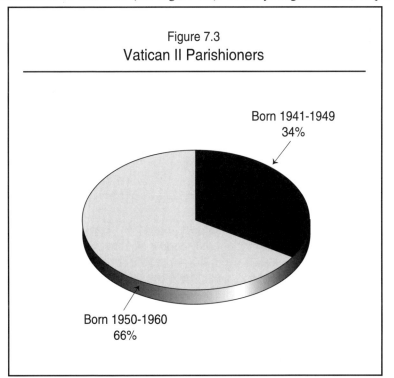

Figure 7.3
Vatican II Parishioners

Born 1941-1949
34%

Born 1950-1960
66%

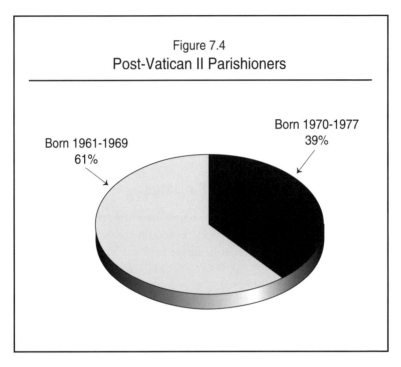

Figure 7.4
Post-Vatican II Parishioners

Born 1970-1977
39%

Born 1961-1969
61%

cent were born between 1961 and 1969; 39 percent were born between 1970 and 1977 (see Figure 7.4). Next, we look at what the three cohorts believe about faith and morals.

Traditional Beliefs and Practices Index

This index is useful for exploring generational differences in regard to pan-Vatican II beliefs such as the Incarnation and Resurrection. It also includes practices such as attending Mass, praying the rosary, praying privately, and going to private confession. There also are items concerning the extent to which parishioners agree that "the Catholic Church is the one true Church" and that "it's important to obey Church teachings even if I don't understand them."

On this index, the most striking difference exists between those belonging to the oldest generation and the two younger cohorts. Fully 66 percent of the pre-Vatican II Catholics scored "high" on this index, compared with 41 percent of the Vatican II Catholics and 37 percent of the youngest cohort. In other words, those who experienced their formative years either during or after Vatican II are much less likely to believe in and practice traditional Catholicism. It is the oldest cohort that stands out as different: the two younger cohorts are roughly similar in their propensity to embrace traditional beliefs and practices.

Table 7.1
Effects of Birth Cohort on Faith and Morals Indices
(percent)

	Faith			Morals	
	Trad. Beliefs/ Practices	Recent Ideas	Recent Practices	Sexual/Rep. Ethics	Social Teachings
	(High)	(High)	(High,Med)	(High)	(High)
Pre-Vatican II Cohort	66	20	8	41	51
Vatican II Cohort	41	32	9	18	45
Post-Vatican II Cohort	37	45	7	13	57

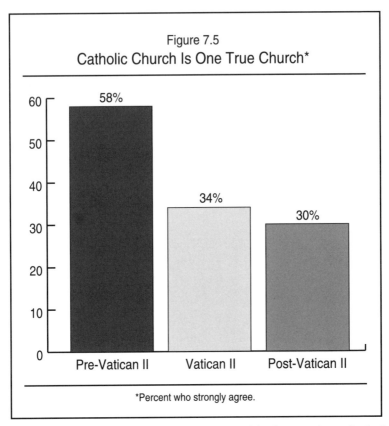

Figure 7.5
Catholic Church Is One True Church*

*Percent who strongly agree.

In looking at cohort differences on the individual survey items included in this index, the story becomes clearer. For example, 72 percent of the pre-Vatican II parishioners claim to attend Mass at least once a week. Fifty-six percent of the Vatican II respondents make this claim; 44 percent of the post-Vatican II Catholics say they go at least once a week. Similarly, 62 percent of the pre-Vatican II respondents receive Communion at least once a week; 45 percent of the Vatican II Catholics and 39 percent of the post-Vatican II respondents make this claim.

Belief items included in this index show the same pattern. For example, 58 percent of the pre-Vatican II parishioners "strongly agree" that the Catholic Church is the one true church. Thirty-four percent of the middle cohort "strongly agree" with this statement; thirty percent of the post-Vatican II Catholics "strongly agree" (see Figure 7.5).

We see the same pattern again with the item asking respondents about the importance they attach to belief in the Trinity: 71 percent of the oldest cohort state that this belief is "very important" to their faith; 58 percent of the middle cohort feel that it is "very important" and 56 percent of the youngest cohort say that belief in the Trinity is "very important" to them.

For some items there is more clearly a linear decline with the post-Vatican II respondents being significantly less orthodox than the middle cohort. For example, when asked whether "it is important to obey Church teachings even when one doesn't understand them," 38 percent of the oldest cohort "strongly agree" with this statement. Twenty-four percent of the Vatican II generation "strongly agree." Only 11 percent of the post-Vatican II Catholics "strongly agree" that it's important to obey teachings when they are not understood (see Figure 7.6).

Perhaps these findings aren't too surprising: we expected that pre-Vatican II Catholics would be more likely to embrace traditional beliefs and practices since they experienced their formative years prior to the changes brought about by the Council. What's surprising, however, is the similarity between the middle generation and the post-Vatican II cohort. Although the boomer Catholics are clearly "between" the two other generations on some items, the overall pattern on items included in the traditional beliefs and practices index shows that it is the two younger generations which are most similar to each other and different from the pre-Vatican II cohort.

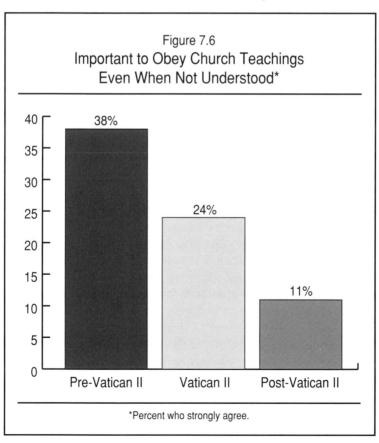

Figure 7.6
Important to Obey Church Teachings
Even When Not Understood*

*Percent who strongly agree.

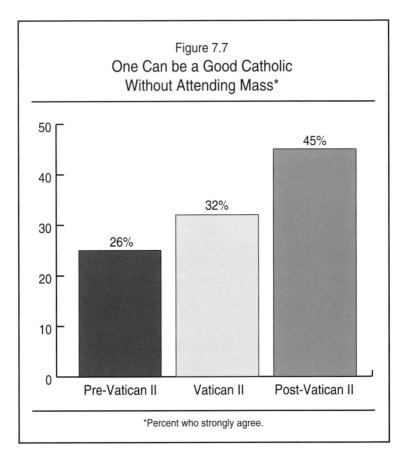

Figure 7.7
One Can be a Good Catholic
Without Attending Mass*

*Percent who strongly agree.

Recent Ideas Index

This index is made up of two items: the extent to which respondents agree that "one can be a good Catholic without going to Mass" and that "women should be allowed to be priests." We expected respondents who experienced their formative years since Vatican II to be the most inclined to score "high" on this index since these ideas have largely come about since the Council. Those who experienced their formative years prior to Vatican II would have been exposed to these ideas later in their lifecourse, and would thus be less likely to accept them. Vatican II Catholics who grew up with one foot in the "old" Church and one foot in the "new" Church were expected to score somewhere between the younger and older generations. This is exactly what we found.

While only 20 percent of those belonging to the pre-Vatican II cohort score "high" on this index, 32 percent of the middle generation, and 45 percent of the post-Vatican II generation score "high." Only 18 percent of those belonging to the youngest cohort scored "low," 31 percent of the

Vatican II generation score "low," and fully 56 percent of the pre-Vatican II generation score "low."

With this index we see an overall linear trend: the tendency to agree and agree strongly that "one can be a good Catholic without going to Mass" and that ordination should be open to women is lowest among those raised prior to Vatican II and highest among those raised in the post-Vatican II Church. The tendency for Vatican II Catholics to embrace post-Vatican II ideas is greater than it is for older Catholics, but less than it is for those belonging to the youngest cohort.

In looking at the items making up this index, the linear trend is most clearly seen in the item measuring agreement with the statement "one can be a good Catholic without attending Mass." Twenty-six percent of the oldest cohort and 32 percent of the middle cohort "strongly agree" with this statement. Fully 45 percent of the post-Vatican II generation "strongly agree" (see Figure 7.7). Conversely, 40 percent of the pre-Vatican II cohort "strongly disagrees" with the statement; 23 percent of the middle cohort "strongly disagree"; and only 14 percent of the post-Vatican II cohort "strongly disagree" that "one can be a good Catholic without attending Mass."

In response to the item measuring agreement that "women should be allowed to be priests," the linear trend is not as clear. Of the pre-Vatican II cohort, 24 percent "strongly agree." Within both the Vatican II and post-Vatican II generations, 41 percent "strongly agree" that "women should be allowed to be priests" (see Figure 7.8). When looking at those who "strongly disagree," 44 percent of the pre-Vatican II parishioners, 30 percent of the Vatican II parishioners, and 19 percent of the post-Vatican II cohort "strongly disagree" with the statement.

Recent Practices Index

We looked at how the three cohorts responded to questions regarding devotional practices that have become more common among Catholics since the Second Vatican Council, such as reading the Bible and attending prayer or faith-sharing groups. In each of the three cohorts, the majority of parishioners score "low" on this index: 92 percent of the pre-Vatican II cohort score "low," 91 percent of the middle generation score "low," and 93 percent of the post-Vatican II generation score "low." Essentially, the three cohorts do not differ significantly on this index. Practices such as reading the Bible and attending faith-sharing groups are so uncommon that it's difficult to see any significant cohort differences at all.

Sexual and Reproductive Teachings Index

The index designed to explore attitudes toward sexual and reproductive behavior produced essentially the same pattern as the index

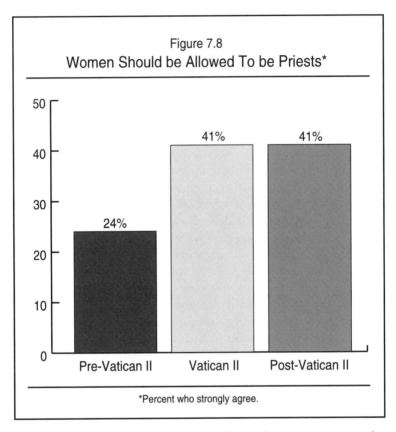

Figure 7.8
Women Should be Allowed To be Priests*

*Percent who strongly agree.

measuring traditional beliefs and practices: the two younger cohorts are similar to one another, but very different from the pre-Vatican II generation. While 41 percent of the pre-Vatican II cohort score "high" on the sexual and reproductive index, 18 percent of the middle cohort score "high," and 13 percent of the post-Vatican II cohort score "high." Pre-Vatican II Catholics clearly are more accepting than those belonging to the two younger cohorts of Church teachings regarding artificial birth control, abortion, homosexual relations, and premarital sex. There is very little difference between Vatican II parishioners and post-Vatican II parishioners when it comes to attitudes regarding sexuality and reproduction.

Looking at the individual items included in this index supports this finding (see Table 7.2). Twenty percent of the oldest generation says that it is "always morally wrong" to use condoms or birth-control pills. Only six percent of the middle cohort, and four percent of the youngest cohort, hold this belief. Ninety percent of the post-Vatican II cohort says that the use of artificial contraceptives is "entirely up to the individual." Eighty-seven percent of the middle cohort believes that it is "entirely up to the

Table 7.2
Effects of Birth Cohort on Deciding the Morality of Sexual and Reproductive Behaviors* (percent)

	Pre-Vatican	Vatican II	Post-Vatican
Artificial Birth Control			
Always morally wrong	20	6	4
Wrong except under certain circumstances	15	8	6
Up to the individual	65	87	90
Premarital Sex			
Always morally wrong	55	26	20
Wrong except under certain circumstances	7	9	9
Up to the individual	37	65	71
Abortion			
Always morally wrong	51	36	31
Wrong except under certain circumstances	29	30	42
Up to the individual	20	34	28
Homosexual Relations			
Always morally wrong	66	42	47
Wrong except under certain circumstances	2	5	4
Up to the individual	32	53	49

* Percents may not total to 100 due to rounding.

individual." Sixty-five percent of the oldest generation feels that the use of condoms and pills is "entirely up to the individual."

The pattern is the same in regard to premarital sex: 55 percent of the oldest cohort believes that it is "always morally wrong" to engage in pre-marital sex; 26 percent of the middle cohort shares this view; 20 percent of the post-Vatican II generation holds the view that premarital sex is "always morally wrong." Thirty-seven percent of the pre-Vatican II generation thinks that whether to engage in premarital sex is "entirely up to the individual." Sixty-five percent of the Vatican II cohort holds this view; 71 percent of the youngest cohort agrees that premarital sex is "entirely up to the individual."

The items tapping attitudes toward abortion and the morality of homo-sexual relations indicate a somewhat different pattern. The two younger cohorts are more similar to one another than either is to older Catholics, but it is the Vatican II generation, not the post-Vatican II cohort, that has the most individualistic views on abortion and homosexuality.

Social Teachings Index

This index includes two items: the extent to which respondents agree that "helping needy people is an important part of my religious beliefs" and that "Catholics have a duty to try to close the gap between the rich and the poor." Somewhat surprisingly, what we find is that parishioners belonging to the Vatican II generation are the least likely to score high on this index: 45 percent, compared with 51 percent of the pre-Vatican II cohort and 57 percent of the post-Vatican II generation. Why is this surprising? Because the prevailing belief among many is that it is the "boomer" generation, or those who experienced Vatican II during their formative years, who are the most concerned about social teachings. Instead, we find that it is post-Vatican II Catholics who are most inclined to embrace the Church's concern for the poor.

In looking at the individual questions that make up this index, it is the item measuring agreement with the statement that "Catholics have a duty to try to close the gap between the rich and the poor" that produces the significant cohort effects we see on this index (see Figure 7.9). If we combine the responses of "strongly agree" and "somewhat agree," it's those belonging to the youngest cohort who are the most likely to agree with the statement (65 percent) and those belonging to the Vatican II cohort who are the least likely to agree (51 percent). Fifty-eight percent of the pre-Vatican II cohort agree that "Catholics have a duty to try to close the gap between the rich and the poor."

In looking at the other item included in this index, we find almost no variance among the cohorts. Between 97 and 99 percent of all three cohorts "somewhat agree" or "strongly agree" that "helping needy people is an important part of [their] religious beliefs."

The overall finding of a U-shape curve on social teachings challenges the often-heard view that Catholics who grew up in the 1960s are more concerned about peace and justice than older and younger parishioners. Despite stereotypes of those belonging to the post-Vatican II generation — the so-called Generation X — as being apathetic in regard to political and economic issues, it is parishioners of this generation who are the most supportive of Catholics working to alleviate the economic inequalities that we currently face in this country.

Intra-generational Variation

Some diocesan and parish leaders have asked whether there are differences within cohorts, especially within the post-Vatican II generation.

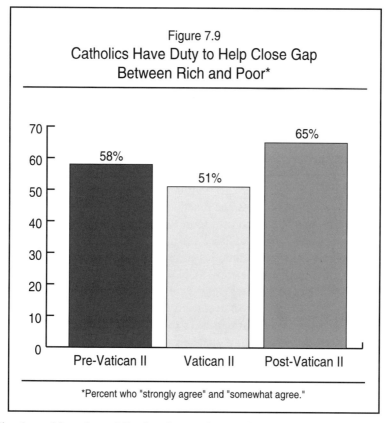

Figure 7.9
Catholics Have Duty to Help Close Gap
Between Rich and Poor*

*Percent who "strongly agree" and "somewhat agree."

They've told us that while they have witnessed a decline in adherence to traditional beliefs and practices among some younger Catholics, they have also met post-Vatican II parishioners who are yearning for a return to the pre-Vatican II Church. These young Catholics seem to embrace the ritual and clearly defined understandings of right and wrong that are characteristic of the "old" Church. Diocesan and parish leaders have told us that this observation has led them to wonder whether there is a "rebound" or "U-shape" effect occurring, with post-Vatican II Catholics moving toward religious sensibilities more similar to those of their grandparents than those of their parents. If this hypothesis is true, we would not see a general decline in acceptance of Church teachings and a weakening of Catholic identity with each successive generation. Rather, we would see a "U-shape" trend, with the youngest parishioners "rebounding" to share the beliefs and practices of the pre-Vatican II cohort.

To explore this hypothesis, we broke the three cohorts into seven smaller birth cohorts: those born before 1920; 1920 through 1929; 1930 through 1940; 1941 through 1949; 1950 through 1960; 1961 through 1969; and 1970 through 1977. This more refined grouping of birth cohorts allows us to further examine the possibility of a "rebound" effect. Also, it allows us to explore differences between older and younger persons within each of the original three cohorts. We can see, for example, if older Vatican II parishioners differ significantly from younger Vatican II parishioners in terms of their faith and morals (see Table 7.3).

Traditional Beliefs and Practices Index

In looking at how the seven cohorts responded to this index, we do not find a "U-shape" or "rebound" effect with the youngest cohorts. Rather, with almost every successive generation there is a general decline in adherence to traditional beliefs and practices. For the pre-Vatican II Catholics born prior to 1920, 82 percent score "high" on this index. Of parishioners born between 1920 and 1929, 77 percent score "high." Fifty-three percent of pre-Vatican II Catholics born between 1930 and 1940 score "high." Within the oldest generation of Vatican II parishioners, those born between 1941 and 1949, 49 percent score "high." Of the baby boomers born from 1950 to 1960, 37 percent score "high."

Next come the post-Vatican II Catholics born from 1961 through 1969. This is the first cohort that does not show a decline in adherence to traditional beliefs and practices: 38 percent score "high" on this index, which is actually one percentage point higher than the boomer generation which came before it. This is not indicative of a "rebound" effect, however; a one-percentage point increase is not significant. It does indicate, however, that the youngest generation of Vatican II Catholics and the older generation of post-Vatican II Catholics are not significantly different from one another when it comes to traditional beliefs and practices. In fact, boomer parishioners born from 1950 through 1960 are more similar to these older post-Vatican II Catholics than they are to the Vatican II parishioners born just prior to them.

In looking at the youngest post-Vatican II parishioners, we find that 35 percent of them score "high" on this index. This is a three-percentage-point decrease from the older post-Vatican II Catholics. We do not see a "rebound" effect here, as these Catholics who were between the ages of 18 and 25 when interviewed are the least likely of all seven cohorts to embrace traditional beliefs and practices.

Recent Ideas Index

Here again, we do not find a "rebound" effect. With only one exception, we find a linear trend toward increased support for the attitudes that "one can be a good Catholic without going to Mass" and "women should be allowed to be priests." The one exception to this general linear trend is the oldest generation of pre-Vatican II Catholics, which is slightly more supportive of these recent beliefs than the pre-Vatican II parishioners born just after them. Twenty-four percent of those born prior to 1920 score "high" on this index; 17 percent of those born from 1920 through 1929 score "high." The next generation of pre-Vatican II Catholics is more supportive of these recent beliefs than those who were born just prior to them: 21 percent score "high."

With the older Vatican II parishioners, we see a rather dramatic increase in support for whether "one can be a good Catholic without going to Mass" and the belief that "women should be allowed to be priests." Thirty-one percent of this generation score "high" on this index. The younger Vatican II parishioners are just as likely to support these beliefs: 31 percent of them also score "high" on this index.

With the post-Vatican II Catholics, we again see an increase in support for these recent ideas. Of the older post-Vatican parishioners, 39 percent score "high" on this index. With the youngest generation, we see even more support for these recent ideas: 55 percent of those born between 1970 and 1977 score "high" on this index.

Recent Practices Index

With this index there really isn't much of a story. Just as when we looked at how the original three cohorts scored on this index, we find almost no significant differences among the seven cohorts. The exception to this is with the oldest group of pre-Vatican II Catholics: only one percent of parishioners of this age group score either "high" or "medium" on this index. Among the other six cohorts, the percentage of respondents scoring either "high" or "medium" ranges from seven to 10 percent. Thus, the very oldest group of parishioners, those born prior to 1920, is significantly less likely than those of any other age group to read the Bible or attend Bible-study or faith-sharing groups. Perhaps this isn't so surprising, as those born prior to 1920 are currently over 76 years old. At this age, parishioners might have poor eyesight, which might limit their ability to read the Bible. Some also might have difficulties getting to and from Bible-study or faith-sharing groups.

Sexual and Reproductive Teachings Index

With this index we once again see a downward trend away from support for Church teachings rather than a "rebound" effect. Among the two

Table 7.3
Effects of Birth Cohort on Faith and Morals Indices (percent)

	Faith			Morals	
	Trad. Beliefs/ Practices (High)	Recent Ideas (High)	Recent Practices (High,Med)	Sexual/Rep. Ethics (High)	Social Teachings (High)
Pre-Vatican II					
Born before 1920	82	24	1	54	65
Born 1920-29	77	17	9	50	56
Born 1930-40	53	21	10	31	42
Vatican II					
Born 1941-49	49	31	8	25	44
Born 1950-60	37	31	10	14	45
Post-Vatican II					
Born 1961-69	38	39	8	17	57
Born 1970-77	35	55	7	9	56

oldest cohorts, about half of the respondents score "high" on this index. With the youngest cohort of pre-Vatican II generation Catholics, we begin to see a dramatic decline: of those born from 1930 to 1940, only 31 percent score "high."

With the Vatican II generation we continue to see the downward trend away from support for the Church's stance on sexual and reproductive issues. Twenty-five percent of those born from 1941 and 1949 score "high" on this index. Only 14 percent of those born from 1950 to 1960 score "high."

The oldest cohort of post-Vatican II Catholics is slightly more supportive than the prior generation of the Church's sexual and reproductive teachings: 17 percent of this generation score "high." While there is a slight increase from the 14 percent of those born just prior to them, a three percentage-point increase is not really indicative of a "rebound." The fact that only nine percent of the youngest generation of Catholics, those born from 1970 to 1977, score "high" on this index is further evidence that there is not a "rebound" occurring.

Social Teachings Index

With this index, there does appear to be somewhat of a "rebound" or "U-shape" effect. Of those born before 1920, 65 percent score "high." Fifty-six percent of parishioners born from 1920 through 1929 score "high" on this index. Of the youngest group of pre-Vatican II Catholics, the percent who score "high" falls to 42. In looking at the Vatican II parishioners, we find that 44 percent of those born from 1941 to 1949 score "high." Forty-five percent of those born from 1950 to 1960 score "high." Of the older post-Vatican II Catholics, those born in or between 1961 and 1969, 57 percent score "high." With the youngest post-Vatican II parishioners, those born in or between 1970 and 1977, 56 percent score "high."

Summary and Conclusions

We find significant generational differences among Catholics. Although some Church leaders have suggested to us that there is a "rebound" or "U-shape" effect, with younger Catholics embracing views and practices similar to those of their grandparents' generation, we do not find it. Rather, it appears that there is a linear trend away from conventional religious sensibilities, with the youngest Catholics being the least inclined to maintain traditional faith and morals. This trend is especially apparent with regard to traditional beliefs and practices, the sexual and reproductive norms, and recent ideas. On each of these three indices, we see a general decline in acceptance of Church teachings and traditional Catholic practices. The one place where we see some rebound is on our social teachings index. There is no real cohort effect on recent practices.

Pre-Vatican II Catholics indicate that they view their faith primarily in institutional terms. For them, the Church is seen as a mediating force in their relationship with God. For these older Catholics, a Catholic identity, participation in the sacraments, acceptance of Church teachings, and overall commitment to the Church are essential to relating with God. They see little difference between involvement with the Church and relating to God because the two are deeply interconnected. Because of this interconnectedness, pre-Vatican II Catholics embrace traditional approaches to faith and morals.

This is less true for Catholics who came of age around the time of Vatican II. In the interviews and focus groups, many described their faith as being less institutionally based than those who came of age before them. Others reflected institutional notions of faith and morals that are similar to the views of pre-Vatican II Catholics.

The post-Vatican II generation is the least committed to the institutional Church. When asked about the essentials of being a "good Catholic," concern with whether an individual is a "good person" dominated their responses. When asked outright whether a "good Catholic" needs to attend Mass regularly and accept various Church teachings, these young Catholics answered no. Similar findings surfaced in bishops' listening sessions with young Catholics and have led to the bishops' recent pastoral letter *Sons and Daughters of the Light* (NCCB, 1996a). Given our results, this letter deserves widespread attention.

Some observers are likely to suggest that our interviews, focus groups, and survey findings simply reflect age effects. Is it possible that as Vatican II generation Catholics get further along in age they will embrace approaches to faith and morals that are more similar to those currently maintained by pre-Vatican II Catholics? Will post-Vatican II Catholics become more committed to the institutional Church as they age? To be absolutely sure of the answers to these questions, we would need to do a longitudinal study with our respondents. But based on the theory of generations discussed earlier, it is very unlikely that Vatican II parishioners will someday reflect the faith and morals of pre-Vatican II Catholics, and that post-Vatican II parishioners will ever embrace the religious sensibilities of their parents and grandparents.

Based on the survey findings, however, we can say that the trend away from traditional beliefs and practices has slowed somewhat. With the traditional beliefs and practices index, we see dramatic shifts between the two younger pre-Vatican II subgroups, and between the older and younger Vatican II parishioners (see Table 7.3). Comparing the younger of the Vatican II parishioners (those born from 1950 through 1960) with the two subgroups of post-Vatican II parishioners, it appears that the downward trend is leveling off. We do not see this leveling off tendency when looking at the recent ideas index and the sexual and reproductive ethics index, however. With both of these indices, the younger subgroup of the post-Vatican II parishioners is significantly less inclined to embrace conventional faith and morals than those just slightly older than them.

8 • Gender Differences
Male and Female Approaches to Faith and Morals

> . . . We do not yet fully understand how complex the re-
> lationship between religion and gender really is.
>
> *Ursula King (1995:5)*

> Womens' versions of certain religions are probably very
> different from mens' versions; a woman may focus on
> those aspects of the group's worldview that speak to her
> social situation.
>
> *Meredith McGuire (1992:112)*

In today's popular culture, it is trendy — even profitable — to make
sharp distinctions between men and women based on a variety of pre-
suppositions. Psychologists from Carol Gilligan (1982) to John Gray
(1992) and others such as linguist Deborah Tannen (1990) speculate about
the causes and effects of gender differences. The assumption is that not
only are women and men different, they are from entirely different planets! At the most extreme, women are stereotyped as highly sensitive vic-
tims who are preoccupied with relationships and overwhelmed with emo-

tion and a monthly hormonal imbalance which interferes with their ability to compete in the real world. On the other hand, men are stereotyped as emotionless, thoughtless, task-oriented robots preoccupied with power and incapable of developing meaningful relationships due to lack of commitment. These views reinforce stereotypes suggesting that women and men are of entirely different species, not different expressions of the same species.

Psychologist Carol Tavris (1996, 1992) insists that the situation is far more complex than this simple dichotomy might suggest. As the roles of men and women in today's society undergo great change, women and men struggle to redefine themselves in relation to a new world whereby old roles no longer suffice to define either gender. Increasing education for women, working outside the home, "soccer moms," divorce, blended families, aging parents, economic necessities, and many more issues come into play when trying to account for gender differences in today's world (Jamieson, 1995).

Although we are unwilling to accept polarizing views of men and women, we can reasonably assume that Catholic women and Catholic men have differing orientations toward their faith and that these differing views are being influenced by the changing role of women in the world (Winter, Lummis, and Stokes, 1994; Pieper, 1993; Greeley and Durkin, 1984; Ulanov, 1981).

Thus, we asked ourselves several questions. Do Catholic women and Catholic men have different views of issues such as the Trinity, Incarnation, Resurrection, and other such doctrines? Are there any topics in which men and women tend to agree? On what issues are men and women most at odds? Is it women or men who most agree with official Church teachings?

We thought there would be some important gender differences on these issues. Assuming that women are more religious than men (Miller and Hoffmann, 1995; Argyle and Beit-Hallahmi, 1975), we expected women to score higher on measures such as traditional beliefs and practices and recent practices. Assuming women are somewhat more compassionate and relational (Wuthnow, 1995), we expected they would embrace the Church's social teachings about peace and justice more than men do. But because women may be more compassionate, we thought they might be more likely to reject the Church's sexual and reproductive ethics, which they might see as too harsh and rigid. Finally, because women have been excluded from power in the Church (McEnroy, 1996), we expected they might be more inclined to agree with recent ideas such as ordaining women.

Sixty-one percent of *all* the people who responded to our national poll are women; 39 percent are men. However, 63 percent of *parishioners* are women, while only 37 percent are men. Therefore, women are more likely

Table 8.1 — Impact of Gender
(percent)

	Faith			Morals	
	Trad. Beliefs/ Practices (High)	Recent Ideas (High)	Recent Practices (High,Med)	Sexual/Rep. Ethics (High)	Social Teachings (High)
Women	49	34	9	23	50
Men	43	30	6	23	51

to belong to parishes, be on parish rolls, and when Mass begins on Saturday evening or Sunday morning, almost two-thirds of those in the pews are women. For that reason alone, it is important to understand how women's views of Church teachings compare with those of men.

Table 8.1 summarizes men's and women's scores on our measures of faith and morals. A first glance seems to show that women and men are more alike than they are different. The percentage differences are rather small. Women are somewhat more likely to accept traditional beliefs and participate in traditional practices (49 percent vs. 43 percent). Also women are a bit more likely to accept recent ideas such as ordaining women (34 percent vs. 30 percent) and to engage in recent practices such as reading the Bible (nine percent vs. six percent). No gender differences are evident on our index of sexual and reproductive ethics. Also, contrary to our expectations, there is virtually no gender difference when it comes to agreeing with the social teachings of the Church (51 percent vs. 50 percent).

Let's take a closer look at our data to see where the similarities and differences are greatest, looking first at the items included in our measure of traditional beliefs and practices.

Traditional Beliefs and Practices Index

The Catholic Church is the one true Church. I still think there is only one truth. The Catholic Church is the truth.
Indiana woman, over 50

The Catholic Church is the true Church that was founded by Christ.
Indiana man, over 50

It's sad to be losing our traditions and heritage.
Indiana man, under 30

I don't know how to say the rosary, and I wish I did.
Indiana woman, under 30

In Table 8.1, we see that women are a bit more likely to score "high" on traditional beliefs and practices. Though only half of parishioners continue to practice their faith in traditionally Catholic ways, women have a somewhat stronger prayer life and somewhat higher rates of participation in conventional Catholic practices.

When we analyze the data more closely (see Table 8.2), paying particular attention to differences in cohort as well as gender, we get a more complex picture. For both women and men parishioners, the pre-Vatican

Table 8.2
Traditional Beliefs and Practices Index
(percent)

	Pre-Vatican II Cohort	Vatican II Cohort	Post-Vatican II Cohort
Total			
Women	69	43	36
Men	61	36	38
Attend Mass once a week or more			
Women	76	58	44
Men	65	52	45
Pray privately once a week or more			
Women	95	90	83
Men	64	79	72

II cohort scores considerably higher than the two younger cohorts. Sixty-nine percent of pre-Vatican II women score "high" on the index while 61 percent of men do. From here, there is a distinctly downward trend in acceptance of traditional beliefs and practices. Both women and men respondents of the Vatican II and post-Vatican II cohorts, our "boomers" and "Xers," score considerably lower on this traditional beliefs and practices index. For women, there is a linear downward trend in which the oldest cohort is most likely to score "high," and the youngest cohort least likely to score "high." Of note is a very slight rebound in the percentages for post-Vatican II men that does not appear for women. Also notable is the fact that women of the older two cohorts accept traditional beliefs and practices in higher percentages than men in the same cohort, whereas the men of the youngest cohort exhibit slightly higher percentages of acceptance than women in the same cohort. Overall, gender differences decline from the pre-Vatican II cohort to the post-Vatican II cohort.

Overall, women are more likely than men to attend Mass once a week or more. Further analysis of the responses reveals that it is the older women who are attending Mass more often and in larger numbers than males of their cohort, and that it is the oldest cohort of both men and women who are filling the pews more often than those in the two younger generations. But the gender differences lessen in each succeeding generation so that both women and men of the youngest cohort are attending Mass in about the same numbers. While older women are more likely to attend Mass than older men, there is no difference between the genders in the youngest cohort. The overall decline in Mass attendance by the middle and youngest cohort is a clear downward trend, and is similar to findings in other recent surveys of Mass attendance (Donahue, 1995; D'Antonio, Davidson, Hoge, and Wallace, 1996).

Another item in the traditional beliefs and practices index is: "How often do you pray privately?" Overall, women pray more often and in higher numbers than men in all three cohorts. But there is a general decline in numbers of women praying. The cohorts of men in our sample exhibit a different pattern. While women exhibit a downward trend from the oldest to the youngest cohort, men exhibit a curvilinear pattern. The middle cohort of men pray more often than their fathers or sons.

Recent Ideas Index

The Pope is too rigid (on the ordination of women) . . .
he's over there; he doesn't see what's going on over here.
Indiana woman, under 30

If I had to follow each and every belief, I wouldn't be in
any religion. I have my own mind.
Indiana woman, under 30

When looking at the recent ideas index measuring the acceptance of unsanctioned movements in the Church, we find only small gender differences. But when cohorts are taken into account, gender differences become considerably more evident (see Table 8.3). There is a clear upward trend toward acceptance of unconventional ideas from the oldest to the youngest cohort. Whereas men of the pre-Vatican II cohort are more likely to score "high" on this index, it is the women of the post-Vatican II cohort who are most likely to score "high." Additionally, gender differences are present for each cohort, but women have moved toward unauthorized ideas in larger numbers and faster than the men of their cohort, so the gender gap reaches almost 20 percentage points in the youngest cohort. The differences between the genders in the oldest cohort indicate that men in the oldest generation are more open to new ideas than women in that cohort. In the middle cohort, women are slightly more likely to accept such views than men of their cohort. In the youngest cohort, however, the women are much more likely to accept recent ideas than the men are.

Individual items in this index more clearly display the generational differences as well as gender differences. We asked if "one can be a good Catholic without going to Mass." Commitment to weekly Mass attendance decreases with each succeeding cohort. The highest percentage of agree-

Table 8.3
Recent Ideas Index
(percent)

	Pre-Vatican II Cohort	Vatican II Cohort	Post-Vatican II Cohort
Total			
Women	18	34	54
Men	24	28	35
Can be a good Catholic without attending mass			
(Strongly agree and somewhat agree)			
Women	45	57	79
Men	49	51	61
Women should be allowed to be priests			
(Strongly agree and somewhat agree)			
Women	40	59	75
Men	42	56	67

ment is by the youngest women. The oldest and the middle cohorts display only modest gender difference, but young women now question the need for Mass considerably more than young men do (79 percent vs. 61 percent).

Respondents also were asked to agree or disagree with the statement "women should be allowed to be priests." The oldest and middle cohorts show very little gender difference, even though there is an increase in the acceptance of women priests between the generations. However, in the youngest cohort it is a much different story. A significant gender difference is apparent, with young women being more inclined to allow women priests than men (75 percent for women vs. 67 percent for men). The trend to embrace the idea of allowing women priests increases faster and in higher percentages for women than for men.

Recent Practices Index

> My faith is strengthened by what I believe and how I interpret it within my spirituality. I don't have to go to Church all the time. I can pray at home.
>
> *Indiana woman, under 30*

> A good Catholic should be willing to learn and grow . . . a good Catholic is a person who's really practicing their faith, not just going to Mass on Sunday.
>
> *Indiana woman, under 30*

There are very small gender differences in recent practices, such as reading the Bible, participating in Bible study, or belonging to prayer groups. Only nine percent of women and six percent of men scored "high" or "medium" on this scale (see Table 8.1). However, controlling for cohort

Table 8.4
Recent Practices Index
(Percent "high" and "medium")

	Pre-Vatican II Cohort	Vatican II Cohort	Post-Vatican II Cohort
Women	11	13	3
Men	1	2	13

(see Table 8.4), we see larger gender differences. Older women participate in these practices more than older men do. On the other hand, young
men participate more than young women do.

Sexual and Reproductive Ethics Index

> I haven't seen anything in the Bible about birth control,
> and I've looked.
> *Indiana woman, under 30*

> Because homosexuality may be biologically caused (ge-
> netic), we cannot put them down for it. They've got to
> live their lives if that is the only way they will be happy.
> *Indiana woman, under 30*

> I didn't think birth control was even an issue anymore;
> maybe it is in Rome, but not here.
> *Indiana man, between 30 and 50*

> It's not necessary to follow the Church's teachings re-
> garding sexuality. It's up to the individuals involved as
> long as no one gets hurt. It depends on the circumstances.
> *Indiana woman, under 30*

Our index measuring attitudes toward Church teachings on sexual and
reproductive ethics issues shows no gender differences. About one-fourth
of all parishioners — male and female — score "high" (see Table 8.1).
Once again, however, this does not tell the whole story. When we look at
individual cohorts (see Table 8.5), we see some real differences between
the cohorts as well as between the genders. The younger two cohorts diverge sharply from the oldest generation; the biggest gender distinction is
found between women and men of the youngest cohort. There is a clear
trend, with the youngest cohort of women being least likely to score "high."
A shift of almost 24 points occurs between the oldest and the middle cohort of women. The difference between the oldest cohort of women and
the youngest is 32 points. For men, as for women, the pre-Vatican II cohort is distinctly different than the succeeding cohorts. Men in the pre-
Vatican II cohort are more than twice as likely to score "high" as their
sons or grandsons. Young men are now more inclined to agree with Church
teachings than young women.

When we look at the low end of our index by gender and cohort
(i.e., those who reject Church teachings of sexual and reproductive issues), there are relatively small differences between men and women in

the oldest and middle cohorts. However, the post-Vatican II cohort of women is much more likely to reject Church teachings on sex and reproductive ethics than post-Vatican II men, by a margin of 23 points. The trend toward low scores is linear for women, but curvilinear for men. For men, the middle cohort stands out as most likely to reject the Church's teachings, in fairly strong numbers. The youngest cohort of men is less likely to reject the Church's sexual teachings than the Vatican II cohort, bringing the young men into wider disagreement with the women in their own cohort.

Table 8.5
Sexual-Reproductive Ethics Index
(percent)

	Pre-Vatican II Cohort	Vatican II Cohort	Post-Vatican II Cohort
Percent "High"			
Women	42	18	10
Men	40	16	18
Percent "Low"			
Women	32	58	64
Men	26	54	41
Homosexual acts:			
Always wrong			
Women	63	39	36
Men	71	49	62
Up to individual			
Women	34	58	61
Men	29	45	34
Abortion:			
Always wrong			
Women	53	35	35
Men	49	38	32
Up to individual			
Women	20	34	35
Men	18	34	19
Premarital sex:			
Always wrong			
Women	61	26	14
Men	44	24	27
Up to individual			
Women	36	65	78
Men	39	66	61

The issue which provokes the greatest gender disagreement is homo-sexuality. This item elicits responses that help explain some of the rebound effect in the youngest cohort of men. For women there is a trend away from Church teachings. For men, however, it is the middle cohort which is least likely to say that homosexuality is always wrong. Young men deny the mo-rality of homosexuality in percentages that resemble the oldest cohort of men more than the middle cohort. This increases the margin of difference to 26 points between the women and men of the youngest cohort.

Similar results show up when we asked if homosexual acts are up to the individual. Women of each successive cohort are increasingly more willing to agree. Men in the middle cohort, however, show a higher will-ingness to agree with the statement than men of the older and younger cohorts. Women and men of the oldest cohort are more similar than women and men of the younger two cohorts. The largest gender difference is seen in the youngest cohort, where women are about twice as likely to accom-modate individual decisions on this issue than men of their cohort.

Less gender difference is evident in the survey question about abor-tion. Cohort differences between the oldest and younger two cohorts are more noticeable than gender differences on this question. There is a down-ward trend away from Church teaching. Half of the pre-Vatican II cohort says abortion is always wrong, but only about one-third of Vatican II and post-Vatican II parishioners are willing to say this.

When asked if the morality of abortion should be up to the individual, a somewhat different pattern appears. For women, the oldest cohort is different than the younger two cohorts. For men, however, a curvilinear a pattern appears again. The oldest cohort of men is very similar to women in the same cohort. Men of the middle cohort are exactly like women in their cohort. However, men in the youngest cohort are much less likely to say that abortion is up to the individual (making the youngest cohort of men nearly identical to the oldest cohort). The gender gap between men and women of the post-Vatican II cohort is 16 percentage points.

In response to the survey item about premarital sex, there is a down-ward trend among women, with each succeeding cohort less likely to say that premarital sex is always wrong. For women, a dramatic 47-point mar-gin separates the oldest cohort of women from the youngest cohort. For the men, there is a slight curvilinear pattern. Pre-Vatican II men are most likely to agree with Church teachings about premarital sex, followed by post-Vatican II men, then Vatican II men.

An increasing upward trend toward individual decisions regarding pre-marital sex is evident among women. However, there is a curvilinear pat-tern for men across the cohorts. Little gender difference is seen in the oldest and the middle cohorts. A 17-point gender difference is found, how-ever, in the youngest cohort.

Social Teachings Index

> It's not important to follow Church teachings on social justice issues.
>> *Indiana woman, under 30*

> What really counts is what's in your heart.
>> *Indiana woman, under 30*

> One of the great things that's happened since Vatican II is all the people involved in peace and justice.
>> *Indiana woman, between 30 and 50*

In Table 8.1, one half of all women and men score "high" on the social teachings index. It is the middle Vatican II cohort that displays no gender differences (see Table 8.6). A gender gap is quite evident in the pre-Vatican II cohort, where women are more likely to score "high." This is consistent with the impression that women are more compassionate. But in the post-Vatican II cohort, the pattern is reversed. Here men are more

	Pre-Vatican II Cohort	Vatican II Cohort	Post-Vatican II Cohort
Table 8.6 **Social Teachings Index** **(percent)**			
Percent "High"			
Women	55	45	53
Men	44	45	62
Percent "Low"			
Women	5	8	16
Men	6	9	8
Helping needy is important (Strongly agree)			
Women	84	79	77
Men	70	78	72
Catholics have duty to close the gap (Strongly agree)			
Women	40	27	32
Men	31	31	38

likely to score "high." Of those scoring "low" the only gender difference is in the post-Vatican II generation where it seems that women are less compassionate than men.

The vast majority of both genders believe in helping the needy. However, the oldest generation of women most strongly embraces the principles of social concerns. Men of the oldest and the youngest cohort are least inclined to express concern for the poor. Another individual item focuses on the social justice teaching: "Catholics have a duty to decrease the gap between the rich and the poor." Fewer respondents are willing to agree with this more controversial language. The largest gender gap is found in the pre-Vatican II cohort, where women score the highest of all respondents. Post-Vatican II women a bit more committed than Vatican II women to closing the gap between rich and poor. Post-Vatican II men are more committed to this goal than either of the other two cohorts of men.

Conclusions

Overall, scores on our five indices show only small gender differences. The big picture indicates that women and men are more alike than they are different — more alike than we expected. Gender alone has not proven to be *the* defining difference in the resulting behaviors, attitudes, and beliefs of Catholics. This finding has several implications for diocesan and parish leaders.

For one thing, parishes and dioceses are not likely to be polarized along gender lines. In most parishes and dioceses, there are more similarities than differences between men and women, especially men and women in the pre-Vatican II and Vatican II cohorts. This common ground provides important opportunities for dialogue and understanding on topics that are of interest to both men and women. There are many more possibilities for mutual respect and growth along gender lines than some leaders might think. If given opportunities to work together on topics of mutual interest — whether these relate to family life or social concerns — there is enough common ground for men and women to work well together. In these days, when there is a presumption that men and women are from different planets, these results should be good news to Church leaders who seek the cooperation of both men and women in their parishes and dioceses.

At the same time, young men and young women do have rather different approaches to faith and morals. Young women are increasingly inclined to disagree with Church teachings, especially on traditional beliefs and practices and on issues such as the ordination of women, the need to attend Mass, and premarital sex. While this pattern of increased dissent also appears among young men, it is not occurring at the same rate, and on some dimensions (e.g. homosexuality, premarital sex), there is some evidence of a rebound effect among young men. Together, these trends produce larger gender differences among post-Vatican II parishioners than among older cohorts. D'Antonio, Davidson, Hoge, and Wallace (1996) found essentially the same thing.

As young men and women diverge on key issues, the Church needs to pay close attention to what they are feeling and saying. Listening is important. So is asking questions about the reasons why they think and act as they do. What conditions have led them to such different views on issues ranging from prayer to homosexuality? Church leaders need to understand the processes by which young men and women are arriving at such different religious perspectives. We will examine these processes again in the last chapter.

Listening to young men and women is important because their loyalty and commitment cannot be taken for granted. As we showed in Chapter 7, there are very clear trends from institutional to individualistic views of faith and morals among young Catholics. Church leaders need to hear the concerns of young men and women if they expect the next generation to remain attached to the Church. In addition to listening, leaders need to find ways of including young men and women in parish and diocesan ministries. Giving them opportunities to discuss policies and plan programs increases their identification with the Church and their sense of having some stake in the Church, both of which tend to foster a Catholic worldview (see Chapter 4).

Because it is easiest to focus on differences, it is the differences that attract public attention. But these differing opinions and beliefs can also be the starting point for new dialogue which begins to reach across the gender barriers toward understanding and acceptance. Gender is an important issue to consider when analyzing why people think and believe and act the way they do. But gender alone is not the "cause" of people's beliefs and attitudes. In Chapter 11 we will examine the extent to which gender affects faith and morals directly, and how much of its effects are through the kind of upbringing women and men have, their lifecourse experiences, and levels of commitment to the Church.

In our next chapter, we look at racial and ethnic diversity, which also plays a role in determining what people think and how they act in regards to faith and morals.

9 • Racial and Ethnic Background

Another Source of Religious Diversity

> No other religious group in America combines as many large, diverse nationality subgroups as do the Catholics; for this reason, there are noticeable ethnic variations in religious styles within the boundaries of this Catholic community.
>
> *Roof and McKinney (1987:123)*

As previous chapters have illustrated, growing up Catholic is not a uniform experience. A variety of personal attributes and both childhood and adult experiences help shape our religious faith and practices. In this chapter we examine how another significant attribute, namely ethnic and racial self-identification, relates to religious beliefs and practices.

Both popular culture and social science have long been interested in how our self-understandings and societal opportunities are influenced by the race and/or ethnic groups we identify with — or which others attribute to us (e.g., Feagin and Feagin, 1993). Stories of the search for one's roots abound in the media; the popularity of the book and television mini-series "Roots" is just one example. And yet we also live in a time when the desire to move beyond group categories seems quite strong. For us, then, the questions become: how closely entwined are religious and ethnic/racial identities today? Are some ethnic/racial groups more closely tied to particular beliefs and behaviors? Are there, in fact, any differences between groups? How much do we learn about the faith and practices of Catholic individuals by knowing which racial or ethnic group they belong to? These are the questions that draw our attention in this chapter.

The Stories of Catholics in America

As school children learn early on, one of the main stories of the United States focuses on immigration. In the case of the collective experience of American Catholics, we know that during the nineteenth and early twentieth centuries the Catholic Church had become "a church of the immigrants" (Dolan and Leege, 1985; see also Dolan, 1992; Greeley, 1977:3-49). The Church became an umbrella for the immigrants, shielding them from the strangeness of the new land and providing them with a variety of institutional supports as they came to be a part of — while often apart from — their new nation. The centrality of the ethnic parish and its school as vehicles for community bonding and building was widely recognized (Dolan, 1992). Perhaps less acknowledged were the limitations, especially the exclusion of people who were "different" (McGreevy, 1996). Even as late as the mid-1960s, the immigrant background of Catholics was significant: "(H)alf the American Catholic adult population was either the first or second generation in this country" (Greeley, 1977:18-19).

But there is a difference between the experiences of European immigrant groups and those of "people of color." Some of the latter are recent immigrants from, for example, Latin America and Asia. Others are members of "colonized" or "conquered peoples," like the Spanish-speaking people who lived in the geographic territory that was to become the United States or like African Americans whose ancestors were forced to come here as slaves. While the experiences of many of the European immigrant groups — for example, the people from England, Ireland, and Germany — led them into mainstream America, the experiences of people of color tell a different story (Feagin and Feagin, 1993). As Greeley (1990:75) has remarked, referring to two of these groups, "America is indeed the land of opportunity, unless you happen to be Hispanic or native-born black." In our study we are interested in looking at both people of color and European-background groups to discover the importance of racial and ethnic identities in their religious beliefs and practices.

To begin the story, however, we need to look at just who our sample is. We asked three questions related to race and ethnicity. First, "Which of the following best describes your race? Are you . . . white, Latino or His-

Table 9.1 Race of Parishioners (percent)	
African American	2
Asian	2
Hispanic/Latino	12
White	81
Other	3
Total	100

panic, African American, Asian, or some other ethnic background (specify)."[1] Table 9.1 shows what we found.

Our sample of parishioners is 81 percent white, 12 percent Hispanic/Latino,[2] two percent each African American and Asian, and three percent "other." As Kosmin and Lachman (1993:120) comment, "We cannot view ethnic and racial categories as a given; they are continually evolving." It is important to recognize as well that these categories mask different realities within the categories (Feagin and Feagin, 1993). The experiences of those Hispanic/Latinos who have Mexican ancestry, for example, are not exactly like those who have roots in Cuba (Badillo, 1994, and Moore, 1994). The same must be said for the different groups within the category of Asian Americans; for example, those with Korean versus those with Chinese backgrounds (Feagin and Feagin, 1993). And, of course, the story of African-American Catholics is a rich and varied one, and includes important regional as well as rural-urban differences in experience (Davis, 1990, and Whitt, 1996).

While acknowledging the variations within the larger category, it is also important to point out that for many people the larger category is an important one (National Black Catholic Congress, 1995; Stevens-Arroyo and Pantoja, 1995; Whitt, 1996). Furthermore, given the size of our sample, we will be examining just the larger categories, that is, Hispanic/Latino, African American, and Asian American. A caution is in order: the numbers are small for the African-American and Asian categories and the reader must bear this in mind as we proceed in the analysis.

Second, we asked the respondents, "What ethnic group or groups are most important in your ancestry?" If more than one ethnic group was mentioned we asked, "Which one of these ethnic groups is most important to you?" By combining these last two questions, we were able to arrive at mutually exclusive ethnic categories.

Table 9.2 presents the data for the five largest ethnic groups, which

Table 9.2 Ethnicity of Parishioners (percent)	
French	7
German	13
Irish	18
Italian	17
Polish	<u>10</u>
Total	65

account for two-thirds of all parishioners. The largest group is Irish (18 percent), followed by Italian (17 percent), German (13 percent), Polish (10 percent), and French (7 percent). What can we learn about the religious beliefs and behaviors by knowing the racial or ethnic group of our respondents? We first discuss the data by racial grouping and then turn to the European-background ethnic groups.

Racial Groups

While the historical usage of the term "race" has been varied (Feagin and Feagin, 1993) and the social, scientific, political, and legal standings of the term are subject to contemporary debate (Lederman, 1996; Peterson, 1995; Wheeler, 1995), in the everyday world of many Americans it is still a socially meaningful term. As noted above, we asked respondents to self-identify on the basis of race, and we use that term in this section for African Americans, Asian Americans, Hispanic/Latinos, and whites.

What do we know about the religious beliefs and behaviors of these groups? While acknowledging the varieties within the groups, we can paint a broad picture of each group. We begin with general information about African Americans, move to Asian Americans, and conclude with Hispanic/Latinos before turning to data from our research.

African Americans

The story of African-American Catholics is not well-known. That the "classic" in the field, *The History of Black Catholics in the United States* by Cyprian Davis, O.S.B., was just published in 1990, gives some indication of how recent it is that systematic attention has been paid to these members of the Church (see also DeRego, 1996; Whitt, 1996; NCCB, 1996b). What we all intuitively know, and what Davis, Whitt, DeRego, and the NCCB report have documented so well, is that segregation scarred the life of the Catholic Church just as it did the nation as a whole. We have among us today many African-American Catholics who can remember sitting in the back of the Church and receiving the Eucharist after their white sisters and brothers, and who continue to feel that they are not full members of the Church. What do we know about the beliefs and behaviors of contemporary African-American Catholics? A review of the current situation indicates that while we have a number of historical works, we are still in need of more national studies of contemporary African-American Catholics and their beliefs and practices.

Blacks number some 12 percent of the population in the United States, about 30 million people. While Bishop J. Terry Steib, the first black Catholic bishop of Memphis, estimates there are between six million and 10 million blacks who do not go to any church (Garlington, 1995), it appears that for African Americans in general, the church is often the hub or social center, the locus of community activity (Cavendish, 1993:4; Feagin and Feagin, 1993:250). As Verba et al. (1995:366) point out, "From the earliest days, the church was the only secondary institution available to African Americans." In their study, Verba et al. (1995:366-368) find that using three measures of religious involvement, African Americans are the most active, compared with Anglo-whites and Latinos. Kosmin and Lachman (1993:130) assert that "National polls about religion have long shown that African Americans are more religious in thought and behavior than other Americans." And our history demonstrates that black churches have often been the source of political activism in attempts to make America in practice more like what it proclaims in theory (i.e., an egalitarian society, free of discrimination, with opportunities for all).

Turning our attention to membership within the Catholic Church, we find that the estimates for the number of Catholics who are African Americans typically range from three percent (Gallup and Castelli, 1987:3; D'Antonio et al., 1989:31) to five percent (D'Antonio et al., 1996:179; Garlington, 1995; Kosmin and Lachman, 1993:127,130). There is a tradition of black Catholic congresses, dating from 1889, with the seventh congress scheduled to occur in 1997 (Davis, 1990; Whitt, 1996). And yet, as Cogley and Van Allen (1986:134) remark, "Until very recently, Negro Catholics were required to conform to standard liturgical uses and white patterns of thought and behavior, while they were effectively cut off from Catholic cultural life by the patterns of social segregation. The result was that no distinctive black Catholicism was ever allowed to flourish in the United States."

While there has been a variety of historical attempts to address this situation, several fairly recent efforts deserve mention. The black bishops, for example, issued their joint pastoral *What We Have Seen and Heard* in

1984. The *National Black Catholic Pastoral Plan* emerged from the National Black Catholic Congress held in Washington, D.C., in May of 1987 (NCCB, 1990a). When Pope John Paul II came to the United States in September of 1987, he held an audience with the 11 black bishops and nearly 2,000 black Catholics in the New Orleans Superdome (Whitt, 1996:612). In 1990 the Secretariat for the Liturgy and the Secretariat for Black Catholics of the National Conference of Catholic Bishops (1990b) released their joint document, *Plenty Good Room: The Spirit and Truth of African American Catholic Worship*, a companion piece to the 1988 document, *In Spirit and Truth: Black Catholic Reflections on the Order of Mass* (released by the Secretariat for the Liturgy) (NCCB, 1988).

A number of researchers have turned their attention to black Catholics as well. John Harfmann, S.S.J., Director of the Josephite Pastoral Center, published his *1984 Statistical Profile of Black Catholics* (Harfmann, 1985). The profile was a follow-up to the 1975 statistical profile and was "an effort to update the statistics and to rank each diocese according to the number of Black Catholics as well as the Black Catholics as a percentage of the total number of Blacks and the total number of Catholics" (Harfmann, 1985:iii). James Cavendish (1993) undertook a reexamination of the data (collected in the early 1980s) from the Notre Dame Study of Catholic Parish Life. In looking for predictors of religiosity among black and white Catholics, Cavendish (1993:45) found that black Catholics were more likely than white Catholics to display higher levels of evangelical and traditional devotionalism, as well as higher levels of reported spirituality. There is a recent study by The National Black Catholic Congress (1995), supervised by Hilbert Stanley, which solicited opinions of African-American bishops, women religious, priests, deacons, brothers, and seminarians, along with a sample of lay persons. Unfortunately, important as this effort is, it is difficult to interpret the findings because, as is noted in the document, the sample is not representative of all African-American Catholics.

Of other national studies on Catholics, the earlier D'Antonio et al. book (1989:40,43,170,172) pointed out several differences when comparing black and white Catholics. First, while whites were more likely to say they were unwilling to leave the Church and more inclined to attend Mass on a regular basis, blacks were somewhat more likely than whites to say the Church was important. Second, blacks were somewhat more likely to donate over $250 a year to the church. Third, blacks were more likely to have an awareness of the bishop's 1986 economic pastoral (and more inclined to agree with it) while whites were more likely to have heard of the bishops' 1983 peace pastoral. Fourth, there was virtually no difference between whites and blacks on frequency of reading the Bible. While the second D'Antonio et al. (1996) book contains a separate chapter on Latino

Catholics (the findings are discussed below), the authors do not discuss findings for African-American Catholics.

Asian Americans

If the African-American Catholic story is not well known, it seems fair to say that the story of Asian-American Catholics is just beginning to be written. We know that, overall, Asian and Pacific Island immigrants "have benefitted greatly from the changes in U.S. immigration laws that have occurred since the 1960s, especially from the elimination of racist immigration quotas and the emphasis on social justice and civil rights" (Feagin and Feagin, 1993:339). Some suggest that since the mid-1980s, this group is the fastest-growing U.S. minority (Feagin and Feagin, 1993:339). According to the U.S. Census, as of 1995 Asians are 3.3 percent of the population, or about 8.6 million people (up from 1.5 percent in 1980) (Holmes, 1996). Kosmin and Lachman (1993:147) estimate that one in four or five Asian Americans is Catholic. They claim that "Catholic leaders tend to underestimate their success with the fast-growing Asian American population. Most Filipino and many Vietnamese immigrants are Catholics" (Kosmin and Lachman, 1993:127). Their estimate is that more than two percent of American Catholics are Asian, with geographic concentrations in California and Washington (Kosmin and Lachman, 1993:127). While there appears to be no other national study documenting the numbers of Asian-American Catholics, individual bishops have spoken about the needs of Asian Catholics in their dioceses (e.g., Grahmann, 1995). A series of national hearings has been held on the Church's response to the Asian presence in the United States (Hall, 1990). The Archdiocese of San Francisco has both a "Pastoral Plan for Filipino Ministry" and a "Chinese Pastoral Plan."

A search of national studies of Catholics yields a dearth of attention to Asian-American Catholics. In D'Antonio et al. (1989), for example, there is no reference in the index to this group, either collectively or separately, although the authors do report that one percent of their sample was Asian. They remark in passing that cultural differences between European ethnic groups are "diminishing somewhat with the Americanization process," adding, "But others — such as the differences between European, Hispanic, and Asian Catholics and among Asian-American Catholics themselves — may be increasingly significant in the years ahead" (D'Antonio et al., 1989:50). There is one entry under "Asian" (in the context of immigration) in their second book (D'Antonio et al., 1996) where again one percent of the national sample was Asian. Greeley's book (1990) on the General Social Survey (GSS) data from the National Opinion Research Center (NORC) has no index references to Asian Americans. We are in great need of studies of Asian-American Catholics.

Hispanic/Latino Americans

Starting in 1990, the U.S. Census Bureau reports Hispanics independently from "race," indicating that Hispanics can be of any race. The 1990 Census reported 22.4 million people of Hispanic origin, while the 1995 estimate is 26.7 million, or 10.2 percent of the U.S. population. Given the difficulties of categories, it is not surprising that the estimates for the number of Catholics who are Hispanic/Latinos are hard to determine. While people often state that between 25 and 40 percent of all Catholics are Hispanic, when national representative samples are examined the number is much lower: 13 percent (D'Antonio et al., 1996:179), 14 percent (Kosmin and Lachman, 1993:127), or 16 percent (Gallup and Castelli, 1987:3).

The relationship of Hispanic/Latinos to the Church is long and complex, one which has become the subject of much systematic study in recent years (Deck, 1989, 1993, 1994; Stevens-Arroyo and Pantoja, 1995). Some encouraging signs of this attention are the creation of the Program for the Analysis of Religion Among Latinos (PARAL) in 1988, and the Notre Dame History of Hispanic Catholics in the United States, begun in 1989. What scholars and pastoral agents point to as factors that cross the various Hispanic/Latino groupings include the following: the importance of the family and within that, the key role of women; the incorporation of "popular" religiosity; devotion to special images of the Mother of God and to select saints; language; the importance of small church communities; and an ethos or worldview (Deck, 1995; Diaz-Stevens, 1994; Gallup and Castelli, 1987:139-148; Holler, 1995; Kosmin and Lachman, 1993:138; NCCB, 1995, 1996c). A number of writers have expressed growing concern over "defections" of Hispanic/Latino Catholics.[3]

While there are a number of fine historical studies, what do we know about contemporary religious practices and beliefs among Hispanic/Latino Catholics? To begin a discussion of religious ideas and practices among Hispanic/Latinos, we must acknowledge that "it is impossible to talk of a single Latino experience" (Stevens-Arroyo, 1994:79). As recently as 1991, John A. Grindel (1991:83) could remark on the absence of a discussion of Hispanic Catholics in his book: "The overview of the present situation of the Catholic Church in the U.S. offered here is primarily an overview of the white, Anglo-Saxon Catholic Church. . . . Given the rapidly growing number of Hispanics in the U.S. Church this absence is more than regrettable. However, to a great extent, the data regarding Hispanics does not exist" (cited in Deck, 1995:103, endnote 15). Partly in response to this situation, the National Conference of Catholic Bishops/United States Catholic Conference, with financial support from the Lilly Endowment, Inc., undertook a study of Hispanic/Latinos that included such topics as Hispanic ministry, the role of Hispanic ecclesial and secular organizations, and Hispanic priests, seminarians, and candidates (see NCCB, 1993).

As for national surveys, there is the 1978 Gallup study of Hispanic Catholics conducted for *Our Sunday Visitor* (discussed in Gallup and Castelli, 1987). The findings suggested that while Hispanic Catholics "appear to be a devout people in many respects, they see the Church primarily as a place of worship, rather than a source of direct help or comfort with personal, family, or community problems" (Gallup and Castelli, 1987:142). They found that for 64 percent of Hispanic Catholics religion was "very important," a finding that was 10 points higher than the response among a sample of Catholics in general at that time (Gallup and Castelli, 1987:143). Referring to a Gallup national sample of Catholics conducted for the Catholic Press Association in 1986, Gallup and Castelli (1987:143-144) note that Hispanics in that study were more likely than other Catholics to read the Bible although they were only half as likely to say they had meditated in the past month.

The Gallup Organization was hired to carry out two other national surveys of Catholics, referred to above (D'Antonio et al., 1989, 1996). The first, conducted in 1987, included only English-speaking adults but it did report a number of ethnic differences when comparing Hispanics to other groups. They (along with Germans) had the lowest score on the item "How important is the Catholic Church to you personally?" Hispanics attended Mass least often and made the smallest financial contributions (D'Antonio et al., 1989:39).

The second Gallup national survey took place in spring of 1993 (D'Antonio et al., 1996). While that survey found some differences between what the authors call "first-wave Catholics" (i.e., those who emigrated from Europe in the nineteenth and early twentieth centuries) and Latinos, the researchers summarized by saying that Latinos' orientation to sexuality and marriage issues was "fairly close to that of the American Catholic laity in general," and that on matters of authority and governance, Latino responses were also similar to those of first-wave Catholics.

The findings of two other studies should be mentioned. Gonzalez and LaVelle (1988) report that only 23 percent of Hispanic Catholics are practicing (cited in Kosmin and Lachman, 1993:139). In their study of the relationships between ethnicity and citizenship participation, Verba et al. (1995) examined the religious activity of Protestant and Catholic Anglo-whites, African Americans, and Latinos. Using three measures of religious involvement (attendance at church services; time spent on social, educational, or charitable activities within a church; and contributions of funds to church), Verba et al. (1995:366) found a "puzzling" pattern for Latinos: "a high level of church attendance coupled with a lower level of involvement in auxiliary church activities." They attribute that lower level to the fact that Latinos are disproportionately Catholic (Verba et al., 1995:367).

Faith, Morals, and Racial Groups

Are there any differences between the racial groups on our five indices? Table 9.3 provides the data for our measures of faith and morals by race.

Keeping in mind the small numbers for African Americans and Asian Americans, what we find is that Asian Americans are, in general, most in line with the official positions of the Church. African Americans, on the other hand, are generally least in conformity with those positions. Hispanic/Latinos and whites fall in between.

On the traditional beliefs and practices index, 78 percent of Asian Americans score "high," compared with 61 percent of Hispanic/Latinos, 44 percent of whites, and 36 percent of African Americans. When we examine the index of recent ideas, we find that no Asian Americans score "high," while approximately one-third of each of the other groups does: 32 percent of whites, 34 percent of Hispanic/Latinos, and 38 percent of African Americans. For the recent practices index, the order is Asian Americans (17 percent), Hispanic/Latinos (14 percent), whites (seven percent), and African Americans (no percent) for our combined high-plus-medium category.

Finally, in examining our two scales for moral issues, the rank order for the "high" category on the sexual-reproductive index is Asian American (29 percent), whites (24 percent), Hispanic/Latinos (19 percent), and African Americans (four percent). The only exception to Asian Americans ranking first is on the social teachings index; here, they rank last (36 percent). On this measure it is the whites who rank first (52 percent), followed by African Americans (48 percent), and Hispanic/Latinos (46 percent).

Racial Groupings and Generational Patterns

Given our special interest in generational patterns, what do we find if we examine the racial data by cohorts? Table 9.4 indicates that the results are different for each group.

Among African-American Catholics, there is a dramatic decrease in support of traditional beliefs and practices. There are no African Americans of any generation in the "high" cell on the recent practices index, and for the sexual-reproductive index it is only the youngest generation that has anyone scoring "high" (and just 10 percent at that). When it comes to

Table 9.3
Faith and Morals by Racial Groups
(percent)

	Faith			Morals	
	Trad. Beliefs/ Practices (High)	Recent Ideas (High)	Recent Practices (High,Med)	Sexual/Rep. Ethics (High)	Social Teachings (High)
African American	36	38	—	4	48
Asian American	78	—	17	29	36
Hispanic/ Latino	61	34	14	19	46
White	44	32	7	24	52

the social teachings index, it is the youngest generation which is leading the way: 90 percent score "high" compared with 27 percent of the Vatican II generation and none among the pre-Vatican II cohort. At least some of these rather dramatic differences are probably linked to the relatively small number of African Americans in our sample.

A look at Asian Americans in Table 9.4 reveals there are no pre-Vatican II members in the "high" cells on any of the indices, a finding that is unique when compared to the other racial and ethnic groups. The pattern that seems to prevail overall is an increasing agreement with Church positions as the generations get younger. In fact, just looking at the youngest generation, we find that on two indices (traditional beliefs and practices, and social teachings), 100 percent of the post-Vatican II generation score high; on the sexual-reproductive index, 66 percent score high; and on recent practices, 56 percent are in the high category. Given the small number of Asian Americans in our study, these results are more suggestive than definitive.

For Hispanic/Latino Catholics there is not a clear pattern. On the traditional beliefs and practices index, the pre-Vatican II generation appears to be unlike the other two. In other words, there is not a straight-line descent across the generations in support for the Church's positions, but rather a "plateau" of sorts with similar percentages for the Vatican II and post-Vatican II generations. On the recent ideas index, there is decreasing support for the Church's position as the generations get younger. On both the recent practices index and the social teachings index, there is evidence of a U-shape pattern: the pre-Vatican and post-Vatican generations are more alike.

For the category of white Catholics, the picture is also a bit complicated. On the traditional beliefs and practices index, the pre-Vatican II generation seems more unlike the other two (that same "plateau" effect we found for Hispanic/Latinos). For the recent ideas index and the sexual-reproductive index, there is decreasing support for the Church's position as the generations get younger. On the recent practices index there is virtually no difference among the generations, while on the social teachings index, the pre-Vatican II and post-Vatican II generations have similar scores (54 percent and 55 percent, respectively), compared with the Vatican II generation (48 percent).

Summary of Findings for Racial Groups

Our research indicates that overall, Asian Americans rank first in support of the Church's official positions. Since our sample size is small and since we have no other national data to compare this to, it is hard to judge the import of this finding except to note it and await further research. The Hispanic/Latinos and whites are somewhat comparable in their beliefs

Table 9.4 — Faith and Morals, Racial Groups, and Generations (percent)

	Faith			Morals	
	Trad. Beliefs/ Practices (High)	Recent Ideas (High)	Recent Practices (High,Med)	Sexual/Rep. Ethics (High)	Social Teachings (High)
African American					
Pre-Vatican II	100	7	—	—	—
Vatican II	27	27	—	—	27
Post-Vatican II	10	82	—	10	90
Asian American					
Pre-Vatican II	—	—	—	—	—
Vatican II	64	—	—	16	11
Post-Vatican II	100	—	56	66	100
Hispanic/Latino					
Pre-Vatican II	100	—	7	24	52
Vatican II	57	27	18	24	39
Post-Vatican II	51	55	10	12	52
White					
Pre-Vatican II	64	22	8	45	54
Vatican II	37	34	8	18	48
Post-Vatican II	33	42	6	11	55

and practices on our measures, which lends support to the national findings reported by D'Antonio et al. (1996). That the African Americans in our sample generally are the least supportive of official Church stands (with the one exception of the social teachings index, where they rank second), seems to conflict with the findings of Verba et al. (1995) and some of those reported by Cavendish (1993). Again, however, our sample is small, this finding should be interpreted cautiously as we await further national research.

When we examine the findings for racial groups by cohort, we discover differences but no clear patterns across the groups. For Asian Americans the highest level of support for the Church's official positions is found among the youngest generation. When looking at the data for African Americans, it appears there is decreasing support for the official stands with each generation (with the exception of the index of Catholic social teachings, where it is the youngest who are most in support). There are less clear patterns for the other two groups. Among Hispanic/Latinos it is the pre-Vatican II cohort which is more supportive of the Church than the other two generations on the traditional beliefs and practices index, while it is that generation, along with the post-Vatican II cohort, that are most supportive of Church positions in the area of social teachings. For whites, there are almost twice as many of the pre-Vatican II cohort who support the Church's position on the index of traditional beliefs and practices. There are almost three times as many among that generation who score high on the sexual-reproductive index compared to the other two cohorts. But interestingly, the oldest and youngest generations score almost identically on the social teachings index (55 percent and 54 percent respectively) and higher than the Vatican II cohort (48 percent).

European-background Ethnic Groups

In contrast to what we have found for the racial groupings, the literature on ethnic groups with European roots is voluminous. A major theme of that work has been whether the various ethnic groups would assimilate into American society, often viewed in Anglo-American terms. That debate has been recast in recent decades, moving beyond the dualistic "melting pot" versus "cultural pluralism" idea. Alba (1990:3), in his *Ethnic Identity: The Transformation of White America*, looked at the changes in the scholarly field and argued that the reassessment ended up obscuring "the enormity of the changes taking place among some ethnic groups." It is his contention that:

> . . . [E]thnicity among whites (more precisely, non-Hispanic whites) in the United States is in the midst of a

> fundamental transformation, whose basic outlines are not
> always perceived clearly, even by knowledgeable observ-
> ers, and whose long-run consequences call for investi-
> gation. This transformation does not imply that ethnicity
> is less embedded in the structure of American society
> but rather that the ethnic distinctions that matter are un-
> dergoing a radical shift. Ethnic distinctions based on
> European ancestry, once quite prominent in the social
> landscape, are fading into the background; other ethnic
> distinctions appear more highlighted as a result. In a
> sense, a new ethnic group is forming — one based on
> ancestry from *anywhere* on the European continent (Alba,
> 1990:3; italics in original).

Is that argument applicable to Catholic ethnics with European ancestry? What do we know about differences and similarities among them?
We will try to highlight fairly recent works that focus on religious patterns
for Catholic European-background ethnic groups and then move to our
research findings.

Cogley and Van Allen (1986) provide some rich descriptive material
on various ethnic groups in their narrative account of American Catholicism. More social scientific kinds of descriptions are provided by various
national surveys. In examining the NORC surveys of the early 1970s,
Greeley (1979) found some ethnic differences for church attendance as
well as for certain beliefs and attitudes. NORC had data on a variety of
items for four European-heritage ethnic groups: German, Irish, Italian,
and Slavic (Polish) groups (along with French for some items). On two
measures, the Germans ranked first; on two other measures, it was the
Irish; on the last measure, it was the Slavic group. The Italians ranked last
on three of the measures; the Irish on one; and the Germans and Poles tied
on the final measure.

On *church attendance*, for example, Greeley (1979:119) reports the
Italians had the lowest percentage for regular Church attendance (45 percent) versus the others, which are all quite similar (Irish, 60 percent; Slavic,
60 percent; French, 61 percent; German, 63 percent). On *belief in life
after death,* the order is German, 85 percent; French, 77 percent; Italian,
75 percent; and Irish, 74 percent (Greeley, 1979:120). When using a scale
for measuring religion as *worldview*, Greeley (1979:124) found the Irish
most "hopeful" (35 percent), followed by Polish (26 percent), German
(20 percent), and Italians (15 percent). And when examining the ethnic
groups on a scale of *certainty of religious conviction*, Greeley (1979:125)
gives this rank ordering of the Catholic European ethnics: Slavic, Irish,
German, Italian. Finally, the data for experiencing a *mystical interlude* are

Irish, 28 percent; Italian, 24 percent; German and Polish, 17 percent each (Greeley, 1979:126).

In analyzing the 1987 national survey findings, D'Antonio et al. (1989:39) report that their data "indicate that ethnicity remains a factor in the extent and nature of Catholics' involvement in the Church." For five items, they provide information on four European-background groups: German, Irish, Italian, and Polish. The items are subjective importance of the Church; reluctance to leave the Church; Mass attendance; contributions; and reading the Bible. On all but the contributions measure, it is the Polish who have the highest percentage, with the Irish generally in second place (D'Antonio et al., 1989:42). The authors report that on the issue of moral authority, "We found the Polish to be the most supportive of church moral authority; no single group can be identified as the least supportive" (D'Antonio et al., 1989:92). The researchers also examined awareness of and agreement with the bishops' pastoral letters on peace and on the economy. The pattern that emerges suggests that it is the Irish overall, followed generally by the Germans, who are most aware and supportive, with the Italians least so. In terms of *awareness* of the peace pastoral the order is: Irish, German, French, Italian, and Polish (D'Antonio et al., 1989:167). For *awareness* of the economic pastoral, the Irish and French are tied for first place, followed by the Germans, Polish, and Italians (D'Antonio et al., 1989:167). In terms of *agreement* with the two documents, their findings indicate this ordering of support for the peace pastoral: Irish, Germans, Poles, Italians, and French (D'Antonio et al., 1989:174). For the economic pastoral, the order of *agreement* is Poles, Irish, Germans, Italians, and French (D'Antonio et al., 1989:174).

Faith, Morals, and Ethnicity

On our composite measure, as Table 9.5 indicates, there are some large differences between the European-background ethnic groups and one clear pattern: on every index, it is the French who rank first. And generally, it is the Italians who rank second. Let's examine each index separately.

With the French in first place on the index of traditional beliefs and practices (54 percent score high), the order that follows is Italians (52 percent), Polish (48 percent), Germans (41 percent), and Irish in last place (36 percent). When we examine our index of recent ideas by ethnic groups, we again find the French most in line with the official positions of the Church: just 27 percent support such ideas as the ordination of women and the belief that you can be a good Catholic without going to Church weekly. The group most in support of the recent ideas is the Germans: 40 percent of them score "high" on this index. In between are the other three ethnic groups: 32 percent of the Irish and 34 percent of both the Italians

Table 9.5
Faith and Morals by Ethnic Groups
(percent)

| | Faith | | | Morals | |
	Trad. Beliefs/ Practices (High)	Recent Ideas (High)	Recent Practices (High, Med)	Sexual/Rep. Ethics (High)	Social Teachings (High)
French	54	27	9	29	66
German	41	40	8	27	45
Irish	36	32	7	20	55
Italian	52	34	7	28	55
Polish	48	34	4	26	38

and Polish score "high." On the index of recent practices, there are virtually no differences among the groups; no more than nine percent of any group scores "medium-high" on these practices.

We find more support for the Church's position on the sexual-reproductive issues, with a range from a low of 20 percent scoring "high" among the Irish to 29 percent among the French. Finally, on the index of social teachings, it is again the French who are most supportive of the Church's position: fully 66 percent of them score "high." The Irish and Italians come next (55 percent each), followed by the Germans (45 percent), and the Polish in last place (38 percent).

Ethnicity and Generational Patterns

As with the racial groups, we now turn to the topic of generational patterns among ethnic groups, examining each group separately. Table 9.6 presents the data.

There seems to be a U-shape pattern with the French respondents. On all but the recent practices index, the pre-Vatican II and the post-Vatican II generations are more like each other than they are like the Vatican II generation. The U-shape also seems to describe the Italian respondents on two of the five indices (traditional beliefs and practices and recent ideas). For the German respondents, the pattern seems to be a straight-line descent in support for the official positions of the Church on three of the indices: traditional beliefs and practices, recent ideas, and sexual-reproductive teachings. For Irish respondents, the pattern on four of the indices (all but the recent ideas scale) is that the pre-Vatican generation is unlike the other two generations: they are more supportive of the official positions. Finally, for the Polish respondents, on two of the indices (traditional beliefs and practices, and recent ideas) it is the pre-Vatican II cohort that is more supportive of the Church's positions than are the other two generations (who are quite similar). There is some hint of a U-shape for the index of sexual-reproductive teachings and a clear finding for the index of social teachings: the youngest generation is unlike the other two in its greater support for the Church's position (51 percent of the youngest cohort score high compared to 35 percent of the Vatican II generation and 30 percent of the pre-Vatican group).

Summary on White Ethnics

Overall, our research indicates that the French are most in line with the Church's positions. This finding seems to contrast with the research reported by D'Antonio et al. (1989), where the French were not in the first place of support for the Church's position on the four items the au-

Table 9.6 — Faith and Morals, Ethnic Groups, and Generations (percent)					
	Faith			**Morals**	
	Trad. Beliefs/ Practices (High)	Recent Ideas (High)	Recent Practices (High,Med)	Sexual/Rep. Ethics (High)	Social Teachings (High)
French					
Pre-Vatican II	88	17	3	69	87
Vatican II	19	36	—	4	46
Post-Vatican II	60	27	—	14	73
German					
Pre-Vatican II	71	21	7	50	51
Vatican II	39	43	17	25	42
Post-Vatican II	9	59	—	2	43
Irish					
Pre-Vatican II	72	23	21	56	63
Vatican II	39	24	4	9	52
Post-Vatican II	21	44	1	9	54
Italian					
Pre-Vatican II	66	32	1	44	59
Vatican II	41	37	9	23	53
Post-Vatican II	55	39	9	18	54
Polish					
Pre-Vatican II	58	21	—	37	30
Vatican II	44	41	—	16	35
Post-Vatican II	43	39	13	28	51

thors mention and, in fact, were in last place on two of them. Greeley's earlier work (1979) included data on French respondents on just one item, where they ranked second. The group that is typically in second place in our research is the Italians. Again, this finding seems to contradict both Greeley's (1979) and D'Antonio et al. (1989), where Italians were more likely to be at the low end among ethnic groups in support of the Church's positions. We should remind the reader, however, that the data in our chapter refer to *parishioners,* which is not the case in the other research cited here.

When we examine the ethnic group data by generations, it appears that for the French, there is a U-shape pattern: the oldest and the youngest cohorts are more like each other and the middle generation stands apart on four of our scales. The U-shape holds for the Italians on two scales, traditional beliefs and practices, and recent ideas. For the Germans, there is a decrease with each generation in support for the Church's official stands on three of our measures: the indices of traditional beliefs and practices, recent ideas, and sexual-reproductive teachings. For the Irish, on all but the index of recent ideas, the pre-Vatican II generation is much more in support of official Church teachings than are the other two cohorts. When we examine the data on the Polish, it seems that the younger two generations are more like each other and different from the oldest generation on both the traditional beliefs and practices and the recent ideas indices, but on the social teachings measure it is the youngest generation most in support of Church teachings (as was true for the African Americans and Asian Americans).

Finally, the data do not provide strong support for Alba's thesis stressing the emergence of a pan-European identity. While there are not always dramatic differences between the five European groups in our study, there are discernible differences in their religious orientations. We are inclined to believe in the continuing significance of separate ethnic identities and their effects on parishioners' views of faith and morals.

Conclusions

While some have argued that racial and ethnic categories are not very meaningful ones, it appears from our study that these identities continue to hold importance. Identification with a racial or ethnic group still helps in accounting for some of the differences among Catholics in their beliefs and practices: race and ethnicity are "real." However, the differences we find among and between racial and ethnic groups are smaller than are the cohort differences.

Yet we cannot assume that European ethnicity is a thing of the past; it persists for some groups. And while our sample sizes for African Americans and Asian Americans are quite small, making our findings more suggestive than definitive, we are intrigued by what we have found. With much of current study focusing on Hispanic/Latinos, we cannot overlook these two groups and their very different experiences.

What do our findings suggest for the Church? First, we need to explore, in our own parishes and dioceses, the salience of racial and ethnic identities. How important are these categories to our own church members in their everyday lives? What strength do they draw from these identities? What challenges emerge if such identities are more or less strong in our own parishes? Second, exploring our racial and ethnic identities can provide guidance for our parish and diocesan lives. If we find racial/ethnic identifications to be meaningful and important to our members, we can seek expressions of that rich heritage in our communal lives. Do our Eucharistic Ministers, for example, reflect the diversity of our congregation? Do we "hear" the Word of God proclaimed, for example, in various languages? Third, where ideas and experiences vary by racial and ethnic groupings, we can initiate fruitful dialogue about why and what this means for all of us. Do we provide programs for conversing with different groups about their experiences of God in their lives? The challenge for the Church, then, becomes one of deepening its knowledge and understanding of the differences among racial and ethnic groups so that two goals are simultaneously met: responding to the needs of various groups while also building the unity Christ prayed for. In this way, we will all make a contribution to the life of the global Church as it enters the twenty-first century.

We turn next to the question of the Catholics in our sample who do not affiliate with a parish. How do they live out their faith? What are they like in terms of their beliefs and practices? How similar or dissimilar are they to the parishioners we have been examining up to this point? The next chapter examines the answers to these questions.

10 • Catholics Without Parishes

Who, and How Different, Are They?

> In any Christian preference group — some church and some don't. Those who church are so different from those who don't that any analysis based on statistical averages of these populations is more likely to mislead than enlighten.
>
> *Ploch and Hastings (1995:514)*

> On a practical level, the only belief that separates many active and inactive Catholics is the belief by active Catholics that they are "in" and the belief by inactive Catholics that they are "out."
>
> *Gallup and Castelli (1987:177)*

Writers do not agree on whether there are significant differences between churched and unchurched; active and inactive; practicing and lapsed; affiliated and unaffiliated; committed and alienated Catholics. Even when they note some differences, they don't always agree on how to interpret them (Hadaway, Marler, and Chaves, 1993; Hadaway and Roof, 1988; Hoge, 1981 and 1988; Hoge and Roozen, 1980; Marler and Roozen, 1993; Ploch and Hastings, 1995; Princeton Religion Research Center, 1988; Welch, 1993; Wilson and Sherkat, 1994). We hope to shed some light on these issues by comparing Catholics who are registered parish members with those who are not registered in a parish.

The focus of this chapter is on whether the Catholics without parishes differ from other Catholics in their approach to faith and morals. We also determine whether some types of people are more likely to be unaffiliated than others and why they are unaffiliated. Finally, we explore the significance of these findings for parish life and the evangelization of the unchurched.

Parishioners and Non-parishioners

According to Canon Law, all baptized Catholics living within the geographical boundaries of a parish fall within its jurisdiction and are technically members. There was a time when the local parish performed many functions for a more or less captive clientele and that rule made a certain amount of sense. In the contemporary urban world with its religious diversity and the mobility, anonymity, and segmented social relations characteristic of the city, the local parish functions more like a voluntary association, requiring one to formally register to become a recognized member. As Marler and Roozen (1993), among others, have noted, the choice of denomination and parish resembles in many ways the consumer choices made in the economic marketplace.

Why, one might ask, is parish affiliation of importance? Organizationally speaking, the parish is the local link with the universal church. For most Catholics it is the heart of the Catholic Church. As Greeley (1990:146) noted, "it is the parish where the people do their living and dying, their loving and their quarreling and their reconciling, their doubting and their believing, their mourning and their rejoicing, their worrying and their praying." It is through the local parish that sacraments are administered, the spiritual needs of the faithful are met, resources are generated for collective enterprises, and the education of the young takes place. For the believer, it is the only place where the most sacred religious rituals take place, such as the sacrifice of the Mass where one can partake of the Body and Blood of Christ. Although some insist you can be a good Catholic without going to Mass, that strikes others as saying one can reject an invitation to the Last Supper and still claim to be a disciple of Christ (Fichter 1954:9-20; Leege and Trozzolo, 1985; Greeley and Durkin 1984:165-181; Greeley, 1990:144-161).

Parishes are still, for the most part, very viable communities. Seventy-eight percent of our parish-affiliated respondents feel that their parish is a very important part of their life. More than half of the unaffiliated who go to a particular parish on a regular basis also feel that way. Moreover, respondents tend to rate their parishes very highly. Over 70 percent of the parish members rate their parishes as excellent or good in terms of "friendliness of the people," "quality of homilies or sermons," "meeting their spiritual needs," and "quality of music at Mass." In these cynical times that is quite impressive. Greeley (1990:154) may be only slightly exaggerating when he claims that "the American neighborhood parish is one of the most ingenious communities that human skill has ever created" (see also Leege, 1987, 1988).

Some writers (Schaeffer, 1996; Linnan, 1996) contend the parish is an obsolete social form that is ill-equipped to meet the needs of the faithful in the modern world. Some comments of our Indiana respondents echo this view:

> I have not been in church for 40 years. My wife (a good, devoted Catholic) passed away [last year] — a service was held in church — I am planning to return and "pray" that my wife is in a better place.

> Have not been to Mass in about three years. Before that I'd always been active. Did not approve of the priest. He had a way of treating you with very little respect, so I just pulled out, but kept up on the monthly offering so I would continue to be a member of the parish.

> I am a convert and since my husband died I know I have not attended Mass the way I should, but the Catholic Church is still the most important part of my life along with my family.

> I grew away from the church during my college years and the first years of marriage. I know I'll go back at some point in the future.

> I was very disappointed in the Pope's recent ruling that women cannot be allowed to be priests. . . . It is because of this and only this that I am giving serious consideration on [sic] leaving the Catholic church.

Gallup and Castelli (1987) estimate that there are 11 to 16 million unchurched Catholics. Twelve percent of these unchurched Catholics say

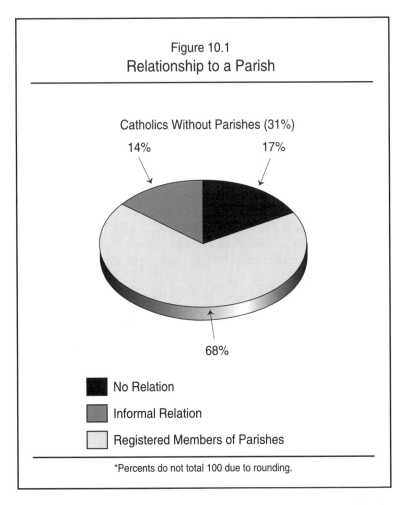

Figure 10.1
Relationship to a Parish

Catholics Without Parishes (31%)
14% 17%

68%

■ No Relation

■ Informal Relation

□ Registered Members of Parishes

*Percents do not total 100 due to rounding.

they have never belonged to the Catholic Church. This suggests that there may be close to two million who have never had formal church membership but still identify themselves as Catholic (Gallup and Castelli, 1987:162-169).[1]

After determining whether the respondents considered themselves Catholic or not, we asked, "Are you currently registered as a member of a Catholic parish near where you live?" Those who responded affirmatively (68 percent of the sample) are considered parishioners. Those who are not registered in a parish (31 percent of the sample) are referred to here as Catholics without parishes (see Figure 10.1). We also asked those who were not registered if they attended a particular parish with any regularity. Forty-seven percent of this group (14 percent of the total sample) indicated an informal affiliation with a parish. The rest (17 percent of the total sample) had neither a formal nor an informal relationship with a parish.

When we compared those with an informal affiliation with those with no affiliation, however, they did not differ significantly in their beliefs and behavior from each other, so we did not pursue that avenue of analysis further. Instead, we compare the registered with those who are not registered.

Do Catholics Without Parishes Have a Different Approach to Faith and Morals?

Differences between parish members and non-members are summarized in Figure 10.2 and Table 10.1. Forty-seven percent of the parish

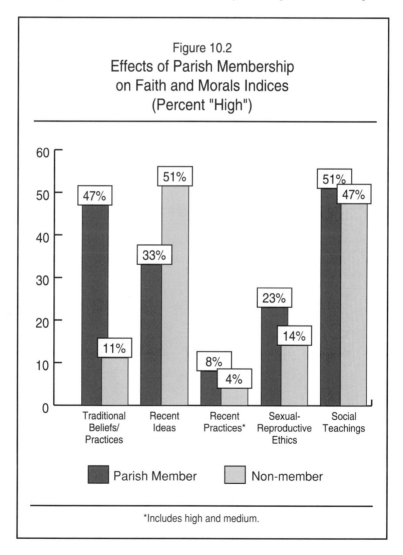

Figure 10.2
Effects of Parish Membership
on Faith and Morals Indices
(Percent "High")

*Includes high and medium.

Table 10.1
Effects of Parish Membership on Faith and Morals Indices, by Cohort
(percent)

	Faith			Morals	
	Trad. Beliefs/ Practices (High)	Recent Ideas (High)	Recent Practices (High,Med)	Sexual/Rep. Ethics (High)	Social Teachings (High)
Total Sample					
Parish Member	47	33	8	23	51
Non-member	11	51	4	14	47
Pre-Vatican II Cohort					
Parish Member	66	20	8	41	51
Non-member	22	39	11	14	39
Vatican II Cohort					
Parish Member	41	32	9	18	45
Non-member	4	54	2	12	43
Post-Vatican II Cohort					
Parish Member	37	45	7	13	56
Non-member	15	53	4	14	53

members score "high" on our measure of traditional beliefs and practices, but only 11 percent of the unaffiliated do. Whereas only eight percent of the members score "low," 39 percent of the unaffiliated do. This indicates a strong relationship between these variables. In fact, the sharpest and most consistent differences in the approach to faith and morals are in the area of traditional beliefs and practices.

We illustrate the differences in the traditional beliefs and practices index by looking at the frequency with which Catholics attend Mass and partake of the Eucharist. These are considered central to the religious life of a Catholic and the Church has even gone so far as to make it a matter of Church law that every able-bodied Catholic who has attained the age of reason is required to attend Mass at least once a week.[2] Table 10.2 compares the frequency of church attendance and Communion reception of parish members and non-members. There is a vast difference between parish members and non-members. If we combine the top two categories and compare the groups in terms of "once a week or more," 58 percent of parishioners attend regularly, while only 13 percent of non-members do. Parishioners are four and a half times more likely to go to church at least once a week. In terms of receiving Communion, parishioners are over five times more likely to receive at least once a week (48 vs. nine percent).

The groups differ not only in their participation in public worship, but also in their private religious behavior. Table 10.3 shows that the unaffiliated are less likely to engage in private prayer, start and end the day with prayer, read the Bible, or say the rosary. The unaffiliated also are much

Table 10.2
Effect of Parish Membership on Mass Attendance and Communion Reception
(percent)

	Mass Attendance		Communion Reception	
	Parish Member	Non-member	Parish Member	Non-member
More than once a week	10	2	7	2
Once a week	48	11	41	7
1-3 times a month	24	20	25	14
Less than once a month	18	67	27	77

Table 10.3
Selected Indicators of Religious Beliefs and Practices
(percent)

	Parish Members	Non-Members
Private religious behavior (At least sometimes)		
Engage in private prayer	95	79
Start and end day with prayer	84	63
Read the Bible	53	33
Say the rosary	57	20
Importance of doctrines (Important)		
Trinity	79	53
Resurrection	92	68
Transubstantiation	88	55
Incarnation	92	69
Mary Mother of God	92	69
Other beliefs (Agree)		
Catholic Church is one true church	59	38
Pope is the Vicar of Christ	82	59
It is important to obey Church teachings they do not understand	52	34
One can be a good Catholic without going to Mass	57	81

less likely to agree on the importance of major doctrines such as the Trinity and the Resurrection. They are much less likely to agree that the Catholic Church is the one true church, that the pope is the Vicar of Christ, and that it is important to obey Church teachings they do not understand. They are much more likely to agree that one can be a good Catholic without going to Mass.

Fifty-one percent of the unaffiliated score "high" on the index of recent ideas such as favoring ordination of women, while only 33 percent of the parish members do (see Table 10.1). Parish members are more likely than the unaffiliated to score "high" or "medium" on the index of recent practices such as Bible reading and participating in prayer groups (eight vs. four percent).

In the case of sexual morals, there is a somewhat greater tendency for parish members to accept church teachings (23 vs. 14 percent). While a little better than one out of five parish members scored "high" on this index, only one out of seven non-members scored "high." There was very little difference between the two groups on the social teachings index. Fifty-one percent of members score high, and 47 percent of non-members do.

Table 10.1 also looks at these relationships while holding cohort constant. For the most part, the relationships described above prevail within each of the three cohorts.

Who Are the Catholics Without Parishes?

The likelihood of being without a parish is related to each of the personal attributes in this study, although not to an equal extent.

Table 10.4 shows that cohort is the most powerful predictor of parish membership. Forty percent of post-Vatican II Catholics are without parishes, compared to 33 percent of Vatican II cohort and only 17 percent of pre-Vatican II cohort. The post-Vatican II generation is almost two and a half times more likely to be without a parish than the pre-Vatican II generation.

Males are somewhat more likely than females to be unaffiliated (36 vs. 29 percent). The gender difference is not great but it is very consistent. In virtually every subgroup examined, males were less likely to belong to a parish than females.

Latinos and African Americans are much more likely than Asians or whites to be unaffiliated, although it appears that much of this difference can be explained by the differences in the age and class composition of the groups. For example, Latinos are disproportionately young — over half of the Latinos are under 35, compared to only one-third of the white respondents. Over 27 percent of the Latino respondents have not gradu-

Table 10.4
Effects of Personal Attributes on Parish Membership
(percent)

	Without a Parish
Total Sample	31
Cohort	
Post-Vatican II	40
Vatican II	33
Pre-Vatican II	17
Gender	
Male	36
Female	29
Race	
White	28
Latino	43
African American	46
Asian	21
Ethnicity	
Irish	28
Polish	19
Italian	32
German	32
French	28

ated from high school, compared to only five percent of the white respondents. On the other hand, almost two-thirds of the Asians are college graduates or higher in terms of education and over 47 percent earned $80,000 or more in income.

Ethnicity does not appear to be an important factor differentiating members from non-members of parishes. With the exception of the Polish origin group, the others are all within four percentage points of each other.

Why Are They Without Parishes?

In explaining the reasons why some groups are unaffiliated and others are affiliated, we follow the model used in the earlier chapters. We start with examining the role of religious upbringing, then major lifecourse experiences, and finally personal interpretations, that is, how one conceives of self and self-interest.

Upbringing

Every faith group strives to transmit its culture and perpetuate its way of life through the socialization of its young. We can gain some insight into the origin of deviance from this goal by examining the nature of one's socialization. Among the factors we examine are the religious atmosphere in one's home when a person was growing up, and one's exposure to formal instruction in Catholic schools (see Table 10.5).

Among the cradle Catholics, it does not seem to matter much whether one's mother was Catholic, but the religiosity of one's family is an important factor in determining whether one joins a parish or becomes unaffiliated. Forty-eight percent of our respondents who reported that their parents rarely talked about religion when they were young are unaffiliated, compared to only 23 percent of the respondents whose parents spoke about religion frequently or very frequently. Both our index of childhood religiosity and our index of parents' religiosity show strong, consistent relationships to unaffiliation — the lower the religiosity, the greater the likelihood of being unaffiliated later in life. This relationship is independent of gender and birth cohort. It remains fairly strong and consistent for each gender and each birth cohort, though is somewhat stronger for women than men, and somewhat stronger for middle-age Catholics than for older or younger groups. So it would appear that parents who rear their children in a religious atmosphere tend to produce adults who have strong attachments to the parish; and those who don't tend to produce adults who distance themselves from the institutional church.

Formal instruction also seems to be effective. The more Catholic schooling, the less likely one is to be unaffiliated later in life. Only 17 percent of the respondents with more than 12 years of Catholic schooling are unaffiliated, but 40 percent of those who had no Catholic schooling are unaffiliated. However at the highest level (more than 12 years), there is a big difference by gender; only nine percent of women are unaffiliated, whereas 27 percent of men are unaffiliated. Catholic schooling seems to pay off for both genders, but the payoff is greater for women. The relationship generally holds up within the three cohorts but was strongest within the pre-Vatican II and the Vatican II generations. Within the post-Vatican II generation, it is weak and inconsistent. If we look at only those with the maximum exposure to Catholic schooling, only eight percent are unaffiliated in the pre-Vatican II and Vatican II generations, compared to 31 percent in the post-Vatican II generation. Clearly, schooling after Vatican II has been less effective in keeping people attached to parishes.

Amount of religious instruction also makes a difference (38 vs. 22 percent), although somewhat less of a difference than Catholic schooling. Interestingly, the type of religion teacher one had also is significant. Those

Table 10.5 — Effect of Religious Upbringing on Parish Membership (percent)

	Without a Parish
Family Background	
Raised as a Catholic	33
Convert	13
Mother Catholic (cradle Catholics only)?	
Yes	33
No	36
Parent's Religiosity	
High	25
Moderate	37
Low	44
Childhood Religiosity	
High	26
Moderate	40
Low	48
Parents Talked About Religion	
Frequently, Very Frequently	23
Occasionally	36
Rarely, Never	48
Religious Education: (cradle Catholics only) Number yrs. in Catholic Schools	
0	40
1-3	39
4-6	36
7-9	29
10-12	23
Over 12	17
Amount of Religious Instruction	
None	38
Some	38
Quite a bit	27
A great deal	22
Type of Religion Teachers	
Mostly priests/sisters	26
Equal number of each	29
Mostly lay	41

who had mostly lay teachers are much more likely than those who had priests or nuns to be unaffiliated (41 vs. 26 percent). This appears to be due in part, though not totally, to the predominance of lay teachers in the post-Vatican II period.

Lifecourse Experiences

Marital status has a big impact. The widowed (22 percent) and the married (24 percent) are least likely to be unaffiliated. The separated (66 percent) , divorced (49 percent), and single (40 percent) are the most likely to be unaffiliated. Clearly, with the exception of widows, being unaffiliated in one social sphere (family) seems to be related to being unaffiliated in another sphere (parish). What accounts for the pattern among widows is not clear. One might think it is a function of the older average age of the widows, but when we control for age, we find that widows remain less likely to be unaffiliated in each of the three birth cohorts.

For each type of marital status, the oldest cohort is the least likely to be unaffiliated. The married and widowed are least likely to be unaffiliated within each cohort. The separated are the most likely to be unaffiliated in each cohort. The impact of separation, divorce, and being single is especially acute in the middle cohort. The combined impact of these two variables is considerable. Only 10 percent of the married, pre-Vatican II generation are unaffiliated, but 78 percent of the separated, Vatican II generation are unaffiliated.

Further analysis indicates that the effects of marital status differ for men and women. Men are more likely to be unaffiliated than women, except for the separated group, where 72 percent of the women are unaffiliated, compared to only 55 percent of men. On the other hand, the impact of being widowed seems to be greater for men. Thirty-seven percent of the widowed men are unaffiliated, but only 19 percent of the widowed women are. Assuming that disaffiliation is an indication of trouble coping with a change in marital status, it seems that men have more trouble coping with widowhood and divorce, while women have an especially difficult time with separation. To what extent general cultural attitudes or parish practices cause these people to become unaffiliated is impossible to say on the basis of our data.

Based on his research with Fee et al. (1981), Greeley (1990:6) claims the greatest determinant of one's religious behavior is one's spouse's religious behavior. Our data also indicate that one's spouse is very important. If one's spouse is Catholic, only 19 percent are unaffiliated. If the one's spouse is not Catholic, 50 percent are unaffiliated. The effect is much the same for men and women. It also doesn't vary by cohort.

It is interesting to note that the incidence of mixed marriages does

Table 10.6 — Effects of Lifecourse Experiences on Parish Membership (percent)

	Without a Parish
Family Lives and Significant Others:	
Marital Status	
Married	24
Single, never married	40
Widowed	22
Divorced	49
Separated	66
Religion of Spouse	
Catholic	19
Not Catholic	50
School-age Children?	
Yes	26
No	34
Significant Other	
Catholic, active, and traditional	21
Other	41
Social Attitudes	
Sex Roles	
Unequal	35
Mixed	28
Equal	36
Poverty	
Individual	31
Societal	31

Table 10.6, continued — Effects of Lifecourse Experiences on Parish Membership (percent)

	Without a Parish
Religious Experiences	
Closeness to God	
High	24
Medium	31
Low	55
Awareness of Vatican II	
High	13
Medium	27
Low	45
Socioeconomic Status	
Education	
> College	35
College	31
Voc/trade, some college	27
High School	27
Occupation	
Executive/Manager	28
Professional	34
White Collar	32
Semi-Skilled	23
Unskilled	47
Income	
> $80,000	28
$50,000 - $79,999	32
$30,000 - $49,999	29
$15,000 - $29,999	34

vary by cohort. Sixteen percent of the spouses of the pre-Vatican II generation are non-Catholic, 32 percent of the spouses of the Vatican II generation are non-Catholic, and 40 percent of the post-Vatican II married respondents have a non-Catholic spouse. A 1989-90 national survey (Kosmin and Lachman, 1993:244) found that 22 percent of Catholic respondents lived with an adult of another faith. Since those results are based on self-identification alone and included non-spouses, it would seem that the real rate of interfaith marriages in 1989-90 was somewhat lower than the reported figure. In our sample collected in 1995, 29 percent of the spouses are non-Catholic (this of course does not include the spouses who converted to Catholicism on the occasion of their marriage or at a later date). It would seem that the rate of interfaith marriages is rising. This growing phenomenon of mixed-faith households and the accompanying difficulties of reconciling conflicting demands seem to contribute to a growing number of couples simply dropping out — withdrawing from any organized religious activity at all. For example, one of our Indiana respondents wrote:

> I come from a strong Catholic background (my mother teaches in parochial schools, I attended Catholic schools, I have a brother who is a Jesuit, and a cousin who is a nun). My wife is from an equally strong Mennonite background (parents serve as missionaries, father has taught at Associated Mennonite Biblical Seminaries, great-grandfather helped found a Mennonite college, grandparents missionaries, grandfather president of the seminary). Our faith life together is a process of integrating these two different traditions. Each of us has found this both challenging and rewarding to learn about each other's faiths. The biggest difficulty is in being able to devote less resources (financial and time) to each, and being somewhat irregular in our commitments to either.

In addition to a spouse of the same faith, the existence of a significant other (role model) who is Catholic, active, and traditional reduces by half the likelihood that one will be unaffiliated. The presence of school-age children in the household also tends to lead to more parish affiliation. Attitudes about sex roles do not make a great deal of difference in whether one belongs to a parish.

The nature of one's religious experiences and level of awareness of Vatican II make considerable difference. If one has had a close personal relation to God over the course of one's life, one is much less likely to be unaffiliated (24 percent) than if one has not (55 percent). Moreover, the more one knows about Vatican II, the less likely one is unaffiliated. These two findings tend to undermine the public image that the unaffiliated are religious rebels inspired by Vatican II.

The social status of the respondent, as measured by education, occupation, and income, also affects participation. In general, the lowest status level in each indicator has the highest level of unaffiliation, but beyond that the relationships do not follow a consistent pattern.

For purposes of illustration, let's look in more detail at completed years of schooling. The lowest educational group (high school dropouts, 44 percent unaffiliated) and the highest education group (college graduates, 35 percent unaffiliated) have the highest levels of unaffiliation. However, when we control for cohort, the picture changes somewhat. The very high level of unaffiliation (85 percent) among the young, high school dropouts accounts for the high unaffiliation level among those with the lowest level of education. For the other two cohorts, education tends not to matter. Cohort tends to have a stronger and more consistent effect than educational level.

The effect of education seems to be in part a function of gender. For males, the greatest unaffiliation level (45 percent) is among those with the most education (some post-graduate education). Among women, the most educated are those with lowest unaffiliation rate (21 percent) and those with the least education (didn't finish high school) have the highest unaffiliation rate (47 percent). These results seem to contradict the view that large numbers of highly educated women are becoming disengaged from their parishes and leaving the Church because of their treatment within the Church. Highly educated men are twice as likely as highly educated women to be unaffiliated.

Personal Interpretations

Table 10.7 makes it clear that self-concepts and self-interests also are very important determinants of parish membership. If one thinks one's parish is a very important part of one's life and/or thinks of oneself as very religious, he/she is much more likely to join and maintain membership in a parish. If one views Catholicism as personally beneficial in terms of services and moral formation, one also is much more likely to be a parish member. Persons with little or no Catholic identity and little or no stake in the Church are most likely to be without parishes.

For example, our index of Catholic benefits (reflecting whether people think their Catholicism gives them a solid moral foundation and whether there is something very special about being a Catholic) strongly influences attachment to parishes. The level of unaffiliation is three times higher among the low scorers than among the high scorers on this index. Sixty-four percent of those who score "low" on the index are unaffiliated, while only 21 percent of those who score "high" are unaffiliated.

Our commitment index combines elements of the self-concept and self-interest measures and illustrates the combined power of these factors. While 31 percent of all Catholics are non-members, only 12 percent of the highly committed are not affiliated with parishes.

In summary, there are a variety of factors that influence the decision to join or not. We think five major conditions foster disaffiliation. The first condition is learning early that religion is not an important part of one's life. These people usually have weak religious backgrounds. They have some residual faith, but they are generally not well informed, are nonpracticing, and perhaps most significantly they are pretty indifferent to the whole matter of religion.

A second condition is social and emotional distress. People caught up in these situations are hurting because of a separation, divorce, or in the case of males, the death of a spouse, and do not seem to find much support within the traditional parish. Some have suggested that the Church can in some instances become a surrogate family, but it appears from our data that all too often local parishes fail to provide any comfort for those experiencing marital problems (Christiano, 1986).

Next is economic distress and minority status. Low education, low occupational status, and low income tend to foster a disproportionate number of unaffiliated Catholics. African Americans and Latinos also fall in this category. It may be that they are too embarrassed to register at the rectory because they can't afford to contribute and they know that new

Table 10.7 **Effects of Personal Interpretations on Parish Membership**	
	Percent Without a Parish
Self-concept	
Parish is important part of my life (% agree)	12
Considers self currently very religious	15
Self-interest	
Stake in Church index (high)	6
Parish satisfaction index (excellent)	16
Catholic benefits index (high)	21
Commitment to the Church index (high)	12

parishioners are usually greeted with a box of envelopes. African Americans and Latinos also may sometimes find that they are treated differently by parishioners because of their race and ethnicity.

A fourth condition concerns transitions, especially among young singles. Dropping out between adolescence and time of marriage is almost a rite of passage in American society (Bellah, et al., 1985; Greeley, 1989). Young singles, out from under parental influences for the first time in their lives, tend to experiment with unchurched status for a while, though marriage and having youngsters of their own tend to draw many of them back to parish life.

Finally, there is marriage to non-Catholic spouses. This is a sizable and growing group that will be difficult to deal with. If parish leaders want to sustain commitment among Catholics with non-Catholic spouses, they may need to explore innovative ways of ministering to interfaith couples. They also may need to place even more emphasis on youth programs stressing the importance of dating and marrying Catholics.

Conclusions

Parishioners and non-parishioners are clearly different populations. There is no question but that aggregating them gives a somewhat distorted view of Catholic beliefs and practices. Even if it makes good sense to keep these groups analytically separate, it would be a mistake to write off the unaffiliated. Many Catholics without parishes are still committed to some elements of the Catholic faith. For example, 59 percent of the unaffiliated agree the pope is the Vicar of Christ, 38 percent say that the Catholic Church is the one true church, and one-third attend Mass with some frequency.

The existence of 20 million or more Americans who consider themselves to be Catholics but do not belong to a parish is in one sense evidence of a certain amount of failure on the part of the institutional church. In another sense, it represents a challenge and an opportunity for serious evangelization of the unchurched. In some cases, it may take little more than a kind word or welcoming hand to bring people back to a fuller involvement with their parish. In most cases, it will take much more than that.

If the efforts to "re-member" the Church are to be successful, pastors and other parish leaders, as well as ordinary parishioners, need to make the poor and minority Catholics feel more welcome in our parishes. This can involve making changes in the liturgy that recognize the language and other cultural differences that may exist within the parish; subsidizing the parochial education of poor and minority children; seeing to it that the poor and minorities are represented on parish committees and councils; and extending a friendly greeting at Mass or social gatherings.

Leaders also will have to do a better job of addressing the needs of those who experience marital problems. In addition to ministries directed to their special needs, it is important that in the everyday life of the parish, they and their children are not inadvertently excluded or made to feel unwelcome. Separation and divorce are traumatic experiences for most people. A parish should be a place of loving support.

It is also important to realize that it is not unusual for many singles to drop out during the teen years and early 20s. Church leaders should strive to maintain open lines of communication and invite them to participate in special programs (e.g. Masses, outings, dances) designed to appeal to them. The American bishops' pastoral letter on youth (NCCB, 1996a) offers many helpful suggestions. Some recommendations may require reallocations of parish and diocesan resources, but such changes may be necessary if Church leaders are serious about transmitting the faith to future generations of American Catholics.

Finally, parish leaders must find ways to minister to Catholics who have little history of religious commitment and little knowledge of the essentials of the faith or the importance of the Church. This is perhaps the hardest group to reach, but even among these people there is often some dormant or residual faith that can be awakened. We offer some suggestions for reaching this group in Chapter 11.

What does the future hold? Obviously no one knows for sure but there are some clear trends. Perhaps the most worrisome is the increase in interfaith marriages. To the extent that this reflects, and leads to more, interfaith understanding, one can't help but be cheered. However, given the tendency for many of these marriages to lead to lower participation and even dormancy in the Catholic partner's faith, it can cause serious problems. Moreover, if as Kosmin and Lachman (1993) note, interfaith marriages are less stable than other marriages, this trend will increase the divorce and separation rate and increase even further the rate of disaffiliation.

Given the positive role Catholic schooling has played in connecting people to the parish church and providing a context for relationships leading to marriages between young Catholics, the decline in parochial school enrollment in recent decades is a disturbing trend. Church leaders need to increase — not decrease — their commitment to Catholic schools and/or invest significantly more resources in parish-based religious formation programs, which also tend to foster higher levels of parish affiliation later in people's lives.

In the next chapter, we recap our findings, explore the interrelationships among the factors that affect parishioners' religious orientation the most, and indicate some of the implications our findings have for Church leaders. We pay special attention to implications for leaders wanting to forge common ground among Catholics and to pass the faith on to future generations.

11 • Pathways to Faith and Morals

Implications for Church Leaders

... As we all attempt to live lives that respond to the deepest stirrings of our being, Catholicism is a good place to be, a place where love and grace are available to saint and sinner alike, a place with a spiritual infrastructure so strong and so varied that we have enormous and continuing assistance as we build our own temporal dwellings upon this earth. We can quibble with this rule or that, this person or that; but for the most part Catholicism embodies good and wise rules, practices, and people that will help to deepen our spiritual and moral selves. The more we practice its ways, the easier they become and the more we benefit (Wilkes, 1996:318).

As Paul Wilkes suggests, millions of "good enough Catholics" feel at home in the Church. Greeley (1990) says, "They like being Catholic," even when they disagree with specific Church teachings. The coauthors of this book feel much the same way. Though we do not agree with the Church, or with one another, on each and every issue of faith and morals, we share a common sense of belonging to a Church that has great meaning in our lives. We want our study to contribute to the overall well-being of the Church.

It is in this spirit that we conclude by addressing three matters. First, we summarize our descriptive findings about the ways in which American Catholics approach matters of faith and morals. Recapping these results, we show where there is the greatest unity and the most diversity in today's Church. Second, having already identified the most important influences at each point in our theoretical approach, now we need to examine the links between these influences and show their combined effects on parishioners' thoughts and actions. We illustrate these combined effects in a picture indicating the major pathways to faith and morals. We also review the processes by which non-parishioners develop religious orientations that are quite different from those of parishioners. Finally, we consider the implications our findings have for Church leaders, giving particular attention to ways of transmitting Catholic faith and morals to future generations of parishioners and Catholics without parishes.

Describing Faith and Morals

In Chapter 1, we documented a trend toward increased diversity in Catholics' beliefs and practices. In Chapter 2, we specified Church leaders' questions about the extent of this diversity. In Chapter Three, we used national data to show how much unity and diversity there is on three dimensions of faith and two dimensions of morals. The data show that parishioners already share some common ground on traditional beliefs and practices and the Church's traditional emphasis on helping the poor, though there is some disagreement on specific issues in each of these areas. There is much less common ground when it comes to recent ideas such as the ordination of women, relatively new scripture-oriented practices such as reading the Bible and Bible study, and sexual and reproductive issues. Some specific findings stand out.

- Two-thirds of Catholics are registered parishioners; one-third are not.

- In general, parishioners are more religiously active and more likely to agree with Church teachings than non-parishioners are. Catholics without parishes are less active in the Church, more inclined to disagree with specific Church teachings, and more willing to embrace ideas that are incompatible with Canon Law.

- Eighty to 90 percent of parishioners report that "pan-Vatican II" doctrines about Mary as the Mother God, the Incarnation, Resurrection, Trinity, and

Real Presence are important parts of their personal faith. These represent the area of greatest consensus among parishioners.

- In an average week, 83 percent of parishioners pray privately, 57 percent attend Mass, and 48 percent receive Holy Communion. Fifty-one percent say they attend Holy Days of Obligation on a regular basis.

- At least half of U.S. parishioners still accept traditional beliefs about the Catholic Church being the "one true Church," the pope being the Vicar of Christ on earth, and the need to obey Church teachings even if one does not understand them.

- Between one-quarter and one-third of parishioners continue to practice traditional devotions such as praying for the intercession of Mary and the saints, saying the rosary, and going to private confession at least two or three times a year.

- Though parishioners are less likely than non-parishioners to disagree with Church teachings, 57 percent of parishioners think it would be a good idea to ordain women. Just as many accept another idea that conflicts with Canon Law, namely that one can be a good Catholic without going to Mass on a regular basis. Even higher percentages of non-parishioners accept these ideas.

- Relatively few parishioners read the Bible (22 percent), attend Bible studies (14 percent), or participate in prayer groups (eight percent) regularly.

- Only a minority of parishioners agree with the Church's sexual and reproductive ethics. The percentage of parishioners saying that each action is "always wrong" drops from 41 percent on homosexual actions to 39 percent on abortion, 33 percent on premarital sex, and only nine percent on artificial birth control.

- Parishioners agree in principle with the Church's social teachings (over 90 percent say that helping the needy is an important part of their own religious beliefs), and 58 percent accept the idea that Catholics have a special responsibility to help close the gap between the rich and poor; 42 percent disagree or are unsure about closing this gap.

- Overall, parishioners' views of faith and morals form a rather loosely integrated Catholic worldview. Several dimensions (e.g., traditional beliefs and practices) cluster together quite well; others (e.g., recent practices and social teachings) overlap somewhat; and some (e.g., recent ideas and recent practices) tend to be at odds with each other.

Explaining Variations

Our other major goal has been to account for the variations on each dimension of faith and morals. Chapter 2 specified a number of Church leaders' questions about the processes by which Catholics arrive at different views of faith and morals. It also outlined the theory we used to explore these questions. That theory included four parts: "personal attributes"; "upbringing"; "lifecourse experiences"; and "personal interpretations." Chapter 2 also described our research design, which included individual interviews, focus groups, a statewide survey of Indiana parishioners, and a national telephone poll. In chapters four through nine, we examined data showing how factors in each part of our model affect the religious orientations of Catholic parishioners. In Chapter 10, we showed how these same factors influence the religious orientations of Catholics without parishes. Now, we combine the most important factors and show how they work together to produce different understandings of faith and morals among parishioners. The results have significance for persons wanting to understand the factors that make it difficult to achieve common ground and pass the Catholic heritage on to future generations.

Parishioners

How do the factors in our model affect each other, and which are the most important influences on our respondents' beliefs and practices? We used a series of statistical tests to examine these questions (see Appendix J for details). These tests show, for example, how personal attributes such

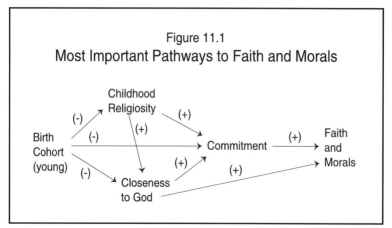

Figure 11.1
Most Important Pathways to Faith and Morals

as birth cohort affect upbringing factors such as childhood religiosity and, in turn, how birth cohort and childhood religiosity affect lifecourse experiences such as closeness to God. They indicate how the factors in our model have both indirect and direct effects on Catholics' beliefs and practices. With these tests, we are able to specify the paths parishioners take to different patterns of faith and morals. We summarize the overall results of these tests in Figure 11.1.

Cohort

Figure 11.1 starts with birth cohort. Cohort affects childhood religiosity, commitment, and closeness to God. Catholics born and raised in the pre-Vatican II Church of the 1930s and '40s report higher levels of childhood religiosity than Vatican II Catholics who are products of the 1950s and '60s and post-Vatican II Catholics who have been raised in the 1970s and '80s. Pre-Vatican II parishioners also have the strongest Catholic identities and a greater sense of the benefits related to being Catholic; Vatican II parishioners have weaker Catholic identities and less attachment to the Church; post-Vatican II are least committed of all. Essentially the same pattern appears with regard to closeness to God. Pre-Vatican II Catholics are most likely to report experiences of the holy; post-Vatican II Catholics are least likely.

We do not deny the possibility that some of these differences are due to age, rather than birth cohort. As young, unmarried Catholics get married and have children of their own, they are likely to become somewhat more involved in the Church, if for no other reason than to set good examples for their children and to make sure their kids are raised Catholic (e.g., Greeley, 1989, 1990).

However, to an even greater extent, these differences reflect the different experiences that age groups have during their formative years (D'Antonio, Davidson, Hoge, and Wallace, 1989, 1996; Williams and Davidson, 1996). Catholics raised in the 1930s and '40s, 1950s and '60s, and 1970s and '80s were raised in very different societal conditions. While the oldest cohort experienced economic depression and World War II during its formative years, the middle cohort experienced the prosperity of the post-war years and the social movements of the 1960s; the youngest cohort experienced the economic polarization and social dilemmas of the last 20 years. The cohorts also experienced three very different types of Catholicism: the pre-Vatican II Church, the Vatican II Church, and the post-Vatican II Church. As a result, they learned very different approaches to religion early in their lives. Other research on cohort effects (e.g., Roof, 1993; Walrath, 1987) also suggests that learning experiences during people's formative years affect their religious outlooks throughout their lives. When and if today's young Catholics become more involved in the Church, they will bring with them the social and religious outlooks they learned during their formative years. Their approaches to faith and morals will never be the same as those currently held by their parents and grandparents.

These cohort differences point to declining levels of childhood religiosity, closeness to God, and commitment to the Church. Young Catholics are less religious in childhood than their parents and grandparents; they report fewer experiences of God's presence in their lives; and they are less committed to the Church. Unless steps are taken, these trends portend a future of dwindling faithfulness among young Catholics, diminishing awareness of God's presence in the lives of Catholic adults, further erosion of Catholic identity, and a declining sense that the Church is worth supporting. These trends, in turn, signal a continuation of recent tendencies to disagree with traditional faith and morals and to embrace religious ideas that are incompatible with Church teachings.

Whether theologically liberal or conservative, members of our research team agree that some elements of this scenario threaten the long-term viability of the Church. Thus, without calling for the reintroduction of outdated beliefs and practices, and without questioning the need to explore ideas that are more suited to conditions at the turn of the new century, we address these concerns in a later section on "action implications."

Childhood Religiosity

Figure 11.1 also shows that childhood religiosity affects closeness to God. The more people learn to be religious as children, the more likely they are to report experiences of the holy later in life. Catholics who experience only limited religious formation in childhood have difficulty experiencing God's love later on.

Childhood religiosity also fosters commitment to the Church. Catholics who learn to be religious when they are young find it relatively easy to claim their Catholic identity. They also come to appreciate the benefits of being Catholic. Lower levels of childhood religiosity are associated with lower levels of commitment later in life.

One might ask, then: What upbringing influences are most closely linked to childhood religiosity? The figures in Appendix J point to the importance of having parents who talked about religion and having religious educators and catechists who are effective in ministry. Young people learn how to be religious when their parents talk with them about religion and when they receive guidance from instructors who know how to nurture religiosity.

Closeness to God

Figure 11.1 also indicates that closeness to God increases commitment to the Church. Persons who learn of God's love and care for them tend to develop strong Catholic identities and are inclined to feel that they have benefited from being part of the Church. Persons who have not had personal experiences of the holy are less likely to think of the Church as an important part of their lives.

Closeness to God also has direct effects on three of the five dimensions of faith and morals. The more God has been an integral part of parishioners' lives, the more they seem ready to agree with the Church's traditional concepts of faith, embrace relatively new devotional expressions such as reading the Bible, and agree with the Church's concern for the poor. These findings support Ludwig's (1995) claim that experiences of the holy are important lifecourse events that foster appreciation of Church teachings. The lack of such experiences increases parishioners' willingness to dissent.

Given its importance, then, what are the antecedents to experiences of being close to God? There are several. As we have said, birth cohort has an influence. So does being female, having parents who talked about religion during one's childhood, and being religious as a child. Males, persons whose parents did not talk about religion, and persons who were not especially religious as youngsters are not as predisposed to experiences of the holy later in life. In other words, the way young people are raised has long-term effects on their ability to experience God in their adult years.

All of these findings point to the learning component of our theory. As we argued in Chapter 2 and as our analyses have shown, Catholics learn faith and morals at different points in time (the cohort effect) and in a variety of settings (the effects of upbringing and lifecourse experiences). At least to some extent, then, Catholics' approaches to faith and morals are natural extensions of what they have learned over the course of their lives.

Commitment

But Catholics are not just products of their environments. In the context of their upbringing and lifecourse experiences, they actively formulate a sense of how important the Church is to them (self-concept), and they estimate the costs and benefits of being part of the Church (self-interest). These interpretations are both communal and personal: they are informed by Catholics' experiences in the Church and, yet, reflect the very personal conclusions that individual Catholics draw from these experiences.

According to our theory, these interpretations also affect Catholics' inclinations to accept or reject Church teachings. The more parishioners identify with the Church and the more they feel the Church meets their social and religious needs, the more they are likely to embrace the Church's worldview. When the Church is not an important part of their identity and they do not feel they have benefited from being Catholic, parishioners do not feel as much obligation to abide by its teachings.

The evidence in Appendix J also supports these claims. Commitment has direct effects on all five dimensions of faith and morals. It is the strongest of all influences on three dimensions (traditional beliefs and practices, recent ideas, and sexual-reproductive ethics) and a statistically significant influence on the other two (recent practices and social teachings). The more committed Catholics are, the more they are inclined toward traditional beliefs and practices, recent practices such as reading the Bible, the Church's sexual and reproductive norms, and its social teachings; they also tend to reject unauthorized ideas such as the ordination of women. These findings point to the overriding importance of Catholic identity and the benefits parishioners associate with being Catholic. Commitment to the Church accounts for more variation on more dimensions of faith and morals than any of the other variables we examined.

Who, then, are the most committed parishioners? They tend to be members of the pre-Vatican II generation, people who were religious as children, people who have had personal experiences of God's love in their adult lives, and people who are relatively well informed about matters such as Vatican II. They also have had parents who talked with them about religion and religious role models as religious instructors.

Catholics Without Parishes

Though there were no appreciable differences between parishioners and non-parishioners on our index of social teachings, there were sizeable differences on the other four dimensions. Forty-seven percent of parishioners score "high" on our measure of traditional beliefs and practices, compared to only 11 percent of non-parishioners. Eight percent of parishioners score "high" or "medium" on our index of recent practices, compared to only four percent of Catholics without parishes. Twenty-three percent of parishioners score "high" on our index of sexual and reproductive norms, compared to only 14 percent of non-parishioners. On the other hand, 51 percent of non-parishioners score "high" on our recent ideas index, compared to only 33 percent of parishioners.

What accounts for the differences between parishioners and Catholics without parishes? Why are non-parishioners so much more willing to disagree with Church teachings? Answers to these questions are found in our theoretical model.

Personal Attributes

Personal attributes account for some of the difference. African Americans, Latinos, and young Catholics are over-represented among Catholics without parishes. Either directly, or indirectly through their effects on upbringing, lifecourse experiences, and commitment, these attributes lend themselves to lower scores on our indices of faith and morals.

Upbringing

Catholics without parishes also are more likely to come from homes in which parents are less religious and less inclined to talk with their children about religion. Non-parishioners also are not as likely to have gone to Catholic schools. They have had less religious instruction than parishioners and are more likely to have had lay teachers than priests and religious. As a result of these family and educational situations, non-parishioners were not as religious when they were youngsters. In a sense, they learned not to appreciate Church teachings early in life.

Lifecourse Experiences

Their adult experiences also tend to be different. They are more likely than parishioners to be separated, divorced, or never married. If they are married, they are more likely to have spouses who are not Catholics. They are not as likely as parishioners to report having a significant other who is an active and traditional Catholic. They are less likely to report experiences of being close to God. Their socioeconomic status is somewhat lower than that of parishioners. In short, they have a number of adult experiences that make it difficult for them to be fully integrated into the life of the Church.

Commitment

Though Catholics without parishes have some sense of being Catholic, their Catholicism is not as central a life interest as it is for parishioners. In addition to having relatively weak Catholic identities, they also feel they have less of a stake in the Church. They don't report as many benefits and don't invest as much time and money in the Church. They are not nearly as committed to the Church as are parishioners.

Action Implications

What implications do these findings have for parish and diocesan leaders? How can our results help bishops, pastors, religious educators, catechists, and others who work for the Church? How can they assist Church leaders in finding common ground and transmitting Catholic faith and morals, especially in the context of American society and the post-Vatican II Church? We have addressed some implications at the end of each chapter, but now we integrate and expand these implications. We start with parishioners, then discuss implications for Catholics without parishes. Our discussion in each section is organized around the key elements in our theoretical model and the pathways shown in Figure 11.1.

Implications for Parishioners

We begin with two important caveats. First, Church leaders have relatively little control over some of the societal influences that foster pluralism in today's Church (e.g., increased individualism in American culture). Thus, there are limits to what Church leaders can do to create common ground and transmit the faith over time. However, leaders have considerable influence in other areas. We focus on conditions over which leaders have some direct control.

Second, Catholics seek and embrace some of the societal changes that contribute to diversity in faith and morals (e.g., the laity's increased prosperity and the Church's emphasis on personal responsibility for one's faith). However, most Church leaders — whether they are theologically liberal or conservative — are likely to agree that there are some changes that need to be addressed because they have adverse effects on the Church. We draw special attention to these conditions.

Personal Attributes

While each of the several attributes we examined has at least some effect on parishioners' faith and morals, the most important attribute we have examined is birth cohort. In one way or another, it affects virtually all dimensions of faith and morals. Catholics who were born and raised in the 1930s and '40s are most likely to embrace traditional beliefs and practices, participate in recent practices, and agree with the Church's sexual and social teachings. They also are least interested in recent ideas such as the ordination of women. Catholics whose formative years were the 1950s and '60s are still quite faithful, but are somewhat more likely to disagree with Church teachings. They also are more inclined than older Catholics to embrace recent ideas that are inconsistent with Canon Law. Young Catholics born and raised in the 1970s and '80s also are faithful in many important ways (especially their appreciation of pan-Vatican II beliefs and their support of the Church's social teachings), but overall they are more likely than either of the other two birth cohorts to question Church teachings and accept recent ideas such as not having to go to Mass to be a good Catholic. They do not express much interest in recent practices such as Bible study and prayer groups. These devotional practices, which require preparation, are collective in nature, and include public disclosure of one's beliefs, may not be as well suited to the post-Vatican II generation's rather individualistic approach to faith and morals as more traditional and private devotions such as the rosary and Stations of the Cross (c.f., *The Catholic Devotional*, 1996).

Race, ethnicity, and gender contribute a bit to pluralism in today's Church, but their impact is relatively small and often tied to cohort effects. We do not suggest that race, ethnicity, and gender are inconsequential. As we have shown in chapters eight and nine, they have effects of their own on faith and morals. However, our evidence quite consistently shows that cohort differences are simply larger than racial, ethnic, and gender differences. Older white males with European ancestry have more in common with older female African Americans than they do with younger white males and younger females of color. Conversely, younger people of color have more in common with younger whites than they do with older people of color and older whites.

An important implication is that in their efforts to appreciate social and cultural diversity in today's Church, parish and diocesan leaders need to pay at least as much attention to cohort differences as they do to racial, ethnic, and gender differences. Meetings that take racial, ethnic, and gender differences into account and overlook cohort differences will fail to address one of the largest communication gaps in the Church today. Church leaders should do everything possible to make sure that Catholics in all three birth cohorts — and who reflect the prevailing views of their cohort — are fully represented at conferences and on committees.

Another implication is that it may be easier to build bridges between Catholics of different races, ethnic traditions, and genders than it is to build them between Catholics belonging to different birth cohorts. Church leaders wanting to forge unity among Catholics should not be surprised to find that methods which work in producing common ground among racial, ethnic, and gender groups may not work with regard to birth cohorts. Pre-Vatican II Catholics have tended to learn through reading; post-Vatican II Catholics have learned through television and computers (Zukowski, 1996). Thus, cohorts have different approaches to learning and communicating, as well as different views of faith and morals. All of these differences are likely to frustrate efforts to forge unity, but they must be taken into account in Church leaders' efforts to forge respect, understanding, and agreement across cohort lines.

Upbringing

If Church leaders want to shape Catholics' views of faith and morals, they need to pay special attention to influences that take place very early in people's lives. The most important of these influences is childhood religiosity. By childhood religiosity, we mean the extent to which youngsters are subjectively and behaviorally involved in the Church. Subjective involvement refers to the salience they attach to religion (i.e., religion's importance in their lives). Behavioral involvement points to their participation in devotional activities such as prayer and public rituals such as attendance at Mass.

Childhood religiosity has some direct effects of its own on the tendency to reject recent ideas, but it has even more impressive effects on lifecourse experiences and levels of commitment, which have significant effects on all five dimensions of faith and morals. The more children participate in religious activities and develop a sense that religion is an important part of their lives, the more they are likely to have close personal relationships with God later in life and the more they are likely to learn about major developments such as Vatican II — both of which foster adherence to Church teachings. Childhood religiosity also promotes Catholic identify and investment in the Church, which also make significant contributions to faith and morals. Early childhood religiosity does not guarantee faithfulness later on, but it sure improves the odds.

What can catechists and religious educators do to nurture childhood religiosity? First of all, they need to think of themselves as key members of a larger network of people, all of whom relate to young people. The network includes parents, school teachers, coaches, school mates, catechists, religious educators, and parish pastors.

Members of this network often relate to children in very different ways. They have very different roles to play in children's lives; they often relate to children on the basis of different values and interests; and they often provide children with different types of guidance. Some are better role models than others; some use reinforcement and approval to motivate youngsters while others tend to rely on punishment. As a result, parents and Church leaders do not always have the same goals or use the same means of getting to there.

Without self-conscious efforts to address the forces that pull parents and Church leaders in different directions, these conditions can produce tensions between them. They can lead parents to think that catechists and religious educators are not realistic, or to feel inadequate in terms of their spiritual responsibilities to their children. They also lead catechists and religious educators to question parents' commitment to their children's religious formation, or to feel disappointed when it seems that parents are shirking their responsibilities.

Like marriage partners or partners in business, parents and Church leaders need to understand the commitments they hold in common; identify areas where they are in disagreement or at odds with one another; and find mutually satisfying solutions to the tensions between them. One way to accomplish these goals is for Church leaders to conduct focus groups with parents on a regular basis. These focus groups should include parents in relatively similar social circumstances. For example, one focus group might be done with dual-career parents. Another might include just single parents. Church leaders might ask parents in each group to discuss three or four topics related to their roles in nurturing children's religiosity. Topics might include parents' religious beliefs and practices; the amount of time parents can afford to give to their children's religious formation; what parents think their own strengths and weaknesses are with regard to the religious formation of their youngsters; what kinds of things parents are most likely to do in the way of family religious rituals; and what parents expect of catechists and religious educators.

Results of these listening sessions will give leaders an indication of the areas where they and parents share common commitments and where they tend to be in conflict. Parents and leaders might identify ways in which they can work together on the difficult task of passing on the faith. They might discover that parents want some help with parenting skills in general, not just religious formation. They might learn that catechists need to offer parents several ways — not just one way — of fulfilling classroom expectations. They might find that some parents can devote more time to religious education if the Church is able to provide day care and snacks for infants. They also might find that some parents have special talents leaders were not aware of, and that they are willing to make contributions leaders had never imagined. In follow-up meetings with parents, Church leaders and parents can build on their areas of agreement and negotiate differences of opinion or expectations. It is important for parents and leaders to arrive at some mutually acceptable set of expectations before launching any program.

Parents have responsibility for their children's social, academic, athletic, and religious formation. However, they often attach more importance to social, academic, and athletic formation than they do to religious formation; and, they often feel they have more expertise in the other areas than they do in religious formation. As a result, they turn to catechists and parish religious educators for support and advice. They may even turn a great deal of their responsibility for religious formation over to church leaders.

Parents have always acted in this way, but their dependency on Church leaders will only increase in the years ahead. There are increased number of dual-career and single-parent families in many parishes; indications that today's parents spend less time with their children than their parents spent with them 20 to 30 years ago; and increased numbers of post-Vatican II parents who are marginally religious and do not feel they know enough about Catholic faith and morals. All of these factors foreshadow an increased tendency to turn to the Church for help. More than ever before, Church leaders will be called upon for expertise.

Ironically, these increased demands will take place at precisely the same time that there are fewer priests and religious and the pool of available teachers includes a growing number of young lay Catholics who do not feel equipped to carry out these responsibilities. Thus, the recruitment and training of religious educators will be more important than at any time in memory. Dioceses and parishes will need to do more than ever before to find competent teachers and to prepare catechists and religious educators for their roles in nurturing childhood religiosity. There also will be a need for more resources to equip these teachers with the skills and materials they will need to do their jobs. Organizations such as the National Conference of Catechetical Leadership, the National Federation of Catholic Youth Ministers, the National Association of Lay Ministers, and the North American Forum on the Catechumenate are wise in addressing the question of how to prepare lay ministers for work in religious education and catechesis.

Whether they are priests, religious, or lay people, catechists and religious educators need skills and resources in at least four areas. First, they need to understand themselves in relation to their role in fostering faith among young people. They need to understand the experiences that have shaped their own approaches to faith and morals. They need to recognize their strengths and their weaknesses with regard to this task. Self-understanding contributes to quality teaching.

They also need to go outside of their own spiritual needs and fully understand the spiritual needs of the young people they are working with. Religious educators make a serious mistake when they shape their teaching around their own spiritual needs, and not the needs of the young people they are teaching.

We once observed a situation where a pre-Vatican II teacher was trying to a convince a class of post-Vatican II Catholics that they could dissent from the Church and still be good Catholics. Though the teacher explained how "probabilism" gives Catholics freedom to form views that are not in accordance with Church teachings, the students were very unhappy with his presentation. Why? The teacher had addressed his birth cohort's struggle with authority; he had not addressed the students' needs. The students said they needed a deeper sense of what the Church stood for. Instead of permission to dissent from the Church, this particular group of young Catholics wanted to learn about the Catholic tradition and its significance in their lives. The class was a classic example of a teacher addressing his own needs and failing to address the needs of his students. Teachers need to bracket their own needs and go out of the way to learn about the needs of their students. There is no one way to do this, but we would recommend being straightforward about it. Ask students what they are looking for in religion.

Catechists and religious educators also need to understand the context in which young people are raised and the most effective ways of educating in this setting. This requires an awareness of students' families, their communities, their schools, and the parishes they attend. How do these contexts foster religiosity? How can Church leaders reinforce these influences? How do the contexts stifle religiosity? How can Church leaders address these conditions? How can they inspire young people to pursue faith in environments that offer so little help?

Finally, leaders need to know content. They need to understand the Catholic faith and how to pass it on to young people. Diocesan and parish leaders need to call upon the most informed parents, asking them to pass their knowledge on to the next generation of Catholics, and rewarding them for doing so. When parents express doubts about their knowledge of the subject matter, leaders need to provide as much preparation as possible. This preparation might include tuition for courses, workshops, and conferences on particular topics. It also might include materials from the United States Catholic Conference and other producers of religious literature and video tapes. The most gifted and experienced leaders — whether clergy or laity — also might lead discussions and training sessions for less prepared teachers. Some form of continuing education is necessary if the Church is to provide leaders who transmit the Catholic heritage to the next generation.

The need for these skills is evident in our individual interviews and focus groups. Both older and younger Catholics expressed concerns that young Catholics are not learning basic truths. While members of the oldest cohort regret some of the authoritarianism and corporal punishment they experienced, they feel they learned a lot about their Catholic heritage. They fear that religious education is not doing the same thing for today's young people. As one person told us:

> When we were growing up, we had the *Baltimore Catechism*. Everything was black and white . . . My daughters were starting school in the '60s, and they went to Catholic school. They brought home a religious book, and everything was kind of abstract. . . . It was all very abstract and they were supposed to pull beliefs out of that. . . . I felt it was easy to believe your religion when you had questions

and answers, and the answers were right there. . . . My kids were not getting that. It was all sort of mush.

Post-Vatican II Catholics prefer their loving God over the punitive God their parents and grandparents learned about, but some young people also have serious doubts about the way they have been taught and what they have taught. Some caution is warranted in this discussion, since we do not know exactly how faithful our post-Vatican II respondents were in attending religious education classes and fulfilling their assignments. However, assuming they were reasonably attentive and responsible, we are concerned about their claims that processes such as making collages and banners were often stressed more than substantive answers to fundamental questions about faith and morals. They feel they were shortchanged in their understanding of scriptures, Church history, core teachings, and Catholic rituals. They say they were taught they are Christians, but they have a difficult time explaining what it means to be a Catholic Christian as compared to a member of a Protestant denomination. They learned that God loves them and wants them to be good people, but they also told us they did not learn what that means in terms of specific behavior. When asked what it means to be a good person, one young Catholic hesitated then said: "I smile at people." Young Catholics have been taught that faith is a matter of personal choice: that they must have a personal relationship with God and that they are to reach their own decisions on matters of faith and morals. They have not been taught to think of their faith in terms of responsibilities to the Catholic tradition, one's diocese, one's parish, or other Catholics. Listen to their words as they reflect on the religious education they received in the 1970s and '80s:

> I don't know what parts of the Mass mean. They didn't really tell us.

> In CCD classes, we just talked about being nice to each other. It wasn't a real dogmatic approach . . . more of a general Christian approach.

> As far as the Bible goes, I couldn't tell you what's in the Old and New Testaments.

These comments lend support to Wilkes' (1996:xix) observation that "an entire generation of Catholic-born children have been raised with little knowledge or understanding of the religious beliefs that shaped their parents and the American Catholic ethos. We are now witnessing the rise of the best secularly educated group of cradle Catholics ever born — and, religiously, the least literate."

One implication, then, is to challenge catechists and religious leaders to think critically about both the processes they use and the substance they transmit to young Catholics. In the pre-Vatican II Church, the priests and religious who were mainly responsible for religious formation were not always equipped with process skills, but they understood content. In the post-Vatican II Church, where there has been — and will continue to be — a heavy reliance on lay teachers, there probably has been more emphasis on process than content. We need a balance of the two. There needs to be a balance between effective learning processes and content that addresses young Catholics' spiritual and morals needs. To this end, leaders might try to identify the best features of religious education programs offered in pre-Vatican II and post-Vatican II years. Without reintroducing the coercion that often accompanied pre-Vatican II religious education, Church leaders might link yesterday's attention to Church teachings with today's emphasis on self-expression. Without resurrecting the harsh discipline of the past, they might find ways to link exercises holding youngsters accountable for Church teachings with ones inviting the expression of students' personal opinions about them.

One step in this direction is to emphasize pan-Vatican II beliefs embedded in the Nicene Creed (which our data indicate are very important to Catholics) and specifically-Catholic teachings (which they yearn to know more about). Shared Christian doctrines such as the Incarnation and Resurrection and uniquely Catholic doctrines such as the Real Presence and Mary as the Mother of God provide a solid foundation for childhood religiosity. Wilkes (1996:158) notes that, "The young people I know are hungry for authentic moral guidelines. No, they will not abide imposed legalisms or the dictums of self-righteous authority but give them rules and guidelines that are right and just and decent, and they will listen."

Leaders also need to provide young people with the means they need to grow in faith and to act on it. Youngsters need prayers to help them talk with God. They need to participate in sacraments, so they can experience a sense of the sacred during their childhood years. But, many young people in our focus groups said they had not been taught prayers or the meaning of the sacraments. They had real difficulty answering when we asked them how they nurture their faith. They told us they didn't know specific prayers. They didn't think of Mass as an opportunity to grow in faith. By urging young people to attend Mass, rewarding them for participating in other parish activities, and teaching them how to pray, educators increase the chances that young people will develop close relationships with God, become aware of major developments in the Church, form strong Catholic identities, and realize the benefits of being Catholic — all of which promote adherence to Catholic teachings about faith and morals. The more catechists put childhood religiosity at the center of religious formation, the more effective they will be in promoting a Catholic worldview.

But parents are still the primary influence in young people's lives. Church leaders need to reassure parents that they are "good enough Catholics" (Wilkes, 1996) and urge them to do their best. Leaders also will need to remind parents that — regardless of how religious or competent they might feel personally — they need to devote as much time and attention to the religious formation of their children as they do to their children's social, athletic, and academic formation. Parents need to practice their faith, so children will have models to imitate. They also need to keep up with developments in the Church, just as they keep up with changes in their children's social lives, schools, and sports teams. Parents need to talk with their children about religion, making religion as much a normal part of family conversation as other aspects of children's lives. Parents also need to lead the way in family religious activities including grace at meals, Advent and Lenten ceremonies, telling stories about saints, hanging religious pictures in children's rooms, and saying bedtime prayers. These activities provide children with a sense of security and love, and they provide opportunities to learn about one's faith. They also are relatively inexpensive and don't require a great deal of time.

Dioceses and parishes need to provide parents with skills and abilities to do these things. They can develop adult religious education programs to keep parents current on developments in the Church — and helping parents see that participation in these programs sets a good example, indicating to children that religious formation is a lifelong process. Church leaders can emphasize the importance of teaching parents how to talk with their children about religion — showing them that it does not require sophisticated theology or special credentials. They also can provide parents with ideas, stories, pictures, and prayers that they can incorporate into their family lives without a great deal of difficulty and at relatively little cost.

Dioceses and parishes will need significant resources to accomplish these tasks. To produce these resources, Church leaders will need to raise additional money and/or reallocate current funds. These needs point to an important dilemma. Murnion's (1992) study of lay ministers indicates a stratification of Catholic parishes. Some are affluent, have educated and multi-talented members, and have lots of other resources to work with (e.g., lots of money, great facilities, the latest equipment). Other parishes have far fewer resources to work with. These inequalities can foster very unequal opportunities to grow in faith. They don't guarantee unequal outcomes, but they certainly contribute to that possibility. To give all our kids a more even chance to experience God in their childhood years, dioceses and parishes may want to form partnerships that allow them to share teachers, classrooms, and materials.

Our experiences in the course of this study indicate that religious educators and catechists are quite willing to explore these substantive and procedural issues. We have been impressed by their readiness to consider the limitations of recent educational policies and to consider modifications. Indeed, many are already doing so (e.g., Duggan and Kelly, 1991; Johnston, 1991).

Lifecourse Experiences

We also have shown that several lifecourse experiences affect the way lay people think of faith and morals. Chief among these are experiences of being close to God and, to a lesser extent, awareness of Vatican II. If Church leaders want to affect the way Catholics approach faith and morals, they need to nurture experiences of the holy and knowledge of major developments in the Church. Nurturing reliance on Almighty God and awareness of recent events such as Vatican II are not only antidotes to the isolation and loneliness that often accompany modern life; as Ludwig (1996) suggests, they also contribute to parishioners' readiness to value Church teachings.

One step in this direction is to cultivate environments in which adult parishioners can learn that God and the Church are integral parts of their lives. Dioceses and parishes are two environments over which Church leaders have some control and which can play important roles in promoting close relationships with God and the Church. Diocesan and parish leaders need to devote special attention to the ways in which these settings communicate a sense of the holy and knowledge of developments such as the publication of encyclicals and pastoral letters. Leaders ought to seize every available opportunity for adult religious formation.

At the diocesan level, bishops and other leaders should continue to use diocesan newspapers to explain God's presence in people's lives and to interpret important developments in the Church. Programs such as RENEW and Christ Renews His Parish also are important steps in the right direction. But, given cohort differences in learning styles (Arkinson, 1995; Zukowski, 1996), diocesan leaders also should experiment with contemporary means of communication. It is quite easy to insert videotapes and cassette tapes into homilies, parish education programs, and parishioners' home VCRs. We think than an Indiana bishop who uses e-mail to carry on conversations with young people in his diocese also is on the right track.

At the parish level, weekend Masses provide one of the best opportunities to nurture a sense of the sacred and to educate parishioners. Liturgists and clergy need to design worship experiences and homilies that center on parishioners' relationships with God and their knowledge of Church teachings. According to Vatican II (Flannery, 1992:18-19; 172-173), homilies are to focus on interpretations of scripture. In recent years, there has been increased emphasis on experiential and story-telling forms of interpretation that are often refreshing and quite persuasive. However, they also can be ahistorical and seldom provide opportunities to forge connections among scripture readings, conciliar documents, and recent encyclicals — all of which communicate God's love and interpret his presence in the modern world. We have seen young Catholics' eyes light up when homilies explain ways in which the Church has tried to interpret scriptures and their relevance to everyday life in different eras and in different parts of the world. In line with Fee et al. (1981) and Greeley's (1990) emphasis on the importance of good preaching, we believe that training in, and use of, various homiletic approaches are steps toward fostering close relationships with God and parishioners' awareness of major developments such as Vatican II.

Adult education and action programs also offer important opportunities to achieve these goals. As diocesan and parish leaders design programs, they need to remember that parishioners learn in many different ways. As Myers' (1980:16) has observed, "we are as likely to act ourselves into a way of thinking as to think ourselves into a line of actions. . . . Individuals are as likely to believe in what they have stood up for as to stand up for what they believe."

Thus, leaders should offer some traditional educational programs that provide information and promote attitude change as steps in the direction of ultimately changing people's behaviors. Speakers' programs in which experts explain the Church's teachings on issues such as the Incarnation, ordination, abortion, and economic justice give parishioners opportunities to think themselves into new ways of acting.

We call special attention to educational programs relating to Vatican II. As Vatican II (and other developments, such as the American bishops' pastoral letters on peace and economic justice) recede into history, there is a risk that its significance will be lost (D'Antonio, Davidson, Hoge, and Wallace, 1989, 1996). We already see that many Catholics — especially young ones — have little or no knowledge of the Council and what it meant. Our data suggest that this is a real loss for the Church and its efforts to achieve the goal of *aggiornamento*. When priests do not talk about Vatican II in their homilies and other Church leaders do not promote knowledge of the Council, they create a vacuum in which ideas that are quite contrary to Church teachings can flourish. Unawareness permits — may even encourage — dissent. From our data, it seems that awareness encourages appreciation of Catholicism's worldview. Though clergy and lay leaders have many different interpretations of Vatican II

(Komonchek, 1995), our data suggest that promoting awareness of Vatican II is important in its own right, but also contributes to appreciation of the Church teachings in the areas of faith and morals. This finding concurs with McBrien's (1994:xli) reminder that "the more history we know, the less likely we are to distort the reality of Catholicism by shaping it to our own predispositions or by identifying it with one razor-thin slice of its long and richly diverse history."

Leaders also should provide action-oriented programs that start with behavioral commitments and are geared ultimately to changing people's attitudes. Social outreach programs and peace ministries are good examples. Previous research indicates that parishes invest relatively few resources in such programs (Leege and Trozzolo, 1985; Leege, 1986; Rafferty and Leege, 1989; Gremillion and Leege, 1989; Davidson, Mock and Johnson, 1997). For example, very few parishes have a full-time staff person in social ministry, designing community-oriented opportunities for social service and advocacy. Most spend less than five percent of their budgets on outreach programs. The lack of programs of this type deprives some parishioners of opportunities to act themselves into new ways of thinking.

But, attitude change does not necessarily lead to behavior change and behavior change does not automatically lead to attitude change. Thus, traditional educational programs should give participants some behavioral options which Church leaders are prepared to facilitate, and action-oriented programs should include opportunities for participants to interpret new behavioral experiences in spiritual and moral terms that might foster attitude change.

In designing any parish or diocesan program, then, leaders need to incorporate elements of prayer, study, faith sharing, support, and outreach. Though programs may focus more attention on one or two of these elements, they are likely to be most successful when all five elements are included. Bible study groups may concentrate on scripture study but, if they are to produce behavior change, they also need to include opportunities for prayer, faith sharing, support, and outreach. Likewise, social ministry programs may concentrate on outreach but, if they are to foster attitude change, they also need to include prayer, study, faith sharing, and support. Small church communities and programs such as RENEW, Christ Renews His Parish, and RCIA are most successful when they incorporate all of these elements and do not focus on one to the exclusion of the others (Hornsby-Smith, 1990; Kelly, 1991; Baranowski, 1996; Appleby, 1997).

Previous research indicates that at least half of parishioners are not involved in any Church activities (Raftery and Leege, 1989). Our study of Indiana parishioners indicates the same thing. Thus, if Church leaders are to affect Catholics' lives, they need to get beyond parish-based ministries and into other environments, where most Catholics spend even more of their time.

Church leaders have special opportunities to influence Catholics' family lives. The Church already participates in marriage preparation. There is growing concern that there is not much follow-through with young couples. As Fee et al. (1981) have suggested, Church leaders could meet with young couples after they are married, encouraging them to understand their relationship with God, their right to petition the Creator for help, and His willingness to answer their prayers. Through such conversations, Church leaders could also help young couples gain a sense of the sanctity of their marriage. They also could gain a sense of God's presence in their lives and developments in the Church that are intended to support their relationship.

Church leaders also must appreciate the fact that most Catholic adults spend a great deal of time in social environments that have little or nothing to do with parish and family life. Among others, these settings include colleges and universities, workplaces, retirement communities, fitness and recreation centers, hospitals, and special-purpose organizations addressing issues of social justice. Church leaders have far less control over what takes place in these community contexts, but those who minister to, and with, adults in these settings have had important effects in Catholics' lives. They have helped many people experience God's presence in these environments, and they have had opportunities to show how events such as Vatican II relate to these settings. Though this type of outreach often takes special people, innovative forms of ministry, and creative resourcing, it can make a real difference in the lives of Catholic adults.

Our focus groups and survey data suggest two other steps leaders can take to help adults experience the holy, no matter what environments they are in. One is provide spiritual exercises and prayers to help people talk with God about their needs; the other is to teach people how to listen and respond to God's call. Young Catholics say they have been taught that God loves them, but they, more than other birth cohorts, say that they have not been taught prayers to communicate with God. When we asked them how they nurture their faith, they provided only vague answers. They think of God as their friend, but feel they have not learned how to respond when God does not seem to answer their prayers or when the Creator expects behavior that is at odds with the expectations of their friends and peers. As Fee et al. (1981) and Greeley (1990) have argued, close relationships with God have many positive implications in the lives of adult Catholics.

Commitment

As we have said, people are not just products of their environments. They interpret the things that happen to them during their childhood and adult years. They create their own identities and assess the costs and benefits of various courses of action. They act on the basis of self-concepts and self-interests, which combine to form a very powerful influence on faith and morals.

Because parishioners vary in the extent of their identification with the Church and draw different conclusions about the costs and benefits of being Catholic, they are inclined to form different approaches to faith and morals. As the range of identities and cost-benefit outcomes has increased in recent years, so has the extent of religious pluralism in the Church.

Church leaders wanting to forge common ground and transmit Catholicism to the next generation need to understand and respect the identities and cost-benefit calculations giving rise to this diversity. Leaders should not deny, dismiss, or disregard them; they must accept and comprehend them. They must appreciate the roles that self-concept and self-interest play in fostering different religious perspectives. They must see how differing identities and interests quite naturally lead to spiritual and moral diversity.

But, self-concepts and self-interests are never permanent. Lay people change their hearts and minds all the time. Church leaders can play — some would say, have a duty to play — a role in these changes. In so doing, they can affect the way American Catholics think about faith and morals.

Leaders who want to forge common ground and perpetuate a Catholic worldview need to take religious identity and religious self-interest seriously. Knowing full well that parishioners will respond to their efforts in quite different ways, we feel leaders should stress the value of a strong Catholic identity and the need to invest time and money in the Church in exchange for the benefits it provides. The more Church leaders promote a strong Catholic identity and a willingness to support the Church with time and money, the more they will increase the laity's inclinations to value Church teachings. To the extent that leaders promote only a general sense of being Christian — or, worse yet, communicate that being Catholic is not particularly important — they reduce the likelihood that Catholics will feel any need to take Church teachings seriously. To the extent that they neglect members' need to support an organization that serves their needs, they also undermine any sense of accountability to the Church.

In the wake of Vatican II, Church leaders have tried to get beyond the ghetto mentality of the 1930s and '40s and have made a self-conscious effort to emphasize commonalities among all Christians. Most of these efforts to establish better relations with other faith groups are to be applauded, because they tear down some unnecessary barriers between Catholics and other faith groups. However, it is a mistake to stress common Christian heritage without also calling attention to what gives Catholics their distinctive identity. It also is a mistake to rob Catholics of a sense of belonging to a Church that deserves — indeed, needs — their support. Such mistakes leave Catholics — especially young Catholics, who live in a much more ecumenical world — feeling vulnerable. They report feeling unprepared when members of other faiths (who often have a very clear sense of what makes their faith special) criticize Catholicism or ask questions that Catholics can't answer. We believe it is quite possible to stress both the commonalities among Christian faiths and a specifically Catholic identity. It also is possible to be ecumenical and expect parishioners to invest their time, talents, and treasures in the Church. It is quite possible to foster pride in and support of one's own tradition without promoting antipathy toward other religious groups. If it is done correctly, achieving a balance of commitment to the Catholic Church and respect for others will foster adherence to Catholic faith and morals without engendering prejudice or discrimination against others.

Implications for Catholics Without Parishes

Our results also have implications for parish and diocesan leaders in evangelization ministries oriented toward Catholics without parishes. Once again, our discussion of these implications follows the lines of our theoretical framework.

Personal Attributes

Though it would require some work, one step could be a census of all people within a territorial parish. Another step could be to ask current parishioners for the names, addresses, and phone numbers of people they know who are not registered in a parish. Telephone calls from pastors and staff persons in specific ministries would be natural next steps. Follow up visits and conversations might lead to the identification of other Catholics without parishes.

Once non-parishioners have been contacted and invited to participate, parishes need to be welcoming to African Americans, Latinos, and young people — all of whom are over-represented among Catholics without parishes. In addition to being hospitable toward racial minorities and young people, Catholic parishes also need to include these groups in all levels of Church life. If and when members of these groups express an interest in parish life, they ought to be included on parish committees that match their interests and expertise. They need to be fully represented on parish staffs, parish councils, and committees related to youth education, adult education, social concerns, parish finances, and liturgy — to name just a few ministries. They also need to be invited into leadership positions at the diocesan level.

Whites and older Catholics need to make serious efforts to include racial minorities and young non-parishioners at all levels of Church life and to make sure that, once in positions of influence, their views — which are likely to differ somewhat — are treated with courtesy and respect.

Given the race and cohort biases of many parishes, such efforts will be a real challenge. Alienated people of color and post-Vatican II Catholics may be reluctant to participate. They are likely to have limited identification with the Church and may feel that the social and emotional costs of participating outweigh the benefits. Parish leaders must learn the nature of these trepidations and address them. Without advocating the reestablishment of "national parishes," the Church would be wise to provide people of color and young Catholics with a network of spiritual and social services (e.g., sacraments, social solidarity, care in times of crisis) that is a modern-day equivalent to the services that European immigrants found so beneficial earlier in the twentieth century. Then, together, parish leaders and Catholics without parishes should explore forms of participation that are consistent with existing religious identities, which non-parishioners find rewarding, and that are as consistent as possible with the values and interests of others in the parish.

Inclusion of people of color and young people also might pose some difficulties for others in the parish. Leaders and other parishioners may encounter attitudes and behavior that they are unaccustomed to and/or that they are inclined to reject. When confronted with such circumstances, they would be wise to withhold judgment. Then, as they work toward common goals in programs they care about, they should discuss the social and religious experiences that lie behind their different views. The ensuing dialogue might be stressful at times, but it also is likely to be an opportunity for the development of mutual respect among members of a very pluralistic Church.

Upbringing

Church leaders also need to address the upbringing experiences that encouraged non-parishioners to be marginal to the Church. Conversations with non-parishioners might explore their parents' religious behaviors, their own religious experiences, and the implications these background influences have on the current relationship to the Church. Exploration of these influences also might foster some appreciation for their need to set good religious examples for their children. In these conversations, Church leaders must be prepared to offer all the support and all the other resources non-parishioners need to grow in faith and offer their children spiritual and moral guidance. They will need parish and diocesan ministries that encourage parents and children to participate together in religious activities and that give parents good reasons to talk with their children about religion. Religious education — in Catholic schools as well as in parish settings — seems indispensable. Catechesis provides a special opportunity for leaders to link families, schools, and parishes in a unified effort aimed at religious formation. Churches must be prepared to provide scholarships and to give young non-parishioners opportunities to learn from some of the parishes' best catechists and educators.

Lifecourse Experiences

Non-parishioners who have limited educational backgrounds, lower status jobs, and only modest family incomes need to be invited into parish life and made to feel welcome — in many of the same ways we mentioned above with regard to racial minorities and young Catholics. They are likely to feel some of the same reluctance, but the Church must make every effort to incorporate them into parish life as fully as it can. Such efforts must include a commitment to treating persons of limited means with the same understanding and respect that churches give to more prosperous members.

Though Church leaders cannot control who Catholics choose to marry, especially in today's more ecumenical world with its increased levels of interfaith marriage (McCutcheon, 1988), they certainly can help young Catholics think carefully about the importance of having a spouse who shares their faith. Not only do same-faith marriages foster somewhat higher levels of adherence to Church teachings among adults, they also contribute to the religious formation of young Catholics (Nelsen, 1990). Parish and diocesan leaders need to make teenagers and young adults fully aware of how important a Catholic spouse can be in one's own attachment to a parish and in transmitting Catholic faith and morals to succeeding generations. Some young Catholics — especially those who have little or no identification with the Church — will resist the idea of using religious affiliation as a factor in selecting a marriage partner. However, Church leaders should persist, knowing that the more they encourage Catholics to marry other Catholics, and the more effective they are in communicating the benefits of religious compatibility, the more likely Catholics are to pass the faith on to their children.

Parishes also need to confront the fact that they tend to be oriented toward families that include both parents, children, and even extended family members. These family norms often make it difficult for singles and separated and divorced Catholics to feel as if they fit in. Without abandoning the Church's commitment to families, diocesan and parish leaders need to find ways to increase unmarried Catholics' identification with the Church. They also need to provide homilies, worship experiences, and parish programs that benefit unmarried persons, especially those who feel their lives have not turned out the way they or the Church had hoped.

We also note that non-parishioners report fewer experiences of being close to God during the course of their adult lives. Some of this difference can be traced to family influences and the lack of religious education in Catholic schools and parishes. Some of it also is linked to difficulties, such as marital discord and economic hardship. If clergy, religious, and lay leaders are to help non-parishioners capture a sense of the holy in their lives, they need additional contact with them — especially at key moments, such as illness and death, when God's presence can be understood most readily. Making sacraments and social services available to non-parishioners on a regular basis also increases leaders' long-term opportunities to cultivate an awareness of God's presence in their lives.

Commitment

Leaders also need to address non-parishioners' religious self-concepts and self-interests. The good news is that non-parishioners still consider themselves Catholic and have had at least some positive experiences in the Church. The bad news is that they tend not to think of religion as an especially important part of their lives, and they probably have had some negative experiences along the way. Simply telling non-parishioners that they ought to place higher priority on their faith and that they should appreciate the benefits of being Catholic is not likely to go very far. What is likely to be more effective is asking non-parishioners to tell their stories about why they still think of themselves as Catholic and building on the positive experiences they describe. The building process almost certainly will involve some encounter with painful incidents that have diminished their Catholic identities. These encounters must be taken seriously and addressed but they also should be seen as opportunities to nurture new understandings of what it means to be Catholic in today's world. With such efforts, some non-parishioners might be inclined to "re-member" the Church.

Conclusions

We have tried to study American Catholics' beliefs and practices in a way that would be helpful to parish and diocesan leaders. We have found that there is considerable common ground in today's Church. Unity is most apparent among parishioners and in the area of pan-Vatican II beliefs such as the Incarnation and the Resurrection, but there also are comparatively high levels of agreement on other issues relating to traditional beliefs and practices and social teachings. There also are more similarities than one might otherwise expect in the religious orientations of parishioners belonging to different racial, ethnic, and gender groups.

We have also learned that there is considerable disagreement among parishioners on issues of sexual and reproductive ethics, that Catholics are quite divided over unauthorized ideas such as the ordination of women, and that they have not yet embraced new devotional practices such as reading the Bible or Bible study. In addition to important differences between pre-Vatican II, Vatican II, and post-Vatican II parishioners, there also are sizeable differences between the two-thirds of all Catholics who are registered parishioners and the one-third who are Catholics without parishes. Non-parishioners are far less active and much more inclined to disagree with Church teachings, except in the area of social teachings, where they are quite similar to parishioners. These social and religious divisions represent the biggest challenges to persons seeking common ground and wanting to pass the faith on to future generations of American Catholics.

We also have specified the processes by which Catholics arrive at different understandings of faith and morals. While we have identified many factors that account for at least some of the differences among Catholics, four influences seem most important: birth cohort, levels of childhood religiosity, lifecourse experiences of (not) being close to God, and degrees of commitment to the Church. Focusing on these variables, we have explored some of the implications our results might have for Church leaders. We have warned against actions that disregard the social and religious conditions that lie beneath the pluralism in today's Church, but we also have identified some steps leaders might take to promote greater unity in the years ahead. Without advocating strict compliance with all Church teachings, we also have recommended some courses of action that assist in passing the faith along to future generations of American Catholics. We hope these reflections are useful to the faithful Church leaders we have met in the course of this study, and to others who we meet for the first time through the pages of this book.

Appendix A
Members of the Research Team

Project Office

James D. Davidson
Andrea S. Williams
Sherry Leuck

Diocesan Coordinators

Richard Lamanna
Kathleen Maas Weigert
William Whalen
Sister Patricia Wittberg
Jan Stenftenagel

Diocesan Advisors

Monsignor Ferdinand J. Melevage
Robert Vasoli
Father Robert Sell
M. Desmond Ryan
Father Michael Madden

Independent Advisors

Roger Finke
John Tropman
Joseph Tamney
Lawrence Cunningham
Thomas Ryba

Appendix B
Research Design

Interviews

Each member of the leadership team did one or two interviews. There was no pretense that the interviewees would be a representative cross-section of Indiana Catholics. We simply contacted people we knew and others whom we didn't know, making sure that they were of different races, ethnic groups, genders, and ages. The purposes of these interviews were to ask a few general questions related to our theoretical framework, and to get a feeling for the different ways in which Catholics think and talk about their religion. Our goal was to listen and learn.

Focus Groups

In summer 1993, we contacted selected parishes in each diocese, again not pretending that these were a representative cross-section of all parishes. However, we made sure the parishes reflected both urban and rural settings, included people with different racial and ethnic characteristics, and included lay people of all ages. We asked pastors of these parishes to provide names, addresses, and phone numbers of parishioners who might be willing to meet with us in focus groups and talk about Catholicism.

We conducted three focus groups in each diocese. One focus group included pre-Vatican II Catholics (people who were 50 years of age or older). Another included Vatican II Catholics between the ages of 30 and 49. The third was for post-Vatican II Catholics between the ages of 18 and 29. Each focus group contained eight to 10 people and lasted two hours. Leadership team members, who were trained in focus group methodology, moderated the groups, giving participants 15 to 20 minutes to discuss each of six questions. The questions dealt with the participants' religious upbringing, their Catholic identities, the meaning they attach to "church," and the role the Church has played in their lives.

Davidson and Williams listened to tape recordings of all focus groups. Diocesan coordinators and advisors listened to tapes of focus groups in their respective dioceses. Each member of the leadership team independently took notes concerning frequently used words, each group's answers to each question, and memorable moments or quotations.

Team members shared their notes at the leadership team's next meeting. The team's goals were to specify themes which cut across all three generations and to identify patterns which distinguished each birth cohort from the other two. Davidson and Williams then summarized the team's findings in a report which was sent to all team members.

One of the things the leadership team observed was a shift from an institutional approach to faith among pre-Vatican II Catholics to a more individualistic concept of faith among post-Vatican II Catholics. With this shift in mind, Williams listened to all 15 tape recordings twice more. Our goal was to document this shift (Williams and Davidson, 1996).

Questionnaire Survey

The interviews and focus group results helped us design a statewide questionnaire survey. Having listened to Catholics talk about faith and morals, we were now more familiar with their beliefs and practices, and the words Catholics in Indiana use to express their views about the Church. We could devise a questionnaire which was sensitive to their concerns and used language with which they were comfortable.

We stratified Indiana's 490 parishes on the basis of their racial and ethnic compositions, then drew a 10 percent sample of parishes. We used a proportionate-to-size random sampling procedure to select 49 parishes which would give every registered Catholic in Indiana an equal chance of being selected (Babbie, 1989). The pastors and staffs of these 49 parishes provided parish rolls, which were "cleaned" to exclude persons under the age of 18, non-Catholics who were married to Catholic spouses, and elderly persons who were physically or mentally unable to participate in our survey.

From these rolls, we selected one percent samples of parishioners from the three largest dioceses (Indianapolis, Gary, and Fort Wayne-South Bend) and two percent samples from the two smallest dioceses (Lafayette and Evansville). In late April and early May 1994, we sent a letter addressed to each respondent and signed personally by the project director and research assistant, a questionnaire, and a carefully chosen prayer card to each of 4,807 parishioners. About two weeks later, we sent all 4,807 persons a postcard, thanking those who had responded and urging the others to return their questionnaires. Three weeks later, we sent all non-respondents a second copy of the questionnaire and another personalized letter urging them to participate. About a month later, we sent non-respondents a third letter, explaining that we needed to hear from everyone, not just the most active Catholics. Persons with Spanish surnames received one letter in English and one in Spanish. Finally, in late August, we sent all non-respondents a fourth personalized letter and another copy of the questionnaire. This time, persons with Spanish surnames received a questionnaire in Spanish.

We closed off returns at the end of September 1994. Despite all of our efforts to clean the rolls, 145 of the people we contacted could not be reached at the addresses the parishes gave us or were ineligible for the study because they were non-Catholic or too old and infirm. When these persons were deleted, the adjusted total of persons contacted was 4,662. We received responses from 2,886 persons (a 62 percent return rate). However, despite all our personalized letters and careful instructions, 250 people asked other people (usually their spouses) to answer the questions and send the questionnaires back to us. We analyzed these surrogate returns, and found bias in the direction of higher levels of commitment and more traditional views, so we deleted them from our returns (Williams and Davidson, 1995). When all was said and done, we had received legitimate responses from 2,636 persons (57 percent of eligible respondents). The responses of the two smallest dioceses then were reproduced (multiplied by two) so they were properly weighted in the statewide analyses. Results were distributed through meetings with bishops and other Church leaders, and a series of news releases published by the five diocesan newspapers in Indiana.

National Telephone Poll

Members of the research team wrote a set of questions that would address the issues included in each cell of our theoretical model. Response Analysis, a professional polling company in New Jersey, developed a national sample and conducted the interviews. The sample design for the national survey was developed to minimize screening costs while, at the same time, yielding an achieved sample that accurately represents the target population. Over-sampling of Hispanic Catholics (and to the extent possible, black Catholics) also was a design goal.

The sampling approach was based on information collected as part of the "Churches and Church Membership in the United States, 1990" study (Bradley et al., 1990). Data from this study were available from The Roper Center and provided estimates of the number of Catholics at the county level. These county-level estimates were used in conjunction with data from the U.S. Census and information on the estimated distribution of working residential telephone numbers across exchanges, to develop a stratification of all telephone exchanges serving the continental U.S. A secondary stratification of exchanges within certain strata was overlaid on the base stratification in an attempt to increase the chances of finding Hispanic and black households.

Using a disproportionate allocation sampling model, exchanges serving areas with higher concentrations of Catholic households were over-sampled, while exchanges serving areas with lower concentrations of Catholics were under-sampled. Within the designated area codes and exchanges, telephone numbers were randomly generated using a random digit dialing (RDD) sample procedure. Response Analysis Corporation purchased these RDD samples from Survey Sampling, Incorporated.

The likelihood of contacting a respondent at each sampled telephone number was maximized by using an extended call-rule, in which a minimum of 10 attempts were made to contact each household, and a call-rotation algorithm that ensured that the sample was cycled through a specified number of week-night, weekend, and weekday calls.

The likelihood of completing an interview with each eligible respondent was maximized by a flexible interviewing schedule so that callback appointments could be made at the respondents' convenience, and a refusal conversion effort in which households that initially refused to participate were recontacted several weeks later in an effort to encourage their cooperation in the survey.

The interviewing team was comprised of English-speaking and bilingual (English/Spanish) interviewers who were selected based on their previous experience with similar projects. All interviewers attended a training session specifically designed for this project.

The interviewer began by giving his/her name and saying the following:

> "I'm calling from Response Analysis Corporation in Princeton, New Jersey. As part of a major research project being conducted by Purdue University, we are calling a random sample of American households. We are not selling anything. We just want to ask you some questions about religion. All of your answers will be strictly confidential. No one on the research team will ever reveal that you were called, or that you participated in this study."

Then, the interviewer asked: "What is your present religion, if any?" If the person answered Catholic, the interviewer asked: "Are there any other adult members of your household, that is, persons age 18 or older, who are also Catholic?" If the person said "yes," the interviewer asked: "Including yourself, how many adult members of your household are Catholic?" After recording that number, the interviewer said: "To make sure we get a random mix of people, we want to select one person in your household to answer a few questions about being a Catholic. The way we do that is to ask this question: "Which of the Catholic adults in this household will be the next to have a birthday?" If that person was home, the interview proceeded. If the person was not home, the interviewer scheduled a callback.

If the person on the phone was Catholic but also said he/she was not very active in the Church, the interviewer said: "We want to talk with all

Catholics, regardless of how active they are" and the screening process continued. If the person was not Catholic, he/she was asked if any adult member of the household was and the process continued. If nobody in the household was Catholic, the interview ended.

A total of 1,058 interviews were completed between May 18, 1995, and July 5, 1995. Ninety-eight percent of interviews were conducted entirely in English; two percent were done at least partly in Spanish. The average interview lasted 23 minutes.

Once the datafile was fully cleaned, weights were developed to correct for disproportional sample allocation and to balance the sample based on the demographic profiles obtained in the "Churches and Church Membership in the United States, 1990" study. Disproportionality was a result of the under- and over-sampling built into the sample design.

Typically, national survey data are weighted to reflect the demographic distribution of all households in the continental U.S. as reflected in the U.S. Census. The weighting plan for this survey differed from what might be considered to be "typical" in that the demographic profile to which the data were balanced is that of Catholic households in the continental U.S. rather than all households. Differences between the demographic profile of this and other national survey data may be due in part to differences in the demographic profile of Catholic households as compared to all U.S. households.

Appendix C
Faith and Morals Indices

Pan-Vatican II Beliefs (alpha = .90)

Would you say that the belief that . . . is very important, fairly important, somewhat important, or not very important to you personally?

There are three persons in one God

Jesus physically rose from the dead

In Mass the bread and wine actually become the Body and Blood of Christ

Jesus was completely divine like God and completely human like us in every way except sin

Mary is the Mother of God

Pan-Vatican II Practices (alpha = .81)

How often, if ever, do you. . . ? More than once a week, once a week, two or three times a month, once a month, less than once a month, almost never or never.

Attend Mass

Receive Communion

Pray privately

How often, if ever, do you. . . ? Regularly, sometimes, rarely, never.

Attend Holy Days of Obligation

Pre-Vatican II Beliefs (alpha = .71)

Please tell me whether you agree or disagree with this statement. Is that strongly or somewhat?

The Pope is the Vicar of Christ

The Catholic Church is the one true Church

It's important to obey Church teachings even if I don't understand them.

Pre-Vatican II Practices (alpha = .71)

How often, if ever, do you. . .? More than once a week, once a week, two or three times a month, once a month, less than once a month, almost never or never.

Pray the rosary

Start and end the day with a prayer

Practice devotions to Mary or a special saint

About how often, if ever, do you. . . ? Once a month or more, several times a year, once or twice a year, never, or almost never.
Go to private confession with a priest

Recent Ideas (r = .31)
Please tell me whether you agree or disagree with this statement.
Is that strongly or somewhat?
One can be a good Catholic without going to Mass
Women should be allowed to be priests

Recent Practices (alpha = .64)
How often, if ever, do you. . . ? More than once a week, once a week, two or three times a month, once a month, less than once a month, almost never or never.
Read the Bible
Attend Bible study
Attend prayer groups or a faith sharing groups

Sexual and Reproductive Ethics (alpha = .75)
In your opinion, is this behavior always wrong, wrong except under certain circumstances, or is it entirely up to the individual?
Use of condoms and birth control pills to prevent pregnancy
Engage in premarital sex
Choose to terminate a pregnancy by having an abortion
Engage in homosexual acts

Social Teachings (r = .24)
Please tell me whether you agree or disagree with this statement.
Is that strongly or somewhat?
Helping needy people is an important part of my religious beliefs
Catholics have a duty to try to close the gap between the rich and the poor

Appendix D

Correlations Among Dimensions of Faith and Morals

	Pan-Vatican II Practices	Pre-Vatican II Beliefs	Pre-Vatican II Practices	Recent Ideas	Recent Practices	Sexual-Rep. Ethics	Social Teachings
Pan-Vatican II Beliefs	.57	.47	.45	-.30	.24	.33	.27
Pan-Vatican II Practices		.46	.64	-.44	.43	.41	.29
Pre-Vatican II Beliefs			.43	-.42	.14	.47	.36
Pre-Vatican II Practices				-.43	.48	.42	.29
Recent Ideas					-.31	-.50	-.08
Recent Practices						.33	.26
Sexual-Rep. Ethics							.26

Appendix E
Self-concept, Self-interest, and Commitment Indices

Self-concept (alpha = .72)
After I read each statement, please tell me to what extent you agree or disagree.

I could be just as happy in some other church; it wouldn't have to be Catholic (disagree)

My parish is an important part of my life

I cannot imagine myself being anything other than Catholic

How religious are you now? Would you say you are very religious, fairly religious, somewhat religious, or not very religious?

Catholic Benefits (r = .40)
After I read each statement, tell me whether you agree or disagree.

Being Catholic has given me a solid moral foundation

There is something very special about being Catholic which you can't find in other religions

Parish Satisfaction (alpha = .80)
How would you rate your parish in terms of . . . . Would you say it is excellent, good, fair, or poor?

Friendliness of the people

Helping you make decisions in work or family

Quality of the homilies or sermons

Meeting your spiritual needs

Quality of music at Mass

Stake in the Church (r = .34)
As I read each statement, please tell me whether you agree or disagree with that statement.

I donate a lot of time to the church

I give more than my fair share of money to the church

Commitment to the Church (alpha = .61)
After I read each statement, please tell me whether you agree or disagree.

I could be just as happy in some other church; it wouldn't have to be Catholic (disagree)

I cannot imagine myself being anything other than Catholic

I donate a lot of time to the church

I give more than my fair share of money to the church

Appendix F

Effects of Self-concept and Self-interest (percent)

	Faith			Morals	
	Trad. Beliefs/ Practices (High)	Recent Ideas (High)	Recent Practices (High,Med)	Sexual/Rep. Ethics (High)	Social Teachings (High)
All Parishioners	47	33	8	23	51
Self-concept					
High	74	17	12	38	60
Medium	26	46	4	10	38
Low	1	58	5	3	39
Self-interest					
Catholic Benefits					
High	65	24	10	32	59
Medium	17	44	5	12	34
Low	7	58	2	2	36
Parish Satisfaction					
High	64	27	14	32	58
Medium	37	33	4	17	44
Low	11	49	5	16	52
Stake in the Church					
High	75	19	17	46	62
Medium	50	33	7	24	52
Low	24	40	3	8	41

Appendix G
Indices of Closeness to God, Awareness of Vatican II, and Sex-Role Attitudes

Closeness to God (alpha = .83)

Now, I have a list of religious experiences that some people have had at one time or another. As I read each one, please tell me how often, if ever, you have had this religious experience or feeling. Many times, several times, a few times, never.

That you sensed the presence of God in a very special way

That God has taken care of you when you've really needed help

That God has answered your prayers

That God has forgiven your sins

Awareness of Vatican II (alpha = .76)

Now, I have some questions about Vatican Council II, a meeting of bishops which took place in Rome from 1962 to 1965. Would you say . . . many times, a few times, never or almost never?

How often have you heard a priest discuss Vatican II from the pulpit?

How often have you talked informally with other people about Vatican II?

And, how often have you read articles or books about Vatican II?

Sex Role Attitudes (alpha = .68)

Now, I'd like to get your opinion on some issues concerning men, women, and family life. I have a list of statements that some people have made about these issues. As I read each one, please tell me whether you agree or disagree with the statements. Is that strongly or somewhat?

When children are young, it is better if the husband is the breadwinner and the wife stays home and takes care of the home and the children.

Most men are better suited emotionally for politics than are most women.

There are still many laws and customs that are unfair to American women.

It is more important for a wife to help her husband's career than to have a career herself.

Most leaders of the women's movement are too radical for me.

Appendix H
Indices of Parents' Religiosity and Childhood Religiosity

Parents' Religiosity (r = .36)
When you were growing up, about how often did your mother/father attend religious services? Did she/he go:
> More than once a week
> Once a week
> Two or three times a month
> Once a month
> Less than once a month
> Almost never or never

Childhood Religiosity (alpha = .63)
Next, I'll read a list of religious practices. As I read each one, please tell me how often you participated in this religious practice when you were growing up. More than once a week, once a week, two or three times a month, once a month, less than once a month, almost never, or never?
> Attend Mass
> Pray Privately
> Go to Communion

How religious were you during your childhood? Would you say that you were. . . ?
> Very religious
> Fairly religious
> Somewhat religious
> Not very religious

Appendix I

Relative Importance of Religious Upbringing, Familial, and Educational Factors (betas)

	Faith			Morals	
	Trad. Beliefs/ Practices	Recent Ideas	Recent Practices	Sexual/Rep. Ethics	Social Teachings
Mom Catholic	.14**	ns[1]	.07*	ns	ns
Dad Catholic	ns	ns	ns	ns	ns
Closeness to Mother	.08*	ns	.08**	.09**	ns
Closeness to Father	.10**	ns	-.14**	ns	ns
Parents' Religiosity	.09**	ns	ns	.07*	ns
Childhood Religiosity	.27**	-.15**	.11**	.10**	.07*
Parents talk about religion	.19**	-.10**	ns	ns	.17**
Years of Catholic school-ing	ns	-.08**	.16**	-.06*	ns
Type religion teachers[2]	.11**	-.19**	ns	.15**	ns
Amount of CCD	.11**	-.08**	.15**	.11**	ns

*=p≤ .05
**=p≤ .01
ns = not significant
[1]ns = not significant
[2]Mostly priests and nuns = 1; Equal mix of priests, sisters, and laity = 2; Mostly laity = 3

Appendix J
Pathways to Faith and Morals:
Results of Lisrel Analyses

We conducted five lisrel analyses, one for each dimension of faith and morals. Lisrel analyses are like path analyses; they estimate the direct and indirect effects of variables (Joreskog and Sorbom, 1993; Baldwin, 1989; Francis, 1988). Our results are summarized below and illustrated in five figures. The larger the beta coefficients in each figure, the stronger the relationship between variables.

Traditional Beliefs and Practices

In chapters four through nine, we identified six factors that seem to be especially important in fostering traditional beliefs and practices. These factors are: being born in or before 1940; having parents who talked about religion; being religious as a child; having a significant other who is an active and traditional Catholic; having personal experiences of God over the course of one's life; and being committed to the Church. Other factors having smaller effects include: being female; being Asian or Hispanic; being French or Italian; having a Catholic mother; having mostly priests and sisters for religious instruction; having a great deal of religious education; being close to one's mother and father during childhood; having religious parents; having a Catholic spouse; being a homemaker; having a relatively small family income; having traditional views of men's and women's roles in society; and being aware of Vatican II.

Now we select all four personal attributes (birth cohort, gender, race, and ethnicity); the two most important upbringing factors (parents talking about religion and childhood religiosity); the two most important life-course experiences (being close to God and having a significant other who is an active and traditional Catholic); and commitment to the Church. We do not deny that the other variables mentioned above continue to play some role, but we call special attention to personal attributes and the most important factors in other cells of our model because we want to identify the main paths to traditional beliefs and practices. We put these variables into a type of analysis that delineates their combined effects on traditional beliefs and practices. The most significant effects are shown in Figure J.1.

Two factors stand out above all others. Commitment to the Church has the largest direct effect (b=.40): parishioners who have strong Catholic identities and feel that the benefits of being Catholic outweigh the costs are most likely to accept traditional doctrines (such as the Incarnation and the Real Presence) and participate in traditional practices (such as attending Mass and saying the rosary). Closeness to God also has a direct effect

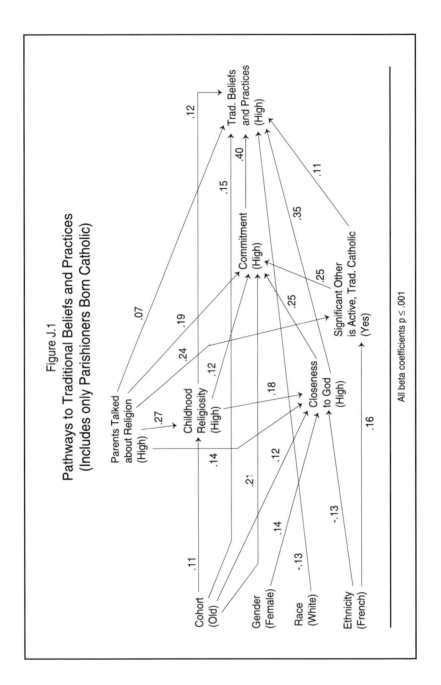

Figure J.1

Pathways to Traditional Beliefs and Practices
(Includes only Parishioners Born Catholic)

All beta coefficients p ≤ .001

of its own (b=.35): people who feel that God has been a part of their lives are most likely to gravitate toward traditional religious orientations.

In addition to commitment and closeness to God, five other factors also foster traditional beliefs and practices, though their effects are considerably smaller. We mention these in the order of their importance. Being born and raised in the pre-Vatican II Church increases one's tendency toward traditional beliefs and practices. Birth cohort has this direct effect of its own (b=.15), but it also contributes to childhood religiosity, commitment, and closeness to God — all of which have additional effects. Race has a direct effect of its own, with people of color — especially Latinos and Asians — being more inclined toward traditional beliefs and practices than other Catholics (b=-.13).

The more religious parishioners were when they were young, the more likely they are to accept traditional beliefs and engage in traditional religious practices when they are older (b=.12). Childhood religiosity tends to be characteristic of older Catholics (b=.11) and parishioners whose parents talked with them about religion when they were young (b=.27).

Having a significant other who is an active and traditional Catholic also fosters traditional beliefs and practices (b=.11). Persons who admire an active and traditional Catholic come from families in which parents talked about religion (b=.24) and tend to have French ancestry (b=.16).

Having parents who talked about religion during one's childhood is important for two reasons. It has a direct effect of its own (b=.07), fostering traditional beliefs and practices, but it also fosters childhood religiosity (b=.27), closeness to God (b=.14), and Catholic significant others (b=.24) — all of which contribute to commitment and lead to traditional beliefs and practices.

These results also help us identify parishioners who are not as inclined toward traditional beliefs and practices. They are parishioners who lack strong Catholic identities and do not feel they have benefited much from being Catholic. They also have not had many experiences of being close to God during the course of their lives. They tend to be young whites. They were not particularly religious as children. They do not think of an active and traditional Catholic when asked to identity someone they admire. Finally, their parents were not inclined to talk with them about religion during their childhood years.

Recent Ideas

So far, our analysis shows that six traits predispose parishioners to recent ideas that are at odds with Canon Law. Parishioners who are most likely to gravitate toward dissenting ideas about ordination and Mass attendance have been born and raised in the post-Vatican II Church; had

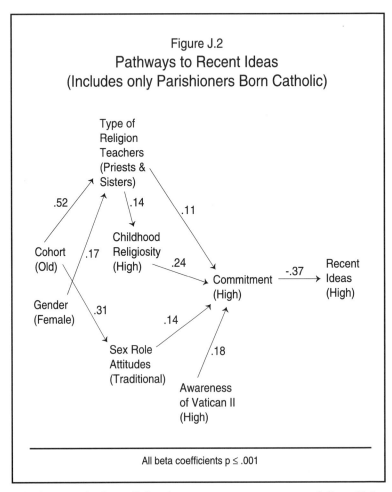

Figure J.2
Pathways to Recent Ideas
(Includes only Parishioners Born Catholic)

All beta coefficients p ≤ .001

mostly lay people for religion instructors; were not especially religious when they were children; question the roles men and women play in society; are not very aware of Vatican II; and feel little attachment to the Church. Other influences having smaller effects include being female; belonging to racial and ethnic groups other than Asian and French; not having much religious instruction during childhood; not attending Catholic schools; having parents who did not talk about religion; not having a significant other who is an active and traditional Catholic; and not having many personal experiences of God during the course of one's life.

Figure J.2 shows the most important pathways to recent ideas. Commitment is the only variable that has a strong effect of its own (b=-.37). The more committed parishioners are, the more they reject ideas such as the ordination of women; the less committed they are, the more willing they are to agree with such ideas. Having mostly priests and sisters for religious education; being religious as a child; having traditional views of men's and women's roles in society; and being aware of Vatican II have indirect effects through their contributions to commitment, but they do not have direct effects of their own.

Recent Practices

To this point, we have seen that Asian and Hispanic parishioners participate in these practices more than blacks and whites. Lay persons with the most Catholic schooling and religious education also favor these practices. So do parishioners who have had frequent experiences of being close to God and who know the most about Vatican II. The most committed parishioners also engage in these practices. Several other factors also have some impact, but are not as important as the ones listed above. Less influential factors include: having Catholic parents; being close to one's mother and father during one's childhood; being religious as a child; having a Catholic spouse; being a homemaker; and having school-age children.

We now examine the combined effects of our four personal attributes; years of Catholic schooling; amount of religious education; closeness to God; awareness of Vatican II; and commitment to the Church. According to the results shown in Figure J.3, parishioners who are most aware of Vatican II also are most inclined to participate in the scripture-oriented devotional practices that Church leaders have stressed in the post-Vatican II years (b=.37). Parishioners who have had close personal experiences of God (b=.20) also are inclined toward these practices. So are people of color (b=-.17) and people who are high in commitment (b=.13).

Awareness of Vatican II springs mainly from Catholic schooling and experiences of the holy. Women, pre-Vatican II Catholics, and people with the most religious education are most likely to report close personal experiences of God. Birth cohort, closeness to God, and awareness of Vatican II contribute to commitment.

Sexual and Reproductive Ethics

So far, our analysis has shown that people who feel most committed to the Church are most likely to agree with its sexual teachings. Other key factors promoting adherence to the Church's sexual and reproductive norms are being raised during the 1930s and '40s; having mostly priests and nuns for religious education; having a great deal of religious instruction in childhood; having traditional views of the roles men and women play in society; and being aware of Vatican II. Lesser influences include being close to one's mother during childhood; having religious parents who talked about religion; being religious as a child; not going to Catholic schools;

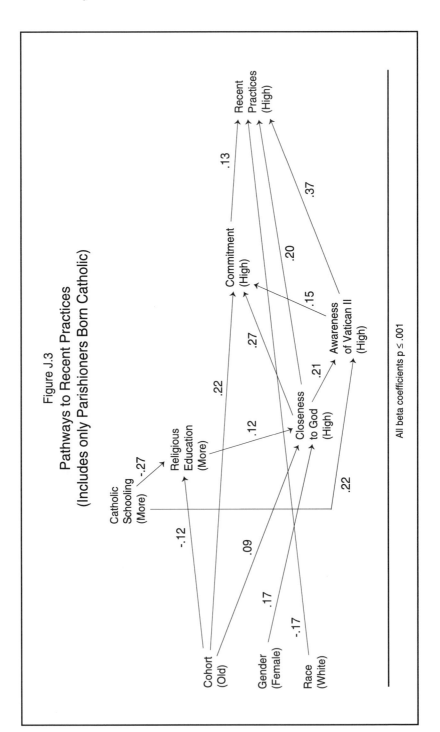

Figure J.3
Pathways to Recent Practices
(Includes only Parishioners Born Catholic)

All beta coefficients p ≤ .001

having a Catholic spouse; having a significant other who is an active and traditional Catholic; having a relatively small family income; and experiencing God's presence in one's life.

The most important pathways to agreement with the Church's sexual and reproductive norms are shown in Figure J.4. Commitment tends to foster agreement with the Church's sexual teachings more than any other influence (b=.37). Having mostly priests and sisters for religious instruction also contributes directly to adherence to Church norms in this area (b=.10). Parishioners who are most likely to quarrel with the Church's views on sexual and reproductive issues have the weakest Catholic identities, are least inclined to feel they have benefited from being Catholic, and tended to have lay people for religious education.

Commitment is rooted in religious education (b=.15). Post-Vatican II Catholics have more years of religious education than pre-Vatican II Catholics (b=.14). Women (b=.15) and older Catholics (b=.52) are most likely to have had priests and sisters for religious instruction.

Social Teachings

Results so far suggest that those who are most inclined to agree with the Church's views on issues such as closing the gap between the rich and poor tend to be white and French; were religious as children and have parents who talked to them about religion; have had frequent experiences of being close to God; know more than other Catholics do about Vatican

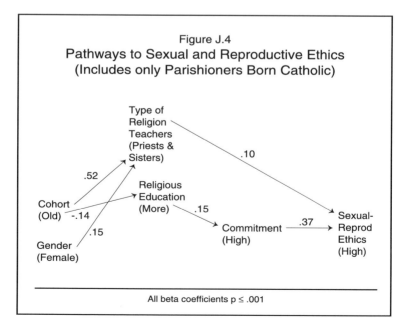

Figure J.4
Pathways to Sexual and Reproductive Ethics
(Includes only Parishioners Born Catholic)

Type of Religion Teachers (Priests & Sisters)

Religious Education (More)

Cohort (Old)

Gender (Female)

Commitment (High)

Sexual-Reprod Ethics (High)

.52

-.14

.15

.15

.10

.37

All beta coefficients p ≤ .001

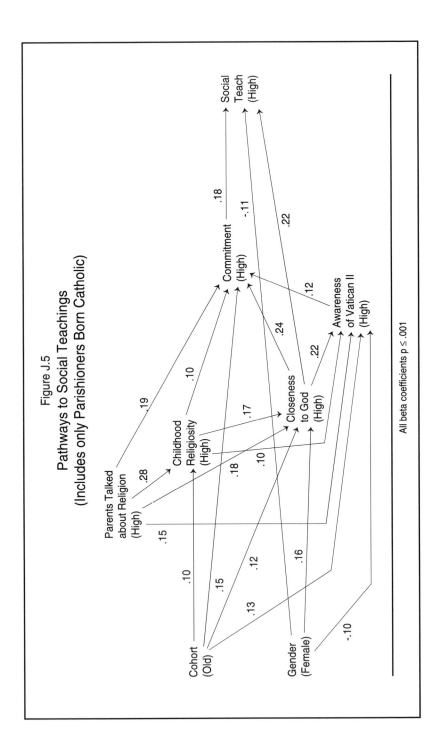

Figure J.5
Pathways to Social Teachings
(Includes only Parishioners Born Catholic)

All beta coefficients p ≤ .001

II; and are highly committed to the Church. Lesser influences include having a significant other who is an active and traditional Catholic; and having traditional views of men's and women's roles in society.

The big story in Figure J.5 is that three factors play especially important roles in predisposing parishioners to agreeing with the Church's social teachings. The most socially conscious parishioners have had experiences of being close to God (b=.22); tend to be highly committed to the Church (b=.18); and are men (b=.11). Women, people who have only limited attachment to the Church, and people who have had few experiences of God's presence in their lives are most likely to disagree with the Church's concern for the poor.

Closeness to God results from several factors, including being female (b=.16), belonging to the older birth cohort (b=.12), having parents who talked about religion (b=.18), and childhood religiosity (b=.17). Commitment is the product of parents who talked about religion (b=.19); childhood religiosity (b=.10); belonging to the pre-Vatican II cohort (b=.15); closeness to God (b=.24); and awareness of Vatican II (b=.12).

Notes

Chapter 1

1. We are concerned with faith and morals as they are viewed by Catholic lay people. Faith includes beliefs and practices expressing Catholics' understandings of God and the Church. Morals concern Catholics' conceptions of the rightness or wrongness of social behaviors. From time to time, we refer to priests and sisters, but we do not examine the beliefs and practices of clergy. Our analysis does not deal with consensus and conflict among religious.

2. Some terms we use may be interpreted quite differently by readers with different worldviews. For example, religious liberals tend to think positively about "pluralism" as tolerance of many different views, even views that are not in compliance with Church teachings (e.g., McBrien, 1983). Conservatives tend to be suspicious of the term, believing that it often is used inappropriately to justify beliefs and practices which are not in accordance with Church teachings (e.g., Hitchcock, 1979). As we explain in more detail in Chapter 2, our research team includes both theological liberals and theological conservatives, and we try hard to strike a balance in our interpretation of history and current developments in the Church. As a team, we do not make value judgments about the desirability or undesirability of trends such as the increasing diversity we document in this chapter (though individually we do). As a team, we also have agreed to use the terms unity, uniformity, and consensus more or less interchangeably to refer to a rather distinct tendency for Catholic lay people to concur in belief and/or action. We use the concepts pluralism, diversity, and dissensus interchangeably when referring to a wide range of views and actions. We ask readers to appreciate our effort to present a balanced analysis using a variety of concepts which we think have similar meanings and, when used interchangeably, enliven our prose by giving us flexibility in word selection.

3. There weren't as many studies of Catholic beliefs and practices in 1930s and '40s as we have today. The ones that were done tended to be small and focused on specific communities; there were none of the large national studies that we do today. Thus, we cannot be absolutely sure exactly what Catholics believed and how they actually practiced their faith between the 1930s and 1950s. However, when we piece together the studies which were done, we get a fairly clear picture of some diversity in the midst of overall unity.

4. Given the pressure to conform in the 1930s and '40s, Catholics who disagreed with Church probably kept their dissenting views to themselves, rather than expressing them publicly as much as they do today. However, when given the opportunities to express their views anonymously and confidentially, as they were in research studies, Catholics were willing to indicate their disagreements, as well as their agreements, with Church teachings. Thus, the studies reported in this chapter are probably quite reliable indications of the extent to which Catholics actually adhered to the official teachings of the Church 50 to 60 years ago.

5. As European Catholics were being absorbed into the American mainstream, a new wave of Catholic immigrants — this time from Latin America and Asia — began to arrive (Dolan, 1985; Fitzpatrick, 1987; D'Antonio, Davidson, Hoge, and Wallace, 1996). Their socioeconomic diversity and the various Hispanic and Asian cultures they brought to the United States contributed to the religious pluralism which grew out of this period in American Catholic history.

6. Some forms of social and cultural bias still exist against Catholics, who have still not achieved parity in their access to positions among the nation's power elite and cultural elite (Davidson, 1994a ; Davidson, Pyle, and Reyes, 1995; Pyle, 1996).

7. Vatican II is interpreted broadly by some Catholics who believe that particular developments are in "the spirit of Vatican II" even though they were not discussed at the Council and do not appear in official Council documents. Other Catholics interpret Vatican II more narrowly, insisting that we only attribute to Vatican II effects which can be traced back to specific Council documents. In our analysis, we have tended toward the narrower understanding.

8. As Nicgorski (1992) has noted, pluralism is a mixed blessing: "It is rooted not only in freedom but also in human fallibility, self-centeredness, and natural diversity." As we said in endnote two, our research team did not judge pluralism as being either essentially good or essentially bad. Our goals as a research team are to describe it and examine its antecedents among American Catholic lay people.

9. For other excellent overviews of the trend to diversity, see Bausch (1985); Dolan (1985); Dolan, Appleby, Byrne, and Campbell (1989); and O'Meara (1996).

Chapter 3

1. In our Indiana survey we also found high levels of agreement on a series of pan-Vatican II belief items. For example, 95 percent of Hoosiers believe there is a heaven; 93 percent say saving their souls is very important; 91 percent believe there are three persons in one God; 81 percent say belief in the Trinity is important to them personally; and 79 percent believe there is a hell.

2. When we had three or more items to work with, we used Cronbach's alpha to determine reliability. On all six such indices, the results meet the commonly accepted criterion of .6 or higher. When we were limited to two items, we selected items that had the highest correlations and addressed one basic concern. In the case of recent ideas, that issue was acceptance of ideas that are not found in canon law. In the case of social teachings, it was concern for the poor.

3. Each of the three segments encompasses one-third of the possible scores on the scales (high=top third; medium=middle third; low=bottom third).

4. To visualize correlations, think of two circles. The higher the correlation, the more the two circles overlap. The smaller the correlation, the less they overlap. To get a sense of how much the circles overlap, simply multiply the correlation coefficient by itself. Thus, a coefficient of .7 means there is a 49 percent overlap. A coefficient of .0 indicates no overlap. A negative correlation means the two circles actually repel each other. The larger the negative correlation, the more tension there is between the two. Correlations indicate the extent to which two beliefs and practices are associated with one another. They do not indicate which belief or which practice "caused" the other. Thus, they tell us how often responses are found together, but they do not tell us anything about causal direction.

5. The alpha score for this overall index is .91.

6. Polarization does not seem to be as great among parishioners as it is among high-profile spokespersons for groups such as A Call to Action and Catholics United for the Faith.

Chapter 4

1. The correlation between these two items was .23.

2. All the correlations between our various measures of self-concept and self-interest are positive: self-concept and Catholic benefits (r = .58); self-concept and parish satisfaction (r = .45); self-concept and stake in the Church (r = .40); Catholic benefits and parish satisfaction (r = .31); Catholic benefits and stake in the Church (r = .25); parish satisfaction and stake in the Church (r = .43).

Chapter 5

1. When asked whether Vatican II has had positive or negative effects on the Church, 65 percent of parishioners indicate that they "don't know enough about it to say one way or the other." Seventeen percent say the Council "helped the Church much more than it hurt it." Five percent say it "hurt the Church much more than it helped it." Ten percent say "its positive and negative effects were about equal."

2. In all but three cases we cross-tabulate individual lifecourse questions and our religious outcome variables. In the other three cases (relationship with God, awareness of Vatican II, and sex role attitudes), we combine several items to form indices which we then run against our measures of faith and morals (see Appendix G for more statistical details on the indices).

3. The fact that traditional sex-role attitudes correlates with the absence of school-age children is explained, at least in part, by the fact that traditional sex-role attitudes and the absence of school-age children are both tied to birth cohort. We will examine the effects of cohort in chapters seven and 11.

4. The fact that awareness of Vatican II is linked with support of Church teachings challenges the view, held by some, that Catholics who are most aware of Vatican II are most likely to dissent from Church teachings. It also challenges a perception, held by some others, that those who are least informed are most inclined to support Church teachings.

Chapter 6

1. There was, in fact, no precedent for teaching children as an acceptable activity for religious orders prior to the sixteenth and seventeenth centuries. The few medieval monasteries which had schools used them primarily to develop literacy in their own novices. When the first apostolic orders of women began teaching young girls in the 1600's, they justified this novel activity as *an ascetic and penitential discipline*: "The

teaching sisters seem to have taken up their vocation as a new form of mortification, comparable to but less venerable than washing the feet of beggars" (Quoted in Wittberg, 1994:135).

2. Though parish and diocesan leaders tend to use concepts such as "religious education" and "catechesis," many lay people still use the term "CCD" to refer to religious instruction they received in their parishes. We use these terms interchangeably to refer to parish-based religious instruction, as compared to education that takes place in Catholic schools.

Chapter 9

1. Two percent of all interviews were done partially or fully in Spanish.

2. We use the term "Hispanic/Latino" in this chapter. One of the newest journals in theology, which had its debut in November 1993, is called the *Journal of Hispanic/Latino Theology*. There is no total agreement on which terms to use. For a discussion of the issues involved in which labels are used, see Stevens-Arroyo (1994) and Stevens-Arroyo and Pantoja (1995).

3. Greeley (1990:123), for example, writes, "The loss of almost one out of ten members of its largest ethnic group is an ecclesiastical failure of unprecedented proportions." See also Gallup and Castelli (1987:142).

Chapter 10

1. Gallup and Castelli (1987:viii) reported that 20 percent of Catholics "say they are not church members." While, at first blush, it may appear that the percentage of non-parishioners is growing, our methodology is different from Gallup and Castelli's, so no direct comparisons can be made. However, these two different results suggest the need for further research that replicates the methods used in one or the other of these two studies.

2. *Catechism of the Catholic Church* (1995), 2181, cites the *Codex Iuris Canonici* (Canon Law), canons 1245, 1246, and 1247.

References

Abbott, Walter, ed., 1966. *The Documents of Vatican II.* New York: America Press.

Adorno, T. W., Else Frenkel-Brunswick, Daniel J. Levinson, and R. Nevitt Sanford, 1950. *The Authoritarian Personality.* New York: Harper and Brothers.

Alba, Richard D., 1990. *Ethnic Identity: The Transformation of White America.* New Haven and London: Yale University Press.

Alston, Jon P. and William Alex McIntosh, 1979. "An Assessment of the Determinants of Religious Participation." *The Sociological Quarterly*, 20 (Winter): 49-62

Appleby, R. Scott, 1997. "Catholicism and American Culture: Keeping the Faith in Late Modernity," paper presented at FADICA conference. Palm Beach, Fla., January.

Argyle, Michael and Benjamin Beit-Hallahmi, 1975. *The Social Psychology of Religion.* London: Routledge & Kegan Paul.

Arkinson, Harley (ed.), 1995. *Handbook of Young Adult Religious Education.* Birmingham, Ala.: Religious Education Press.

Babbie, Earl, 1989. *The Practice of Social Research.* Belmont, Calif.: Wadsworth Publishing Company.

Badillo, David A., 1994. "Latino/Hispanic History Since 1965: The Collective Transformation of Regional Minorities." Pp. 50-76 in Jay P. Dolan and Allan Figueroa Deck, S.J. (eds.), *Hispanic Catholic Culture in the U.S.: Issues and Concerns.* Notre Dame, Ind.: University of Notre Dame Press.

Baldwin, Beatrice, 1989. "Methods, Plainly Speaking: A Primer in the the Use and Interpretation of Structural Equation Models." *Measurement and Evaluation in Counseling and Development*, 22: 100-112.

Bandura, Albert, 1977. *Social Learning Theory.* Englewood Cliffs, N.J.: Prentice-Hall.

Baranowski, Arthur, 1996. *Creating Small Church Communities* (third edition). Cincinnati, Ohio: St. Anthony Messenger Press.

Bausch, William J., 1985. *Pilgrim Church*. Mystic, Conn.: Twenty-Third Publications.

Bellah, Robert N., Richard Madsen, William M. Sullivan, Ann Swidler, and Steven M. Tipton 1985. *Habits of the Heart: Individualism and Commitment in American Life*. Berkeley: University of California Press.

Bernardin, Cardinal Joseph, 1984. "Religion and Politics: The Future Agenda." *Origins*, (November 8):321-328.

——, 1988a. *Consistent Ethic of Life*. Kansas City, Mo.: Sheed and Ward.

——, 1988b. "Euthanasia: Ethical and Legal Challenge." *Origins*, 18 (June 9):52-57.

——, 1988c. "Voters and the Consistent Ethic." *Origins*, 18 (September 1):186-189.

——, 1990. "The Consistent Ethic of Life After Webster." *Origins*, 19 (April 12):741, 743-748.

Blanshard, Paul, 1951. *Communism, Democracy, and Catholic Power.* Boston: Beacon Press.
——, 1958. *American Freedom and Catholic Power* (revised edition). Boston: Beacon Press.

Blau, Peter, 1964. *Exchange and Power in Social Life*. New York: John Wiley and Sons.

Bradley, Martin B., Norman M. Green, Jr., Dale E. Jones, Mac Lynn, and Lon McNeil, 1990. *Churches and Church Membership in the U.S., 1990*. Atlanta, Ga.: Glenmary Research Center.

Briody, Elizabeth K. and Teresa A. Sullivan, 1988. "Sisters at Work: Career and Community Changes." *Work and Occupations*, 15:313-333.

Bruce, Steve, 1995. "The Truth About Religion in Britain." *Journal for the Scientific Study of Religion*, 34:417-430.

Burns, Gene, 1992. *The Frontiers of Catholicism: The Politics of Ideology in the Liberal World.* Berkeley: University of California Press.

Casanova, Jose, 1994. *Public Religions in the Modern World.* Chicago: University of Chicago Press.

Catechism of the Catholic Church, 1995. New York: Doubleday.

Cateura, Linda Brandi, 1989. *Catholics USA.* New York: William Morrow and Company, Inc.

Cavendish, James C., 1993. "Predictors of Religiosity for Black and White Catholics." Department of Sociology, University of Notre Dame, Notre Dame, Ind.

Chalfant, H. Paul, Robert E. Beckley, and C. Eddie Palmer, 1994. *Religion in Contemporary Society* (third editon). Itasca, Ill.: Peacock Publishers.

Chancellor, Loren E. and Thomas P. Monahan, 1955. "Religious Preference and Interreligious Mixtures in Marriages and Divorces in Iowa." *American Journal of Sociology,* 61:233-239.

Charon, Joel M., 1989. *Symbolic Interactionism* (third edition). Englewood Cliffs, N.J.: Prentice-Hall.

Christiano, Kevin J., 1986. "Church as a Family Surrogate: Another Look at Family Ties, Anomie, and Church Involvement." *Journal for the Scientific Study of Religion,* 25: 339-354.

Cogley, John and Rodger Van Allen, 1986. *Catholic America, Expanded and Updated Edition.* Kansas City, Mo.: Sheed and Ward.

Cook, Karen S. (ed.), 1987. *Social Exchange Theory.* Newbury Park, Calif.: Sage.

D'Antonio, William V., 1988. "The American Catholic Family: Signs of Cohesion and Polarization." Pp.88-106 in Darwin L. Thomas, ed., *The Religion and Family Connection: Social Science Perspectives.* Religious Studies Center Specialized Monograph Series, Volume III. Provo, Utah: Brigham Young University Press.

—— and Joan Aldous, 1983. *Religion and Families*. Beverly Hills, Calif.: Sage.

—— , James D. Davidson, Dean. R. Hoge, and Ruth. A. Wallace, 1989. *American Catholic Laity in a Changing Church*. Kansas City, Mo.: Sheed and Ward.

——, James D. Davidson, Dean R. Hoge, and Ruth A. Wallace, 1996. *Laity: American and Catholic — Transforming the Church*. Kansas City, Mo.: Sheed and Ward.

Davidson, James D., 1975. "Glock's Model of Religious Commitment: Assessing Some Different Approaches and Results." *Review of Religious Research*, 16:83-93.

—— and Dean D. Knudsen, 1977. "A New Approach to Religious Commitment." *Sociological Focus*, 18:251-273.

——, 1977. "Socio-Economic Status and Ten Dimensions of Religious Commitment." *Sociology and Social Research,* 61:462-485.

——, 1985. "Theories and Measures of Poverty: Toward a Holistic Approach." *Sociological Focus,* 19:177-198.

——, 1994a. "Religion Among America's Elite: Persistence and Change in the Protestant Establishment, 1930-92." *Sociology of Religion*, 55:419-440.

——, 1994b. "Practicing Catholicism: Personal and Institutional Commitment," paper presented at annual meeting of Religious Research Association. Albuquerque, N.M., November.

——, 1995. "Alienation in the Church Today," paper presented at North American Forum on the Catechumenate. Chicago, April.

——, Ralph Pyle, and David Reyes, 1995. "Persistence and Change in the Protestant Establishment, 1930-1992." *Social Forces*, 74:157-175.

——, 1996. "Identity and Various Subcultures in the Church Today." Pp. 45-60 in William Friend, James D. Davidson, Jr., Angela A. Zukowski, and Michael J. Himes, *Evangelization, Culture, and Catholic Identity*. Saint Leo, Fla.: Saint Leo College Press.

——, Alan K. Mock, and C. Lincoln Johnson, 1997. "Through the Eye of a Needle: Social Ministry in Affluent Churches." *Review of Religious Research*, 38:247-262.

Davis, O.S.B., Cyprian, 1990. *The History of Black Catholics in the United States*. New York: Crossroad.

Deck, S.J., and Allan Figueroa, 1989. *The Second Wave: Hispanic Ministry and the Evangelization of Cultures*. New York: Paulist Press.

——, 1993. "Hispanic Ministry." Pp. 168-176 in T. Howland Sanks and John A. Coleman (eds.), *Reading the Signs of the Times: Resources for Social and Cultural Analysis*. New York: Paulist Press.

——, 1994. *Hispanic Catholic Culture in the U.S.: Issues and Concerns*. Notre Dame, Ind.: University of Notre Dame Press.

——, 1995. " 'A Pox on Both Your Houses': A View of Catholic Conservative-Liberal Polarities from the Hispanic Margin." Pp. 88-104 in Mary Jo Weaver and R. Scott Appleby (eds.), *Being Right: Conservative Catholics in America*. Bloomington, Ind.: Indiana University Press.

Demerath III, N.J. , 1965. *Social Class in American Protestantism*. Chicago: Rand McNally.

DeRego, Jr., Frank R., 1996. "A House Divided: A Resource Dependency Theory of U.S. Catholic Bishops' Response to Black Evangelization and Black Leadership from the Antebellum Period to the End of Reconstruction." Department of Sociology and Anthropology, Purdue University, West Lafayette, Ind.

Diaz-Stevens, Ana Maria, 1994. "Latinas and the Church." Pp. 240-277 in Jay P. Dolan and Allan Figueroa Deck, S.J. (eds.), *Hispanic Catholic Culture in the U.S.: Issues and Concerns*. Notre Dame, Ind.: University of Notre Dame Press.

Dinges, William D., 1983. "Catholic Traditionalist Movement." Pp. 137-158 in Joseph H. Fichter (ed.), *Alternatives to American Mainline Religion*. New York: Unification Theological Seminary.

Dolan, Jay P., 1978. *Catholic Revivalism: The American Experience*. Notre Dame, Ind.: University of Notre Dame Press.

——, 1985. *The American Catholic Experience*. Garden City, N.Y.: Image Books.

—— and David C. Leege, 1985. "A Profile of American Catholic Parishes and Parishioners: 1820s to the 1980s." *Notre Dame Study of Catholic Parish Life*, Report No. 2. Notre Dame, Ind.: University of Notre Dame.

——, R. Scott Appleby, Patricia Byrne, and Debra Campbell, 1989. *Transforming Parish Ministry: The Changing Roles of Catholic Clergy, Laity, and Women Religious*. New York: Crossroad.

——, 1989. "A Question in Search of an Answer." Pp. 307-320 in Dolan, Appleby, Byrne, and Campbell, *Transforming Parish Ministry: The Changing Roles of Catholic Clergy, Laity, and Women Religious*. New York: Crossroads.

——, 1992 (orig. 1985). *The American Catholic Experience: A History from Colonial Times to the Present*. Notre Dame, Ind.: University of Notre Dame.

Donahue, William A., 1995. *Catholic League's Survey of Adult Catholics*. New York: Catholic League for Religious and Civil Rights.

Dorr, Donald, 1983. *Option for the Poor: A Hundred Years of Vatican Social Teaching*. Maryknoll, N.Y.: Orbis Books.

Dudley, Roger L. and Margaret G. Dudley, 1989. "Religion and Family Life Among Seventh Day Adventists." *Family Science Review,* 2:359-372.

Duggan, Robert D. and Maureen A. Kelly, 1991. *The Christian Initiation of Children*. New York/Mahweh: Paulist Press.

Ebaugh, Helen Rose, 1991. "Vatican II and the Revitalization Movement." Pp. 3-19 in Ebaugh (ed.), *Vatican II and U.S. Catholicism*. Greenwich, Conn.: JAI Press.

Edmonds, Patricia, 1993. "U.S. Catholics Often at Odds with the Pope." *USA Today*, August 10:1-2.

Ellis, John Tracy, 1969. *American Catholicism*. Chicago: University of Chicago Press.

Feagin, Joe R. and Clairece Booher Feagin, 1993. *Racial and Ethnic Relations*, fourth edition. Englewood Cliffs, N.J.: Prentice Hall.

Feagin, Joe R., 1975. *Subordinating the Poor*. Englewood Cliffs, N.J.: Prentice-Hall.

Fee, Joan, Andrew Greeley, William McCready, and Teresa Sullivan, 1981. *Young Catholics*. New York: Sadlier.

Fendrich, James M. and William V. D'Antonio, 1970. "Dogmatism and Religious Involvement." Pp. 333-346 in William T. Liu and Nathaniel J. Pallone (eds.), *Catholics/U.S.A.* New York: John Wiley and Sons.

Fesquet, H., 1967. *The Drama of Vatican II: The Ecumenical Council, June 1962-December 1965*. New York: Random House.

Fichter, Joseph H., 1951. *Southern Parish, Dynamics of a City Church*. Chicago: University of Chicago Press.

——, 1952. "The Profile of Catholic Religious Life." *American Journal of Sociology*, 58:145-149.

——, 1953. "The Marginal Catholic: An Institutional Approach." *Social Forces*, 32:167-173.

——, 1954. *Social Relations in the Urban Parish*. Chicago, Ill.: University of Chicago Press.

——, 1973. *One Man Research: Reminiscences of a Catholic Sociologist*. New York: John Wiley.

Finke, Roger and Rodney Stark, 1992. *The Churching of America, 1776-1990*, New Brunswick, N.J.: Rutgers University Press.

Fitzpatrick, Joseph P., S.J., 1991. "The Church and Social Issues: Institutional Commitments." Pp. 155-168 in Helen Rose Ebaugh (ed.), *Vatican II and U.S. Catholicism*. Greewich, Conn.: JAI Press.

——, 1987. *One Church, Many Cultures*. Kansas City, Mo.: Sheed and Ward.

Flannery, Austin (ed.), 1992. *Vatican Council II: The Conciliar and Post Conciliar Documents, Volumes I and II.* Grand Rapids, Mich.: William B. Eerdmans Publishing Co.

Foley, Leonard March, 1993. "Vatican II: The Vision Lives On!" *Catholic Update.* Cincinnati, Ohio: St. Anthony Messenger Press.

Fox, Thomas, 1995. *Sexuality and Catholicism.* New York: George Braziller.

Francis, David J., 1988. "An Introduction to Structural Equation Models." *Journal of Clinical and Experimental Neuropsychology*, 10: 623-639.

Friedan, Betty, 1963. *The Feminine Mystique.* London: Victor Gollancz.

Galbraith, John Kenneth, 1958. *The Affluent Society.* Boston: Houghton Mifflin.

Gallup, George, Jr. and Jim Castelli, 1987. *The American Catholic People: Their Beliefs, Practices, and Values.* Garden City, N.Y.: Doubleday and Company.

Garlington, Lela, 1995. "Black Catholics Raising a Host of Questions, Conferees Stress Tuning into Culture." *The Commercial Appeal*, March 19:1B.

Gilligan, Carol., 1982. *In a Different Voice: Psychological Theory and Women's Development.* Cambridge: Harvard University Press.

Gleason, Philip, 1989. *Keeping the Faith.* Notre Dame, Ind.: University of Notre Dame Press.

Glenn, Norval and Ruth Hyland, 1967. "Religious Preference and Worldly Success: Some Evidence from National Surveys." *American Sociological Review*, 32:73-85.

Glock, Charles Y., Benjamin B, Ringer, and Earl R. Babbie, 1967. *To Comfort and To Challenge.* Berkley: University of California Press.

Gonzalez, Robert and Michael LaVelle, 1988. *The Hispanic Catholic in the U.S.* New York: Northeastern Pastoral Center.

Grahmann, Bishop Charles, 1995. "Total Catholic Education." *Origins,* 25 (September 14):206-216.

Gray, John, 1992. *Men Are From Mars, Women Are From Venus: A Practical Guide for Improving Communication and Getting What You Want in Your Relationships.* New York: HarperCollins.

Greeley, Andrew M., 1967. *The Catholic Experience.* Garden City, N.Y.: Doubleday and Company.

—— and William E. Brown, 1970. *Can Catholic Schools Survive?* New York: Sheed and Ward.

——, 1976. *The Communal Catholic.* New York: Seabury Press.

——, 1977. *The American Catholic: A Social Portrait.* New York: Basic Books.

——, 1979. "Ethnic Variations in Religious Commitment." Pp. 113-134 in Robert Wuthnow (ed.), *The Religious Dimension: New Directions in Quantitative Research.* New York: Academic Press.

—— and Mary Durkin, 1984. *Angry Catholic Women.* Chicago: Thomas More Press.

—— and Mary Greeley Durkin, 1984. *How to Save the Catholic Church.* New York: Viking.

——, 1989. *Religious Change in America.* Cambridge, Mass.: Harvard University Press.

——, 1990. *The Catholic Myth: The Behavior and Beliefs of American Catholics.* New York: Collier Books.

Gremillion, Joseph, 1976. *The Gospel of Peace and Justice.* Maryknoll, N.Y.: Orbis Books.

—— and David C. Leege, 1989. "Post-Vatican II Parish Life in the United States: Review and Preview." Report 15, Notre Dame Study of Catholic Parish Life. Notre Dame, Ind.: University of Notre Dame.

Grindel, John A., 1991. *Whither the U.S. Catholic Church?* Maryknoll, N.Y.: Orbis Books.

Hadaway, C. Kirk, and W. Clark Roof, 1988. "Disaffiliation from Mainline Churches. " Pp. 26-46 in *Falling from the Faith,* David G. Bromley (ed). Newberry Park, Calif.: Sage.

——, Penny Long Marler, and Mark Chaves, 1993. "What Polls Don't Show: A Closer Look at U.S. Church Attendance." *American Sociological Review*, 58:741-752.

Hall, Suzanne E., 1990. "A Report on Asian Hearings: A Catholic Response to the Asian Presence in the United States." Washington, D.C.: National Catholic Education Association.

Harfmann, John, S.S.J., 1985. *1984 Statistical Profile of Black Catholics.* Washington, D.C.: Josephite Pastoral Center.

Henriot, Peter, Edward P. DeBerri, and Michael J. Schultheis, 1987. *Catholic Social Teaching: Our Best Kept Secret.* Maryknoll, N.Y.: Orbis Books.

Herberg, W., 1960. *Protestant-Catholic-Jew.* Garden City, N.Y.: Doubleday Anchor Books.

Hitchcock, James, 1979. *Catholicism and Modernity: Confrontation or Capitulation?* New York: Seabury Press.

Hoge, Dean R. and David A. Roozen, 1980. *The Unchurched American: A Second Look.* Special Supplement, *Review of Religious Research,* 21:385-475.

——, 1981. *Converts, Dropouts, Returnees: A Study of Religious Change Among Catholics.* New York: Pilgrim Press.

——, 1986. "Interpreting Change in American Catholicism: The River and the Floodgate." *Review of Religious Research,* 27:289-292.

——, 1988. "Why Catholics Drop Out." Pp. 81-99. in *Falling from The Faith*, David G. Bromley (ed.). Newberry Park, Calif.: Sage.

——, Benton Johnson, and Donald A. Luidens, 1994. *Vanishing Boundaries.* Louisville, Ky.: Westminster/John Knox Press.

Holland, Joe and Peter Henriot, 1983. *Social Analysis: Linking Faith and Justice.* Maryknoll, N.Y.: Orbis Books.

Holler, Stephen, 1995. "Exploring the Popular Religion of U.S. Hispanic/Latino Ethnic Groups." *Latino Studies Journal*, 6:3-29.

Holmes, Steven A., 1996. "Census Sees a Profound Ethnic Shift in U.S." *New York Times,* March 14:A8.

Homans, George C., 1974. *Social Behavior: Its Elementary Forms.* New York: Harcourt Brace Jovanovich.

Hornsby-Smith, Michael, 1990. "Renewing the Face of the Earth? RENEW in an English Diocese." Paper presented at Future of the American Church conference, "From Dream to Reality to Vision: 25 Years After Vatican II." Washington, D.C.

Iannaccone, Laurence R., 1990. "Religious Practice: A Human Capital Approach." *Journal for the Scientific Study of Religion*, 29:297-314.

Jamieson, Kathleen Hall, 1995. *Beyond the Double Bind: Women and Leadership.* New York: Oxford.

John Paul II, 1993. *The Splendor of Truth (Veritatis Splendor).* Boston: St. Paul Books and Media.

——, 1994. *The Gospel of Life (Evangelium Vitae).* Washington, D.C.: United States Catholic Conference.

Johnston, Robert L., 1991. "Religious Education: Who's Failing Our Students?" *U.S. Catholic*, 56:6-13.

Joreskog, Karl and Dag Sorbom, 1993. *Lisrel 8: Structural Equation Modeling with the SIMPLIS Command Language.* Hillsdale, N.J.: Lawrence Erlabaum Associates.

Kane, John J., 1955. *Catholic-Protestant Conflicts in America.* Chicago: Henry Regnery Company.

——, 1960. "Church and the Laity Among Catholics." *The Annals*, 332: 50-60.

Kelly, James R., 1991. "Community and Contentiousness: Lessons from the RENEW Program." Pp. 171-182 in Carl S. Dudley, Jackson W. Carroll, and James P. Wind, *Carriers of Faith: Lessons from Congregational Studies.* Louisville, Ky.: John Knox/Westminster Press.

——, 1991. "Catholic Sexual Ethics Since Vatican II." Pp. 139-154 in Helen Rose Ebaugh (ed.), *Vatican II and U.S. Catholicism*. Greenwich, Conn.: JAI Press.

Kennedy, Mary Jo, 1952. "Single or Triple Melting Pot? Intermarriage in New Haven, 1870-1950." *American Journal of Sociology*, 58: 56-59.

King, Ursula, 1995. *Religion and Gender*. Cambridge, Mass.: Basil Blackwell. Ltd.

Kirkpatrick, Lee A., and Shaver, Phillip R., 1990. "Attachment Theory and Religion: Childhood Attachments, Religious Beliefs, and Conversion." *Journal for the Scientific Study of Religion*, 29:315-334.

Kluegel, James R. and Eliot R. Smith, 1986. *Beliefs about Inequality*. New York: Aldine de Gruyter.

Komonchak, Joseph A., 1995. "Interpreting the Council: Catholic Attitudes toward Vatican II." Pp. 17-36 in Mary Jo Weaver and R. Scott Appleby (eds.), *Being Right*. Bloomington, Ind.: Indiana University Press.

Kosmin, Barry A. and Seymour P. Lachman, 1993. *One Nation Under God: Religion in Contemporary America*. New York: Harmony Books.

Kosnick, Anthony, William Carroll, Agnes Cunningham, Ronald Modras, and James Schulte, 1977. *Human Sexuality*. New York: Paulist Press.

Lamanna, Richard, 1994. "What's Next? Views of the Future." Paper presented at annual meeting of the Religious Research Association. Albuquerque, N.M., November.

Lederman, Douglas, 1996. "Court Rulings Force Colleges to Consider Ending Use of Race in Admissions Process." *The Chronicle of Higher Education*. July 19:A27.

Lee, Richard R., 1992. "Religious Practice as Social Exchange: An Explanation of the Empirical Findings." *Sociological Analysis*, 53:1-35

Leege, David C. and Thomas A. Trozzolo, 1985. "Religious Values and Parish Participation: The Paradox of Individual Needs in a Communitarian Church." Report 4, Notre Dame Study of Catholic Parish Life. Notre Dame, Ind.: University of Notre Dame.

——, 1986. "Parish Organizations: People's Needs, Parishes Services, and Leadership." Report 8, Notre Dame Study of Catholic Parish Life. Notre Dame, Ind.: University of Notre Dame.

——, 1987. "The Parish as Community." Report 10, Notre Dame Study of Catholic Parish Life. Notre Dame, Ind.: University of Notre Dame.

——, 1988. "Who is a True Catholic?: Social Boundaries on the Church." Report 12, Notre Dame Study of Catholic Parish Life. Notre Dame, Ind.: University of Notre Dame.

Lenski, Gerhard, 1963. *The Religious Factor.* Garden City, N.Y.: Doubleday and Company.

Linnan, John E., 1996. "From Current Crisis Springs Future Parish." *National Catholic Reporter,* May 31:6.

Lohkamp, Nicholas, 1991. "Your Conscience and Church Teaching." *Catholic Update* (C1282). Cincinnati, Ohio: St. Anthony Messenger Press.

Lott, Bernice and Albert J. Lott, 1985. "Learning Theory in Contemporary Social Psychology." In Gardner Lindzey and Elliot Aronson (eds.), *The Handbook of Social Psychology* (third edition). New York: Random House.

Ludwig, Robert A., 1995. *Reconstructing Catholicism.* New York: Crossroad.

Luria, Keith, 1989. "The Counter-Reformaiton and Popular Spirituality." Pp. 93-120 in Louis Dupre and Don E. Saliers (eds.). *Christian Spirituality III: Post Reformation and Modern.* New York: Crossroad.

Mannheim, Karl, 1952. "The Problem of Generations." Chapter 7 in Mannheim's collected *Essays on the Sociology of Knowledge*, edited by P. Kecskemeti. London: Routledge & Kegan Paul.

Markey, John J., 1994. "The Making of a Post-Vatican II Theologian: Reflections on 25 Years of Catholic Education." *America*, 171 (July 16-23):16-22.

Marler, Penny Long, 1995. "Lost in the Fifties: The Changing Family and the Nostalgic Church." Pp. 23-60 in Nancy Tatom Ammerman and Wade Clark Roof (eds.), *Work, Family and Religion in Contemporary Society.* New York: Routledge.

Marler, Penny Long and David A. Roozen, 1993. "From Church Tradition to Consumer Choice: The Gallup Surveys of the Unchurched American." Pp. 253-277 in *Church and Denominational Growth*. David A. Roozen and C. Kirk Hadaway (eds.). Nashville, Tenn.: Abingdon Press.

Marty, Martin, 1986. *Pilgrims in their Own Land.* New York: Penguin Books.

McBrien, Richard P. (ed.), 1994. *Catholicism.* New York: Harper San Francisco.

——, 1983. "Roman Catholicism: E Pluribus Unum." Pp. 179-189 in *Religion and America,* Mary Douglas and Steven Tipton (eds.). Boston: Beacon Press.

McCarthy, Timothy G., 1994. *The Catholic Tradition: Before and After Vatican II (1878-1993).* Chicago: Loyola University Press.

McCready, William C., 1981. "Let's Support Catholic Schools, At Any Price." *U.S. Catholic,* 46 (November): pp.12-17.

McCutcheon, Allan L., 1988. "Denominations and Religious Inter-marriage: Trends among White Americans in the Twentieth Century." *Review of Religious Research,* 29: 213-227.

McEnroy, Carmel, 1996. *Guests in Their Own House: The Women of Vatican II.* New York: Crossroads.

McGreevy, John, 1996. *Parish Boundaries: The Catholic Encounter with Race in the Twentieth-Century Urban North.* Chicago: The University of Chicago Press.

McGuire, Rt. Reverend Monsignor Michael A., 1961. *Baltimore Catechism, No. 1* (new revised edition). New York: Benzinger Brothers, Inc.

McGuire, Meredith B., 1992. *Religion: The Social Context* (third edition). Belmont, Calif.: Wadsworth Publishing Company.

McNamara, Patrick H., 1992. *Conscience First, Tradition Second: A Study of Young American Catholics.* Albany, N.Y.: SUNY Press.

Meltzer, Bernard, John W. Petras, and Larry T. Reynolds, 1975. *Symbolic Interactionism: Genesis, Varieties, and Criciticsms.* London and Boston: Routledge and Kegan Paul.

Miller, Alan S. and John P. Hoffmann, 1995. "Risk and Religion: An Explanation of Gender Differences in Religiosity." *Journal for the Scientific Study of Religion,* 34: 63-75.

Moberg, David O., 1962. *The Church as a Social Institution.* Englewood Cliffs, N.J.: Prentice-Hall.

Moore, Joan, 1994. "The Social Fabric of the Hispanic Community Since 1965." Pp. 6-49 in Jay P. Dolan and Allan Figueroa Deck, S.J. (eds.), *Hispanic Catholic Culture in the U.S.: Issues and Concerns.* Notre Dame, Ind.: University of Notre Dame Press.

Mueller, Charles W. and Weldon T. Johnson, 1975. "Socio-economic Status and Religious Participation." *American Sociological Review,* 40:785-800.

Murnion, Reverend Monsignor Philip J., 1996. *Called To Be Catholic: Church in a Time of Peril.* New York: National Pastoral Life Center.

——, 1992. *New Parish Ministers.* New York: National Pastoral Life Center.

Myers, David G., 1980. "Faith and Action: A Seamless Tapestry." *Christianity Today* 24 (November 21), 1980:16-19.

Myers, Phyllis Goudy and James D. Davidson, 1984. "Who Participates in Ecumenical Activity?" *Review of Religious Research,* 25:185-203.

Myers, Scott M., 1996. "An Interactive Model of Religiosity Inheritance: The Importance of Family Context." *American Sociological Review,* 61:858-866.

National Black Catholic Congress, 1995. "A Study of Opinions of African American Catholics." Report to the Board of Trustees, National Black Catholic Congress.

NCCB (National Conference of Catholic Bishops), 1988. *In Spirit and Truth: Black Catholic Reflections on the Order of Mass.* Washington, D.C.: United States Catholic Conference.

——, 1990a. *Here I Am, Send Me: A Conference Response to the Evange-lization of African Americans* and *The National Black Catholic Pastoral Plan*. Washington, D.C.: United States Catholic Conference.

——, 1990b. *Plenty Good Room: the Spirit and Truth of African American Catholic Worship*. Washington, D.C.: United States Catholic Conference.

——, 1993. *Strangers and Aliens No Longer: Part One — The Hispanic Presence in the Church of the United States*. Washington, D.C.: United States Catholic Conference.

——, 1995. *Hispanic Ministry: Three Major Documents*. Washington, D.C.: United States Catholic Conference.

——, 1996a. *Sons and Daughters of the Light*. Washington, D.C.: United States Catholic Conference.

——, 1996b. *Keep Your Hand on the Plow: The Catholic African American Presence*. Washington, D.C.: U.S. Catholic Conference.

——, 1996c. "Communion and Mission: A Guide on the Small Church Communities for Bishops and Pastoral Agents." *Origins,* 25: (January 25):513-522.

Neal, Marie Augusta, 1987. *The Just Demands of the Poor*. New York: Paulist Press.

——, 1990. "Faith and Social Ministry: A Roman Catholic Perspective." Pp. 205-226 in James D. Davidson, C. Lincoln Johnson, and Alan K. Mock (eds.), *Faith and Social Ministry: Ten Christian Perspectives*. Chicago: Loyola University Press.

Nelsen, Hart M., 1990. "The Religious Identification of Children of Interfaith Marriages." *Review of Religious Research,* 32:122-134.

Nicgorski, Walter, 1992. "American Pluralism: A Condition or a Goal?" In F. Clark Powers and Daniel K. Lapsley (eds.), *In Challenge of Pluralism*. University of Notre Dame Press.

Occhiogrosso, Peter, 1987. *Once a Catholic*. Boston: Houghton Mifflin.

O'Dea, Thomas, 1958. *The American Catholic Dilemma*. New York: Sheed and Ward.

Official Catholic Directory, 1960, 1995. New Providence, N.J.: P.J. Kenedy, 1960, 1995.

O'Malley, William J., 1986. "Jesus, the Warm Fuzzy." *America*, 154 (March 15): 204-206.

O'Meara, Thomas F., 1996. "Leaving the Baroque: The Fallacy of Restoration in the Postconciliar Era." *America*, 174 (February 3):10-14, 25-28.

Orbach, Harold L., 1961. "Aging and Religion." *Geriatrics*, 16:530-540.

Orsi, Robert A., 1985. *The Madonna of 115th Street: Faith and Community in Italian Harlem.* New Haven: Yale University Press.

Paul VI, 1968. *Humanae Vitae.* Boston, Mass.: Daughters of St. Paul.

Peterson, Paul E., 1995. "A Politically Correct Solution to Racial Classification." Pp. 3-17 in Paul E. Peterson (ed.), *Classifying by Race.* Princeton, N.J.: Princeton University Press.

Pieper, Jeanne, 1993. *The Catholic Woman: Difficult Choices in a Modern World.* Los Angeles: Lowell House.

Ploch, Donald R. and Donald W. Hastings, 1995. "Some Church; Some Don't." *Journal for the Scientic Study of Religion*, 34:507-515.

Princeton Religion Research Center, 1988. *The Unchurched Americans . . . 10 Years Later.* Princeton, N. J.

Pyle, Ralph E., 1996. *Persistence and Change in the Protestant Establishment.* Westport, Conn.: Praeger Press.

Raftery, Susan R. and David C. Leege, 1989. "Catechesis, Religious Education, and the Parish." Report 14, Notre Dame Study of Catholic Parish Life. Notre Dame, Ind.: University of Notre Dame.

Roberts, Michael and James D. Davidson, 1984. "The Nature and Sources of Religious Involvement." *Review of Religious Research*, 25:334-350.

Rodriguez, Richard, 1982. *Hunger of Memory.* New York: Bantam Books.

Rokeach, Milton, 1960. *The Open and Closed Mind.* New York: Basic Books.

Roof, Wade Clark and William McKinney, 1987. *American Mainline Religion.* New Brunswick, N.J.: Rutgers University Press.

——, 1993. *A Generation of Seekers.* San Francisco: Harper.

Rosenberg, Morris, 1981. "The Self-Concept: Social Product and Social Force." Pp. 593-624 in Morris Rosenberg and Ralph Turner (eds.), *Social Psychology: Sociological Perspectives.* New York: Basic Books.

Rossi, Alice and Rossi, Peter, 1990. *Of Human Bonding: Parent-Child Relations Across the Life Course.* New York: DeGruyter.

Ryan, William, 1981. *Equality.* New York: Pantheon.

Ryba, Thomas, 1994. "Theological Orientations: Pre-Vatican II and Post-Vatican II Beliefs." Paper presented at annual meeting of the Religious Research Association. Albuquerque, N.M., November.

Sandomirsky, Sharon and John Wilson, 1990. "Processes of Disaffiliation: Religious Mobility Among Men and Women." *Social Forces,* 68:1211-1229.

Schaeffer, Pamela 1996. "Parish as Community? Outdated, says Speaker." *National Catholic Reporter,* May 24.

Schoenherr, Richard and Lawrence Young, 1993. *Full Pews, Empty Altars.* Madison, Wis.: University of Wisconsin Press.

Seidler, John and Katherine Meyer, 1989. *Conflict and Change in the Catholic Church.* New Brunswick, N.J.: Rutgers University Press.

Sherkat, Darrin E., and John Wilson, 1995. "Preferences, Constraints and Choices in Religious Markets: An Examination of Religious Switching and Apostasy." *Social Forces,* 73:993-1026.

Stark, Rodney, 1972. "The Economics of Piety: Religious Commitment and Social Class." Pp. 483-503 in Gerald W. Thielbar and Saul D. Feldman (eds.), *Issues in Social Inequality.* Boston: Little, Brown.

Stevens-Arroyo, Anthony M., 1994. "The Emergence of a Social Identity Among Latino Catholics: An Appraisal." Pp. 77 -130 in Jay P. Dolan and Allan Figueroa Deck, S.J. (eds.), *Hispanic Catholic Culture in the U.S.: Issues and Concerns.* Notre Dame, Ind.: University of Notre Dame Press.

—— edited with Segundo Pantoja, 1995. *Discovering Latino Religion: A Comprehensive Social Science Bibliography.* Program for the Analysis of Religion Among Latinos, PARAL Series Volume Four. New York: Bildner Center for Western Hemisphere Studies.

Stolzenberg, Ross M., Mary Blair Loy, and Linda J. Waite, 1995. "Religious Participation in Early Adulthood: Age and Family Life Cycle Effects on Church Membership." *American Sociological Review,* 60:84-103.

Stryker, Sheldon, 1980. *Symbolic Interactionism: A Social Structural Version.* Menlo Park, Calif.: Benjamin/Cummings.

—— and Richard T. Serpe, 1982. "Commitment, Identity Salience, and Role Behavior: Theory and Research Example." Pp. 199-218 in William J. Ickes and Eric S. Knowles (eds.), *Personality, Roles, and Social Behavior.* New York: Springer-Verlag.

Sweetser, Thomas P., 1996. "The Parish: What Has Changed, What Remains?" *America,* 174 (February 17):6-7.

Tannen, Deborah, 1990. *You Just Don't Understand: Women and Men in Conversation.* New York: Ballantine.

Tavris, Carol, 1992. *Mismeasure of Woman.* New York: Simon and Schuster.

——, 1996. "Misreading the Gender Gap." *New York Times,* September 17, 1996:A15.

Taylor, Robert J. and Chatters, Linda M., 1988. "Church Members as a Source of Informal Social Support." *Review of Religious Research,* 30:193-203.

Thomas, John L., 1951a. "Religious Training in the Roman Catholic Family." *American Journal of Sociology,* 57: 178-183.

——, 1951b. "The Factor of Religion in the Selection of Marriage Mates." *American Sociological Review,* 16:487-491.

Turner, Jonathan H., 1991. *The Structure of Sociological Theory* (fifth edition). Belmont, Calif.: Wadsworth Publishing Company.

Ulanov, Ann Belford, 1981. *Receiving Woman: Studies in the Psychology and Theology of the Feminine.* Philadelphia: Westminster.

Verba, Sidney, Kay Lehman Schlozman and Henry Brady, 1995. "Race, Ethnicity, and Political Participation." Pp. 354-378 in Paul E. Peterson (ed.), *Classifying by Race.* Princeton, N.J.: Princeton University Press.

Walch, Timothy, 1996. *Parish School: American Catholic Parochial Education From Colonial Times to the Present.* New York: Crossroad.

Walrath, Douglas A., 1987. *Frameworks: Patterns for Living and Believing Today.* New York: The Pilgrim Press.

Wallace, Ruth A. and Alison Wolff, 1991. *Contemporary Sociological Theory.* Englewood Cliffs, N.J.: Prentice-Hall.

Weaver, Mary Jo and R. Scott Appleby, 1995. *Being Right: Conservative Catholics in America.* Bloomington, Ind.: Indiana University Press.

Weigel, Gustave, 1959. "Inside American Catholicism." *Christianity and Crisis*, 19 (June 8): 79-81.

Weigert, Kathleen Maas, 1994. "Theological Priorities: Salience of Religious Beliefs and Practices." Paper presented at annual meeting of the Religious Research Association. Albuquerque, N.M., November.

Welch, Michael R., 1993. "Participation and Commitment Among American Catholic Parishioners." Pp. 324-345 in *Church and Denominational Growth,* David A. Roozen and C. Kirk Hadaway (eds.). Nashville, Tenn.: Abingdon Press.

Wheeler, David L., 1995. "A Growing Number of Scientists Reject the Concept of Race." *The Chronicle of Higher Education*, February 17:A8, A9, A15.

Whitt, Reginald, 1996. "The Personal Particular Church from the Antepreparatory Stage of the Second Vatican Council to Canon 372, sec. 2, in the 1983 Code of Canon Law and Its Application to American Roman Catholics of African Ancestry." *Canon Law Studies 549.* Washington, D.C.: The Catholic University of America.

Wilkes, Paul, 1996. *The Good Enough Catholic.* New York: Ballantine Books.

Willer, David and Bo Anderson, 1981. *Networks, Exchange, and Coercion.* New York: Elsevier.

Williams, Andrea S., 1994. "Catechism Catholics, Council Catholics, and Christian Catholics: A Theory of Catholic Generations." Paper presented at the annual meeting for the Religious Research Association in Albuquerque, N.M., November.

—— and James D. Davidson, 1995. "Honey, You Fill This Out: Sex Bias in Questionnaire Returns." Paper presented at the annual meeting of the North Central Sociological Association.

——, 1995. "Exploring Generation X." Workshop presented at National Catholic Campus Ministry Association convention in Atlanta, Ga., January.

—— and James D. Davidson, 1996. "Catholic Conceptions of Faith: A Generational Analysis." *Sociology of Religion,* 57:273-289.

Wilson, John and Darrin E. Sherkat, 1994. "Returning to the Fold." *Journal for the Scientific Study of Religion*, 33:148-161.

Wilson, John, 1978. *Religion in American Society*. Englewood Cliffs, N.J.: Prentice-Hall.

Wimberley, Dale W., 1989. "Religion and Role Identity: A Structural Symbolic Interactionist Conceptualization of Religiosity." *Sociological Quarterly*, 30:125-142.

Winter, Miriam Therese, Adair Lummis, and Allison Stokes, 1994. *Defecting in Place: Women Claiming Responsibility for Their Own Spiritual Lives*. New York: Crossroad.

Wittberg, Patricia, 1994. *The Rise and Fall of Catholic Religious Orders*. Albany, N.Y.: State University of New York Press.

Wuthnow, Robert, 1995. *Learning to Care: Elementary Kindness in an Age of Indifference*. New York: Oxford.

Zahn, Gordon C., 1955. "The Content of Protestant Tensions: Personal Experiences and 'Known Facts.'" *American Catholic Sociological Review,* 16:12-22.
——, 1957. "The Content of Protestant Tensions: Fears of Catholic Aims and Methods." *American Catholic Sociological Review,* 18:205-212.

Zukowski, Sister Angela A., 1996. "The Impact of Media on Culture and the Church: Present and Future." Pp. 63-84 in Reverend William B. Friend, James D. Davidson, Sister Angela A. Zukowski, and Reverend Michael J. Himes, *Evangelization, Culture and Catholic Identity*. St. Leo, Fla.: St. Leo College Press.

Index

Our Sunday Visitor...
Your Source for Discovering the Riches of the Catholic Faith

Our Sunday Visitor has an extensive line of materials for young children, teens, and adults. Our books, Bibles, booklets, CD-ROMs, audios, and videos are available in bookstores worldwide.

To receive a FREE full-line catalog or for more information, call **Our Sunday Visitor** at **1-800-348-2440**. Or write, **Our Sunday Visitor /** 200 Noll Plaza / Huntington, IN 46750.

Please send me: __ A catalog
Please send me materials on:
   __ Apologetics and catechetics   __ Reference works
   __ Prayer books   __ Heritage and the saints
   __ The family   __ The parish

Name_____
Address_____Apt._____
City_____State ____Zip_____
Telephone (   ) _____

A73BBABP

Please send a friend: __ A catalog
Please send a friend materials on:
   __ Apologetics and catechetics   __ Reference works
   __ Prayer books   __ Heritage and the saints
   __ The family   __ The parish

Name_____
Address_____Apt._____
City_____State ____Zip_____
Telephone (   ) _____

A73BBABP

Our Sunday Visitor
200 Noll Plaza
Huntington, IN 46750
1-800-348-2440
OSVSALES@AOL.COM

Your Source for Discovering the Riches of the Catholic Faith